The CEO
Within

The CEO Within

*Why Inside Outsiders Are
the Key to Succession*

Joseph L. Bower

HARVARD BUSINESS SCHOOL PRESS

Boston, Massachusetts

Library of Congress Cataloging-in-Publication Data
    Bower, Joseph L.
    The CEO within : why inside outsiders are the key to succession planning /
Joseph L. Bower.
        p.   cm.
    ISBN-13: 978-1-4221-0461-3 (hardcover : alk. paper)
    ISBN-10: 1-4221-0461-3
    1. Executive succession—United States. 2. Directors of corporations—
United States. 3. Industrial management—United States.
    I. Title.
    HD38.25.U6B69 2007
    658.4'02—dc22
                                                                2007014137

The paper used in this publication meets the requirements of the American
National Standard for Permanence of Paper for Publications and Documents
in Libraries and Archives Z39.48-1992.

*For my colleagues at
Harvard Business School,
especially Hugo and John*

CONTENTS

Preface   ix

ONE

Why the Inside Outsider?

1

TWO

The Job Description

21

THREE

Inside Outsiders

57

FOUR

Building Inside Outsiders

81

FIVE

The Succession Process

119

SIX

Why So Many Companies Fail at Succession

165

SEVEN

The Special Case of Family-Business Succession

181

EIGHT

What We Ask of Our Leaders

201

Notes 223
Index   235
Acknowledgments   241
About the Author   243

THIS BOOK is about CEO succession—how it works and how it can be made to work better. In the internal life of the organization, CEO succession is a watershed. For those who want to be the CEO, succession is the game of "king of the mountain" that they have been playing for a number of years. Everyone, including those contestants, knows that the transition has the potential to change their lives radically. And the performance of the company will be affected as well in important ways.

A young turk named Jack Welch took over GE, and soon all the rules had changed. Initially, two hundred thousand people lost their jobs, but over twenty years, the $150 billion of market value was created as well as one hundred thousand new jobs. James Kilts took over Gillette, and three years later, the company was sold to Procter & Gamble. A CEO can make that kind of difference.

Yet for some reason—even though the stakes for the organizations and its people are enormous—there is a norm in nonpolitical organizations that the contest for succession is politics. And good management doesn't involve politics. So talk about succession happens behind closed doors and in lowered voices. Except in very large organizations, CEO succession is usually noted as an event, perhaps reported as a squib in the local newspaper. And even with giant corporations, the topic gets attention only in the year or so before an incumbent is scheduled to retire.

So a process that dominates the news media for two years or more before a transition in the CEO of a government, and that is virtually the organizing theme for the histories of nations, gets very modest attention in the business media—even though many companies today dwarf nations in size. And if we look at books on management, succession gets almost no attention.

I had taught about general management, the work of CEOs, for some forty years when it occurred to me toward the end of a decade's research on the work of corporate leaders that CEO succession had everything to do with a company's ability to sustain high performance over decades. The natural tendency for companies that perform exceptionally well for several years is to regress back to average behavior. The leader who was able to push his or her company to above-average performance gets tired, or competitors figure out how to pass them and do so before they can be stopped. Even great companies like IBM lose their way. So I thought it would be helpful to write a book that described the way companies that handled succession well managed the process.

It was a simple idea—until I started looking carefully at individual instances and at patterns.

To begin, what I found was passion and drama. Although we live in peaceful times, the forces at work looked a lot like what I had read about in the Bible, in Roman and Byzantine history, and in Shakespeare. The main difference was the absence of physical violence—although in the case of family companies, there have been some wild crises. Here in Boston, to help in a law suit against some of his children, a wealthy entrepreneur shot himself as part of a staged attempted murder. Leaving the passion out distorts your understanding of what is going on during succession.

But I also found that some companies had developed ways of managing the succession process that enabled them to provide good leadership. And those findings are what this book is about. Nonetheless, to capture some of the powerful human dilemmas that characterize succession management, I have, on occasion, drawn on well-known examples from political history. And I use lots of metaphors. Near the end, I even quote a poem.

There was another finding that made it harder to provide simple guidance for readers seeking a recipe for their company's succession problems. We talk about CEO successions as if they were a homogeneous class of events, but each instance I examined had unique characteristics that were important. In the specific instance, they were determining. My task was to highlight the basic attributes of the process when it was successful without pretending that the specifics were not also important. Here are the essential ideas: to begin, the process reflects the discipline with which a company is managed and its culture. In other words, succession is not a last-minute add-on. So, second, the process starts early, at least five years—often more—before the incumbent is retiring. Next, an attempt is made to expose as many candidates as possible to those who will be involved in the selection. And, finally, while the CEO manages the process pretty significantly, a small cohort of directors and advisers are involved throughout.

As a good academic, I started looking for statistics to confirm the patterns that I saw in the case histories. I combed the Execu-Comp database and the literature. And then I discovered an appalling statistic: most companies (more than 60 percent) didn't have a process at all! The best search consultants, who had decades of experience, told me that if a company had one good candidate, it was lucky!

That basic fact had everything to do with my choice of methodology. I used the databases as far as they went. But when it came to identifying what worked and what didn't, the data was far too abstract. I argue in this book that the best new CEO is an insider who has developed with an outsider's perspective, that it takes years to develop this kind of odd bird, and that if you are confronted with the decision today and have no such candidate, you have to engage in a two-step process that involves a holding action and an intensive multiyear process of development for the most likely inside outsider.

To make this argument, I turned to my forty-plus years of experience. I've been a professor of general management at Harvard Business School (HBS) for forty-three years. I taught many generations of MBA students during those years; more recently, I've focused on the participants in our school's executive development programs. Specifically, I've designed programs aimed at providing exactly the kinds of broadening experiences that help develop an outsider perspective, experiences that help transform the talented executive from the inward-focused specialist-doer to the outward-focused generalist-manager. In those contexts, I've worked with at least a thousand managers who were on the fast track to the senior levels of great corporations around the world—and were determined to do what it took to stay on that fast track.

I've also conducted research into the specific challenges of general management work and published numerous books and articles based on that research. Like much of the work that is done at HBS, my research has been steeped in the day-to-day realities of business. I have been less interested in the formalities of a theory and more interested in its relevance to practicing managers. And the choice of the word *formalities* is not an accident. There is no trade here between rigor and relevance. Only the language is informal.

This book continues in that vein. I draw extensively on interviews I've conducted over the past decade with some of the world's greatest leaders—some celebrated and others relatively unknown. I use their own words in part because those words are often so compelling and also because they are part of the evidence on which I base my conclusions. When the CEO of an Italian home appliance maker says the same thing as the CEO of a leading U.S. high-tech company, it suggests that what they are describing is probably a general phenomenon.

I bring one more qualification to the table. At Harvard, we are encouraged to serve on a manageable number of corporate boards because, in theory, that will help us understand the real problems faced by management. (Again, relevance trumps formalities.) As a director, I have participated directly in the management of nine CEO successions—some highly successful and others arguably less so. So I write from the vantage point of someone who has celebrated when a collective judgment was borne out and a CEO succeeded—but who has also mourned when an individual came up short or, worse, was brought up short by circumstances.

I've written *The CEO Within* to give more individuals and companies the opportunity to celebrate success.

ONE

Why the Inside Outsider?

A CENTRAL CHALLENGE facing most companies today is picking their next CEO.

Even if a company's CEO has only recently been installed, and even if he or she seems to be doing an outstanding job, the people with a stake in that corporation—including the incumbent CEO—need to be giving serious thought to the all-important question: who will lead us next?

Maybe this sounds like hyperbole. In this book, I argue that it isn't.

Why? One answer has to do with *power*. Even in the wake of the symbolic wing clipping that followed the fiascoes at Enron, WorldCom, Adelphia, and other companies, CEOs today still wield enormous power. Far more than politicians—who usually are hemmed in by the checks and balances of the democratic process—CEOs are masters of their own fate and that of their company. One of the great professors at Harvard Business School once referred to companies as "undemocratic hierarchies run for the pleasure of their boss." And to a surprising degree, CEOs are like the ship captains of old: the absolute rulers of their domains. As such, they play a determining role in their companies' long-term success—or failure.

This doesn't mean subordinates don't count. Of course they do. Operating units make things happen. Especially, they create the options a CEO and his or her team can consider when trying to set corporate direction. And how those teams execute makes a huge difference. Nonetheless, the CEO's decisions can make or break a company.

This may sound contrary to the current view that boards of directors have established themselves as a countervailing power to the CEO. My view sounds contrary because it *is* contrary. Yes, boards are quite capable of intervening in the management of the company, and in certain limited circumstances, they can play a key role in succession. But, as I will argue in these pages, beyond committing the time needed to inform themselves about how the succession is being managed, and beyond validating and back-stopping that process, there is almost nothing they can do to actually *manage* the process. The truth is, managing succession is a pivotal responsibility of the CEO, with huge consequences for the company's long-term success.

The exception to this rule, in which the board plays an active role in managing succession, arises when the incumbent CEO hasn't been effective. Here's the hard and irreducible fact: the process of developing men and women who have the potential to succeed the incumbent takes more than a decade. Yes, board members can and should inform themselves about the process and the candidates, but ultimately, managing talent development is the CEO's responsibility. In fact, I will argue, it's one of the most crucial parts of the job. If the CEO's team has done good work, there will be a number of qualified candidates. At that point the board's voice will be important. Remember, though, that even in these circumstances, much of the information the board has necessarily comes from the CEO.

Again, in cases in which the company is performing poorly and there are no qualified inside candidates, then the board must step in. At that point, however, there is a tacit admission by all parties (or *almost* all parties!) that the incumbent CEO has failed.

The stakes are enormous. Consider this contrast: in 1980, GE and Westinghouse were considered comparable players in the electrical equipment industry. By 2000—a scant twenty years later—GE was a $150 billion behemoth, and Westinghouse, for all practical purposes, was gone.

What made the difference? In GE's case, the company's capabilities were transformed, making it a more focused world-class competitor, turbocharged by a new foundation of integrated financial services businesses. In Westinghouse's case, no such transformation was attempted. The venerable company's portfolio was diversified, rather than focused, with disastrous results. Westinghouse's later attempts to imitate GE's success in finance were even worse.

And what lay behind these differences? I argue that it was those companies' choice of leaders in that twenty-year period. GE Chairman Reg Jones picked Jack Welch to succeed him in 1980. Welch was a stuttering forty-year-old Illinois Institute of Technology chemical engineer PhD from Lynn, Massachusetts, whom many at GE regarded as an outsider. Welch stayed—and flourished—in GE's top job for a full two decades, during which the company's market cap grew by an astounding 6,000 percent.

In that same period of time, Westinghouse burned through six chairmen, most of whom had tenures of only three or four years. By the turn of the century, the once-proud company that had first commercialized electricity, radio broadcasting, radar, frost-free refrigerators, and nuclear power—an astounding record of innovation!—was only a memory.[1]

We live in an era in which teams are celebrated. To the extent that a team adds up to more than the sum of its parts, it's, of course, a good thing. But there are many instances in which a team's failure is used as cloak and cover for a lack of leadership. Jack Welch certainly had a team—an extraordinary team, in fact—but there was no doubt about who was its leader.

Here are two more interesting data points:

- The average tenure of CEOs is dropping. *Now 7 yrs.*

- More and more companies are going outside to find their next leader.

Why is the typical CEO tenure becoming shorter and shorter? There are multiple reasons. Perhaps most compelling, the job is getting harder, so the chances of succeeding are shrinking, so CEOs increasingly tend to fall, get pushed, or jump to a new ship. It used to be sufficient to be a big fish in a small pond—local, regional, or national—but today, most CEOs have to worry about, for example, beating competitors on the other side of the world who may or may not play by the same rules.

There's another reason why the job is harder, and this one is an absolute killer: the heightened expectations of investors. It used to be sufficient to be better than average in your industry; today, you have to be a great performer not in relative terms but in absolute terms.[2] Most stock is held by institutions like insurance companies and pension funds. Their average holding period is now less than a year, and all they want is current return. You may not consider that to be "investing," but they're the shareholders whom contemporary CEOs have to face.

For most corporate leaders, this isn't easy. In fact, it's damn tough. Boards and shareholders are increasingly focused on maximizing shareholder return—not only through share-price increases, but through dividend streams, stock buybacks, and other techniques. It's no longer enough to promise great things in the long run; Wall Street wants a model that generates good cash in the near term.

In short, there are clear performance targets that must be hit. If not, the revolving door of CEOs is very likely to be set in motion, sweeping up the hapless incumbent who is standing in its way.

Meanwhile, the top corporate job is no longer a comfortable sinecure—if indeed it ever was. Today, it's hard, grinding, 24/7 sort of work, often characterized by inhumane hours, jet lag, more intrusive regulators, increasingly skeptical reporters, feistier boards, and so on. The pay is good, but—at least for some CEOs—

the price is too high. They've already reached the pinnacle; do they want to put their health and happiness at risk to stay there? Some say no. Many give that revolving door a shove of their own; they sell the company to a strategic buyer—or more frequently today, a private equity group—and, with a sigh of relief, pocket the gains on their options.

And what about that second data point mentioned earlier, that more and more companies are looking outside for their leaders?

On the face of it, this makes no sense. Everything that we know about the job, in both our heads and our guts, suggests that an insider should have a huge advantage. In fact, in *Good to Great*, Jim Collins makes a compelling argument in support of the case that promoting an insider is a key characteristic of "great" companies.[3]

So we are faced with an interesting dilemma, which can be summed up as follows:

- The CEO's job is critically important.

- Many people who get this important job are not measuring up.

- The way we tend to go about hiring CEOs is—by an ever-increasing percentage—wrongheaded.

Other factors work to diminish the stature of the corporate leader. For one thing, the sheer scale of major companies today makes them seem impervious to singular events like changes in leadership at the top. GE's sales, for example, grew from $450 million in 1940 to $150 billion six decades later. Microsoft, founded in 1975, had a market cap of $500 billion by century's end.[4] At this scale, can the influence of a single individual, or series of individuals, make a difference?

I contend that the answer is yes, definitely.

Meanwhile, the academy has also contributed to undercutting the CEO's stature. The dominant metaphor today among business scholars for describing long-term change in the business world is evolution. In this worldview, companies—and, indeed, whole industries—play the role of species that compete to beat (or eat) each other and to survive large-scale ecological changes. In fact, some business theorists have adopted an almost purely ecological model in which the environment selects which companies will survive.

Companies, in other words, are like mammoths. If the environment changes in ways that are unfavorable, they will simply die out. The gods have spoken, and no merely mortal CEO can alter his or her fate.

A Failure of Leadership

Well, is this worldview accurate? No.

The leading companies in the United States in 1975 looked something like the leading companies in the United States in 1955: more than half were the same. Contrary to the common wisdom, this situation persisted for another fifteen years or so. Then all hell broke loose. By 2000, there was wholesale change, and more than two-thirds of the top companies of 1990 were gone by 2004.

What happened in that intervening quarter-century? A perfect storm of technological change and globalization produced tumultuous economic conditions that contributed to the destruction of many companies. But I contend that those hapless companies went bankrupt, were sold, or were broken up principally because their management could not redeploy resources in productive ways.

So, yes, the ecology changed. But at the root of the wholesale destruction that took place toward the end of the twentieth century among established corporations was a failure of leadership. In fact, academics who have tracked the effect of CEOs have found that when the environment was tumultuous and resources had to be reallocated, the impact of leaders was dramatic—for good and for bad.[5]

I am most familiar with such failures in U.S. companies, although I'm sure there are equivalent stories to be found and told around the world. U.S. tire companies continued to invest in bias-ply technology, and the associated manufacturing capacity, long after bias-ply tires had been made obsolete by radial technology. The only way to make a bias-ply tire stronger is to increase its number of plies, which increases its mass, which increases its heat retention—which, of course, destroys the tire. The result? Firestone was sold to the Japanese. Goodrich was sold to the Italians.

U.S. television manufacturers continued to turn out sets of dubious quality that wholesaled for more than the Japanese sets retailed for. The Japanese sets were more reliable and, some argued, looked better. The result? Magnavox and GTE Sylvania were sold to the Dutch. Motorola's Quasar division and Zenith were both sold to the Japanese.

The same sad story could be recounted in industry after industry—and, in fact, is still being written today. In the 1990s, the telecommunication industry and its equipment suppliers responded to the opportunity posed by the Internet with very poor results. Lucent, the heart of old AT&T, is now owned by Alcatel, a French company. The cement industry is owned by foreign producers, as is integrated steel.

What we see, time and time again, are companies that fail to respond to changing circumstances and that fail to look forward. Yes, bigness sometimes hurts. Scientists speculate that in the case of the biggest dinosaurs, it may have taken several minutes for pain signals to travel from the tip of the beasts' tail all the way to their brain, which is not a good thing for long-term evolutionary success. But bigness need not be a death sentence. Bigness carries with it certain advantages—like economies of scale and scope—that go a long way toward offsetting a big company's ponderousness.

But bad leadership is a death sentence. I contend that the ability of companies to adjust their capabilities and direction over the long term—to meet the challenges of new markets and new competitors—grows directly out of the quality of their leadership.

And if you accept that premise, then logically you have to agree that the success of a company over the longer term hinges on the management of CEO succession and how its leaders are chosen.

Outsiders and Insiders

Where do great leaders come from? At the risk of seeming to state the obvious, great leaders either have to come from inside the company or outside the company. A central premise of this book is that as a rule, the best leaders are people from inside the company who somehow have maintained enough detachment from the local traditions, ideology, and shibboleths that they have retained the objectivity of an outsider. I call these unusual people *Inside Outsiders*, and I'll return to them shortly.

Note the qualifier just used: "as a rule." Great rules are meant to be broken. Sometimes, the best solution lies outside the company. Sometimes, even the reasonably objective insider is a disaster. Let's look at some examples.

When Lou Gerstner arrived at IBM in 1993, he looked like the quintessential outsider. He was a former McKinseyite who had spent eleven years as a top executive at American Express and had then served for four years as the chairman and CEO of RJR Nabisco—in other words, he went from management consulting, to financial services, to tobacco and cookies. Old-time IBMers, as well as many industry observers, were intensely skeptical. Gerstner spent his first six months at IBM simply trying to figure out what the company's possible futures looked like. This was, in part, driven by the company's ecology. Was the IT field going to deliver on its promise of "distributed computing"—that is, a world in which all information was available to everyone all the time, through cheap and ubiquitous technologies? Just as important, would it deliver on its promise of total integration and interoperability? If both prospects were realized—and that was the betting in most corners of the industry and the company at that time— then IBM was indeed a dinosaur. It added no value and ought to be broken up.

But Gerstner didn't buy the conventional wisdom. As he later recalled in his autobiographical account of IBM's turnaround:

Even before I had crossed the threshold at IBM, I knew that promise [of interoperability] was empty. I'd spent too long a time on the other side. The idea that all this complicated, difficult-to-integrate, proprietary collection of technologies was going to be purchased by consumers who would be willing to be their own general contractors made no sense . . .

Now, I must tell you, I am not sure that in 1993 I or anyone else would have started out to create an IBM. But, given IBM's scale and broad-based capabilities, and the trajectories of the information technology industry, it would have been insane to destroy its unique competitive advantage and turn IBM into a group of individual component suppliers— more minnows in an ocean . . .

So keeping IBM together was the first strategic decision, and, I believe, the most important decision I ever made—not just at IBM, but in my entire business career. I didn't know then exactly how we were going to deliver on the potential of that unified enterprise, but I knew that if IBM could serve as the foremost integrator of technologies, we'd be delivering extraordinary value.[6]

What's going on here? Gerstner was an outsider in the sense that he had no high-tech experience. But he did understand the uses of technology in business, and from the consumer's perspective, he was fully prepared to challenge the conventional wisdom. And after half a year of poking around in IBM's attics and closets, he was also prepared to argue *against* the conclusion that Big Blue needed to be broken up. He saw a future in which IBM would be the "foremost integrator of technologies," rather than a collection (or a former collection!) of "minnows in an ocean." He reversed the company's plans to splinter itself up and began laying the foundations for the creation of a powerful service business. It was, indeed, an important decision—hugely important.

Outsiders can make change happen. Some, like well-traveled CEO John Nevin, made a career of it. At Firestone, he quickly shut off corporate investments in the doomed bias-ply tire technology and sold the tire business to Japan's Bridgestone. At Zenith, he sold Panasonic to Matsushita.

But does it always take an outsider to see the need for change? Actually, no. Jack Welch, the maverick insider, sold GE's mining business to the Australians and home electronics business to the French. In an even more dramatic move, which was highly criticized at the time, insider Darwin Smith—then only recently promoted to the post of CEO at Kimberly-Clark—sold off the company's coated-paper mills. While less celebrated than GE's performance under Welch, Kimberly-Clark's performance began to soar once its commodity manufacturing activities were abandoned. In both cases, the divestitures cut a key link to the company's past, and both insiders and outsiders faulted Welch and Smith for selling off the family jewels. But these Inside Outsiders were resolute, and they were right.

Conversely, outsiders do not always get things right. Carly Fiorina was brought in to shake up Hewlett-Packard (HP). Shifts in the markets for IT hardware had undermined HP's strategic position. Rather than consolidating HP's leading position in high-end printers and other computer-related peripherals, Fiorina bought struggling PC maker Compaq. That too was a fundamental choice, and it appears to have been a near-disastrous one. Under Mark Hurd, HP has captured leadership in PCs, but between July 1999, when Fiorina took over, and February 2005, when she resigned, HP lost almost half of its market value.

Getting It Right

Corporate leaders regularly are faced with tough decisions, even if such decisions aren't always of the bet-the-company variety. And the tough truth is, leaders seldom make those decisions as well as they or shareholders would like. It's very hard, moreover, to disentangle the decision from its implementation. And, finally, conventional wisdom about the meaning and "rightness" of the decision continues to evolve long after both the decision and its implementation are largely history.

At the end of the day, however, the consequences of the decision as implemented are what counts. Unlike college math class, you don't get points for getting the idea right. This is one reason why the numerous statistical studies of succession tell us very little.[7]

But that does not absolve those with the task of choosing leaders of their responsibilities. If they do it so badly that the statistical results look like an ecological process, that merely means that they are doing it badly—not that it can't be done.

I return to my opening observation: picking the next CEO is a central responsibility facing companies today. It is key to sustaining success over decades. Having made this observation, we should also note—as I pointed out earlier—that the tenure of CEOs is dropping and that the tendency to go outside for a leader is rising. Average CEO tenure dropped from 9.5 years in 1980 to 7.0 today.[8]

What does this tell us? Among other things, it tells us that the management of succession is getting worse. When insiders fail to perform, the board turns to an outsider. At the same time, the best studies of insiders versus outsiders strongly suggest that insiders come to the CEO job with a huge leg up. In *Good to Great*, as previously noted, Jim Collins makes the case that promoting an insider turns out to be a key characteristic of "great" companies. In Jim Collins' sample, less than 5 percent of the CEOs of "good to great" companies were outsiders, while in the weaker performing comparator companies 30 percent of the CEOs were outsiders. Furthermore, there were twice as many CEOs within the given time frame, indicating shorter tenures, in the weaker performing companies.[9]

My analysis of a much larger sample, the S&P 500, tells a similar story, as shown in table 1-1. This table compares the performance of CEOs who were with their company two or more years before their appointment with that of outsiders. Performance is measured as the total return less the S&P. (Total return is a very crude measure, but it captures the point accurately.)

TABLE 1–1

TABLE 1–1

Standardized company return for companies in sample (company less S&P 500)

	Average (%)	Median (%)	Number of observations
Insider	1.48	−0.15	1,214
Outsider	−0.28	−3.09	600

Source: Standard & Poor's Compustat data, www.standardandpoors.com; the Corporate Library's Board Analyst database, www.thecorporatelibrary.com.

Simply put, insiders perform better than outsiders. And this is not surprising, on the face of it. Most people familiar with the challenges of managing a large organization find it intuitively plausible that an insider could do a better job. After all, the insider knows the organization, its products, its markets, its competitors, and its people. But this same insider might be the one who was inclined in 1993 to go with the conventional wisdom and break up IBM—the conventional wisdom that outsider Lou Gerstner had to fight so strenuously against. Insiders "drink the Kool-Aid," as they say.

To get at the big picture, I looked at the population of successions in the past decade in the S&P 500 companies. I split the sample according to whether the performance of the company before succession was better than or worse than the S&P, and whether the successor was an insider or an outsider. Then I examined whether the postsuccession performance of the company was better than or worse than the S&P over the next three-year period, as in figure 1-1.

The first thing to note is that almost three-quarters of the successors were insiders when the performance was better than the S&P. When performance was worse, outsiders were tapped almost 40 percent of the time, as in figure 1-2.

The next thing to note is that insiders outperformed outsiders in both cases, but especially when the company had had poor prior performance. In other words, the conventional logic that poor

FIGURE 1-1

Post-succession returns for sample companies

		Prior performance was	
		Better than S&P 500	Worse than S&P 500
New CEO was an	Insider	–3.4%	4.5%
	Outsider	–5.0%	–1.3%

performance requires going outside is not justified by this data.

But a final thing to note is that these differences in the median returns are small, and the individual cases show wide swings, as in figure 1-3.

Most boards that I know of have full access to statistics like these. So that begs an obvious question: why do boards go outside if it is so clearly a risky business move? My colleague Rakesh Khurana has devoted a book to a discussion of the search for "charismatic CEOs."[10] My summary of his conclusions is that some boards, facing difficult strategic circumstances in the markets for their company's products and services, lose faith in the capabilities of the insiders who produced those lousy results. They then go off in search of a superhero who can turn lead into gold and transform a dire situation into a winning proposition.

[handwritten margin note: Celebrity CEO,]

Khurana estimates that boards with the lead-to-gold mind-set are disappointed more than half the time. The problem is that their search process leads them to star performers in other com-

FIGURE 1-2

Prior performance of companies in the sample

		Company performance was	
		Better than S&P 500	Worse than S&P 500
New CEO was an	Insider	510	704
	Outsider	178	422

FIGURE 1-3

Examples of companies showing wide variation

		Company performance was			
		Better than S&P 500		Worse than S&P 500	
	Insider	Gateway	−51%	United Airlines	−60%
		Xerox	−40%	NY Times	−39%
		Boeing	+55%	AMR Corporation	+62%
New		Cisco	+48%	Procter & Gamble	+29%
CEO					
was an	Outsider	RJR Nabisco	−68%	ITT Corporation	+17%
		Home Depot	−3%	Barnes & Noble	+10%
		Compaq	−42%	Hershey	+7%
		Honeywell	+35%		

panies, not necessarily an executive with the capabilities needed in the particular situation facing their company.

The CEO Within presents a way to resolve this dilemma and to get out of the trap that it represents. It suggests practical ways to find, recruit, and retain a probable winner for the CEO job.

For example, research suggests that the biggest challenge to a successful CEO transition is developing a pool of candidates from which a highly qualified leader can be chosen. If you say this to high-ranking officers and board members, most nod their heads in agreement. And yet, most companies don't act in ways that embody this principle. Most persist in training managers without building leaders. In other words, they may put a great deal of effort into grooming executives who can head up functions or run business units, but they fall down terribly when it comes to preparing those executives, or others, for the CEO job.

Does that sound like an exaggeration? It's not. Figure 1-4 shows the response of 286 of 1,380 HR managers at leading companies who responded to an online inquiry. A full 60 percent did not have a CEO succession plan in place! And that's why companies wind up looking outside: they have nowhere else to look.

In this book, I propose to pin down exactly what is involved in the CEO job and, hence, the kinds of things that those picking

FIGURE 1-4

Levels at which succession plans are in place at companies polled

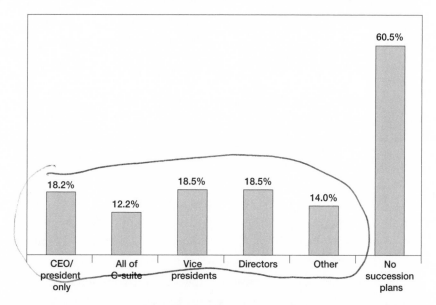

Source: Society of Human Resources Management, "SHRM Weekly Online Poll," December 2003, results reported in Susan Meisinger, "The King Is Dead, Long Live the King!" *HR Magazine* 49, no. 6 (2004).

the CEO must consider. To do so, I will draw on the classic CEO job descriptions that the great management thinkers have provided over the years. I'll also use real-life cases—some celebrated, some not so celebrated—to capture and illuminate these job descriptions. What is "the job"? Who's done it well, and who's done it not so well? How can we generalize about who/what works and who/what doesn't work?

This brings us back to the idea of the Inside Outsider. My contention—not only in this book, but also in my other writings and my teaching at Harvard Business School—is that the best candidate for the CEO job is an individual with a distinctive skill set and mind-set. There are exceptions to every rule, of course, but in general, the candidate most likely to succeed in the CEO post is a person who is both inside and outside the company: the Inside Outsider.

*Insider/outsider
defined*

How can you be both? By *insider,* I mean a person who has grown up, professionally speaking, primarily within the confines of the company. He or she knows it intimately. By *outsider,* I mean someone who has retained a degree of detachment from the company. He or she is skeptical when confronted with the company's unadulterated ideology—its self-serving, and often self-deluding, bromides. He or she is outside the mainstream of the company and is therefore able to bring what might be called "peripheral perspectives" to bear.

Am I advocating the elevation of eccentrics, misfits, and other marginal types? Of course not. But based on my years of formal and informal research into how corporations actually work, the successful CEO from inside must be able to look at his or her corporate inheritance as if he or she had just bought the company. Yes, they can and should take advantage of the intimate working knowledge—of people and systems, of suppliers and customers, of regulators and the competition—that they have gained through their tenure as a manager. At the same time, they must draw heavily on their understanding of the new world to which the company must respond. They must do so unencumbered by all the cognitive and emotional baggage that very often comes as the result of a long tenure within a single organization. The imperatives of the world ahead must be their drivers.

Having established the peculiar requirements of the job, I then look at what's involved in building executives who make good candidates: recruitment, development, selection, and transition. The starting point, of course—the sine qua non—is a certain personal makeup, which tends to involve big doses of smarts, high personal integrity, and good humor. Right after good humor comes good health, which I believe to be linked in important ways to good humor. The ability to laugh at oneself, it seems, wards off all kinds of physical ailments and psychological evils.

Last but not least in the personal makeup arena is a healthy dose of competitiveness. We in the university setting spend a lot of our time and energy focusing on what might be called the "in-

tellect of business"—the cerebral, cool, passive aspects of enterprise—mainly because these are the easier aspects to describe,
capture, and quantify. But much of business is all about the pas-
sionate aspects of our human nature: the noisy, extroverted, aggressive side that we inevitably bring with us to the office and that
we draw on to climb the corporate ladder. CEOs tend to have a
whole lot more passion in their makeup than your average guy or
gal on the street; highly successful CEOs tend to have even more. *Passion*

Although *The CEO Within* will give only short shrift to this
side of corporate life—the passion side—I wanted to mention it
early and invite you to put my subsequent advice through this
screen: how does the intellect of a brilliant succession process intersect with the passion of a half dozen highly ambitious individuals,
five of whom are guaranteed to lose the single most important
competition of their lives? It's not an easy question to answer, but
it's one that we should keep in mind throughout the following
chapters. Remember, not too long ago, people killed for these
jobs—sometimes even killing their parents to get into the medieval
equivalent of the corner office.

What about the contributing factors that aren't intrinsic to
the individual? First and most important, great leaders need to have
mastered their business. Mastery grows out of prolonged exposure to a single business across a variety of assignments. For the
most talented individuals, this eventually involves the transition
from specialist-doer to generalist-manager (which at Harvard we
generally shorten to "general manager"). Their view must be ho-
listic, cumulative, and longitudinal. They must have an understanding of the various general management challenges posed by
businesses in different stages of development, and they must
bring that understanding to bear on all kinds of novel and baffling
challenges.

That distinctive view and that broad-gauge understanding have
to come from more than one kind of general management assignment. That means that the company has to be organized so that
there are multiple general management jobs—that is, not just the

CEO job, but other opportunities for would-be CEOs to test their wings and prepare to soar.

This kind of on-the-job training may be combined with intensive mentoring or coaching or with university-based general management programs (I have designed and helped teach several such programs). Again, the overall goal, however accomplished, is to develop a unique and powerful perspective: that of the Inside Outsider.

Who Is This Book For?

This book is directed primarily at the men and women who are personally involved in the development and selection of CEOs.

That means different things at different companies. A partial list of the potential players includes board members, incumbent CEOs and their leadership team, senior HR managers, HR consultants, and the executive development/search community. All these players have a personal stake in finding and recruiting CEOs and in making sure those hires succeed in their formidable new assignments. The board of directors, in particular, should find useful advice here about how its members can be helpful in this all-important process without stepping on people's operational toes.

In my experience, companies that do a poor job of developing potential CEOs sometimes do so because they are badly organized or managed—just as a disorganized restaurant can turn great ingredients into a bad meal. For that reason, I think that *The CEO Within* also speaks to another whole group of corporate leaders—the kinds of people who worry about how information flows within the organization and how strategy and structure intersect. Certain kinds of consultants deal mainly with corporate-level leaders; these people too should understand how some of their most important clients are chosen and what that choice says about the companies they are serving.

Further down in the organizational ranks are whole cohorts of people who should benefit from understanding the ideas contained in *The CEO Within*. Even though a company can have only one CEO at a time—and hopefully will only have a new one every decade or two—that doesn't keep lots of people within the organization from aspiring to the top post. Even among those who don't have aspirations for the corner office, many people want to understand how their next boss (or their boss's next boss) will be picked. After all, few events will have more impact on their professional lives, either directly or indirectly. Even if this book does nothing to improve the CEO selection process—which I certainly hope is not the case!—it can help make that process more transparent to those who have a stake in it, and that would be a good thing.

Similarly, many students at Harvard Business School and at other leading business schools aspire to be CEOs someday. I hope this book helps them think about the kind of real-world experiences they need to obtain after they embark on their managerial careers; I also hope it helps them think about the kinds of companies they want to sign up with in the first place. And if they someday make it to the CEO post, or have the privilege of serving on another company's board, I hope they take their succession-planning responsibilities to heart.

Toward the end of the book, I touch on the interests of still another audience: the family-business community. Most companies in the United States are (or began as) family businesses. Their succession challenges are especially daunting because the dynamics and psychodramas of succession—difficult enough in the "normal" business context—can be greatly exacerbated by intergenerational conflict and sibling rivalry. *Insider* takes on a whole new meaning in the family-business context, and wise families go to great lengths to provide the next generation with significant outsider experiences.

The final chapter of the book returns to the theme with which I opened this chapter: leadership matters, and the way we have been picking leaders isn't working very well. Part of the problem is that we are increasingly picking leaders as if they are interchangeable parts to be discarded when they're not performing well to make room for a new one purchased in the market.

Chapter 3 takes a close look at Inside Outsiders and why their odds for success are better. Chapters 4 and 5 then examine the processes needed to build and select the right Inside Outsider. Chapter 6 explains why these processes are so hard to develop and maintain, and chapter 7 makes it clear why these tasks are even harder for family-controlled companies. But another big piece of the problem is that the CEO job in today's large corporations is very demanding—huge scale, complex operations, and brutal demands for current performance make for a perilous mission. Understanding the dimensions of that mission is the task of the next chapter.

The Job Description

He'll sit here and he'll say, 'Do this! Do that!'
And nothing will happen. *Poor Ike—*
it won't be a bit like the Army.
He'll find it very frustrating.

—HARRY S. TRUMAN[1]

A N ACQUAINTANCE of mine—who used to run one of the world's largest and most influential management consulting firms—often provoked his audiences by saying that he had never met a corporate general manager who was competent to do the job.

Having captured his audience's attention, he then explained what he meant by that provocative assertion. No, it wasn't that he didn't know any skilled executives; actually he had worked with dozens of brilliant corporate leaders. But the CEO's job, he went on to say, was simply bigger than any one individual.

Despite this fact, of course, somebody had to fill CEO posts and the other challenging jobs at the upper reaches of management. And of those who took the jobs, he explained, some of them beat the odds and succeeded.

Obviously, this is a bracing hypothesis. It is a very different perspective on the CEO's job than we normally encounter. This one emphasizes the job's inherent difficulty, the likelihood that the incumbent will make mistakes, and the relatively long odds against success. And, for our purposes, it's a very useful perspective. If we can figure out why the job of a leader is so hard, we should be able to better pick effective leaders.

Toward that end, let's consider the words of the late Ken Andrews, a former colleague of mine at Harvard and one of the leading exponents of the craft of general management: "Chief executives, presidents . . . are first and probably least pleasant persons who are responsible for the results attained in the present as designated by plans made previously. Nothing that we will say . . . can gainsay this immediate truth."[2]

The plaque on Harry Truman's desk read, "The buck stops here."[3] As amended by Andrews, that plaque would read, "The buck stops here, *even if I didn't start it.*" Whether or not the leader set in motion the activities that produced the present results—and whether or not environmental shifts made losses inevitable—the leader is responsible for the results during the time of his or her stewardship.

That is why, as a rule, CEOs are thought of as doing a good job during times of economic prosperity and as performing badly during recessions. When the sun is shining, CEOs have to do all they can to make hay, as much and as quickly as possible, and do whatever they can to extend the hay-making season. (And at the risk of overextending the metaphor, they have to use inherited hay-making equipment, at least in the early part of their tenure.) When it's raining, conversely, CEOs have to make do. They have to take whatever corrective action they can so that the planned results, or some semblance of the planned results, can still be attained.

So executives have to own their results. In addition, wrote Ken Andrews, executives have to "see as their second principal function the creative maintenance and development of organizational capability that makes achievement possible." In other words, they have to deploy the organization's resources in such a way that builds its capacities.

This activity, Andrews noted, leads in turn to a third key function: "The integration of the specialist functions which enable their organizations to perform the technical tasks in marketing, finance . . . which [functions] proliferate as technology develops and tends to lead the company in all directions. If this coordination is successful . . . general managers will probably have performed the task of getting organizations to accept and order priorities in accordance with the company's objectives. Securing commitment to purpose is a central function of the president as organizational leader."

But we've haven't yet finished adding to our growing pile of CEO responsibilities. We still have to attend to issues of strategy and vision. As Andrews put it: "The most difficult role . . . of the chief executive of any organization is the one in which he serves as the custodian of corporate objectives . . . The presidential functions involved include establishing or presiding over the goal-setting and resource allocation processes of the company, making or ratifying choices among strategic alternatives, and clarifying and defending the goals of the company against external attack or internal erosion."

Let's recap the scope of the leadership challenge implied by these tasks. To be responsible for today's results, which grow out of yesterday's plans, means you are riding someone else's wave. In addition, you are owning results that are inevitably shaped by unforeseen events. In the last week of August 2005, for example, Hurricane Katrina reshuffled the deck for millions of people (and corporations) in New Orleans, on the U.S. Gulf Coast, and around the world. Less dramatically, blizzard conditions in the northeast United States forced a rethinking of corporate and individual plans. As a CEO, you can't argue with Mother Nature; you can only scramble to accommodate her.

Meanwhile, industry sectors and regional and national economies continue to evolve. For example, an odd conjunction of high productivity and international competition has made consumer markets throughout the world hypercompetitive. The surprise acquisition of Gillette by Procter & Gamble may alter the balance of power between retailers and suppliers and may compel mighty Wal-Mart to rethink aspects of its strategy. Similarly, the merger of Kmart and Sears, as well as that of Federated and the May Department Stores, may have changed the face of U.S. department store retailing. In such a context, achieving results planned even a year ago—let alone five years ago!—is remarkably difficult.

And borders are increasingly porous. In most markets today, there are powerful competitors with operations around the globe. The Gerdau Group and Mittal, steel producers based in the Third World countries of Brazil and India, are now challenging leaders in major markets such as France, the United States, and the United Kingdom—and not just as importers, but as owners of important local operations. Samsung is pushing Sony, Matsushita, and Motorola. Indesit (formerly Merloni Elettrodomestici) is pushing Bosch and Electrolux, with Haier (based in China) and Arçelik (based in Turkey) right behind. This is a new world.

Even tougher. It's no longer enough to make good products efficiently. World-class companies have to make the best products at the lowest possible cost, which means that they have to cut costs and cut them relentlessly. At the same time, they have to innovate and retain their capability to work toward future objectives.

If companies can't do all these contradictory things and still make a profit, they will lose. They will be beaten by other companies and squeezed out of their long-standing markets. Or, thanks in part to the existence of huge and liquid financial markets, they will be taken over by their competitors.

All in all, it's a complex and daunting picture. In this turbulent context, what makes organizational achievement possible? The answer, which is deceptively simple, has two parts. First, the organization must recruit and develop a management team with the skills and ability to work in relative harmony. Second, the organization in which these executives are deployed must be capable of delivering the operating excellence required for competitiveness and the innovation required for sustained growth.

This may sound easy, but it's not—for all the reasons cited earlier. The devil, as they say, is in the details. Do you look inside or outside the organization for these team members? How do you deal with things, like cost cutting and innovation, that tug in different directions?

To begin exploring the answers to these questions, I've chosen companies in four categories:

- *Outside/good.* A company (ad agency Ogilvy & Mather) goes outside for a new leader, with good results.

- *Outside/bad.* A second company (Apple Computer) goes outside, with less happy results.

- *Inside/good.* A consumer products company (Brown Group) finds strong leadership inside the organization.

- *Inside/bad.* Finally, a U.K. retailing icon (Marks & Spencer) looks inside and comes up short.

Collectively, these four stories—to which we'll return to from time to time throughout the book—give us insight into the challenges of the CEO's job. They instruct us about the kinds of levers that are available to be pulled (or not pulled) in the corporate context. They introduce real-world ways of thinking about critical corporate functions—for example, succession planning. (To that end, I'll include extensive quotes from the principals wherever possible.) And, finally, they give us insight into the desirable characteristics of the Inside Outsider.

Outside/Good:
Charlotte Beers at Ogilvy & Mather

The first of our four cases involves advertising agency icon Ogilvy & Mather. Founded in 1948 by industry legend David Ogilvy, the agency made its mark in the ad world by selling products with both fictional characters (the "Hathaway man") and real-life company spokespeople (Commander Whitehead of Schweppes). A subsequent ad for Rolls-Royce ("At 60 miles an hour, the loudest noise in the new Rolls-Royce comes from the electric clock"), as well as Ogilvy's own writings (*Confessions of an Advertising Man*, among others), cemented the agency's reputation.[4]

In the mid-1970s, Ogilvy retired to Touffou, a sixty-room, fourteenth-century chateau a hundred miles southwest of Paris, an event that some mark as the beginning of the agency's subsequent twenty-year decline. Ogilvy's firm was purchased in 1992 by the marketing-services holding company WPP, led by Martin Sorrell. For many inside the organization, the event was tumultuous, even cataclysmic. From the banks of the river Vienne, retired David Ogilvy felt compelled to weigh in: "God, the idea of being taken over by that odious little jerk really gives me the creeps. He's never written an advertisement in his life."[5]

Sorrell's lack of relevant experience was only one issue facing WPP's newly acquired agency. The bidding war that had preceded the firm's takeover had led to a very high purchase price of $864 million, which meant that the agency now had to perform at correspondingly high levels. Meanwhile, though, good account executives were leaving—and taking accounts with them. As is so often the case in times of trouble, the people with good options elsewhere left, and those with no other good options stayed.

Soon after the takeover, Ogilvy CEO Ken Roman resigned. His replacement was Graham Phillips, a twenty-four-year veteran from the account management side of the business who had a reputation for being a very good manager. But the bleeding continued. In 1989, the agency lost Shell and Unilever; in 1990, Seagram's Coolers and NutraSweet; and in 1991—a particularly bad year—Campbell Soup withdrew its $25 million account, Roy Rogers pulled its $15 million account, and American Express announced that it was moving its $60 million account. At the end of 1991, with confidence inside the firm shaken, revenue 40 percent off budget, and an anemic 4 percent operating margin, Phillips resigned.[6]

Charlotte Beers, CEO of the Chicago agency Tatham-Laird & Kudner, was named as his successor—the first CEO hired from outside the ranks of Ogilvy.[7] Beers had entered the agency business at J. Walter Thompson's Chicago office, rising quickly to become senior vice president for client services. In 1979, she was recruited to be COO of Tatham-Laird, where she was named

CEO in 1982 and board chair in 1986. Billings tripled during her tenure, and the industry took notice. In 1987, she became the first woman to be elected chair of the American Association of Advertising Agencies.

Why was she picked for the Ogilvy job? To begin with, there was no internal candidate who looked plausible. (The internal candidates appeared to be part of the problem, rather than the solution.) Beyond that, she had a strong track record as a builder of a creative agency and a great reputation in the industry at large, which meant that her presence could fill a gaping credibility gap. For his part, Martin Sorrell was certain that Beers would be the right person in the right place at the right time:

> Why did I pick Charlotte Beers? She had the attention span of a gnat, but she was fantastic. And she had tremendous personality. And she embodied that much-abused word, *charisma*. People thought I was half mad—if not completely mad—because Charlotte had run a small- [or] medium-sized . . . Chicago-based advertising agency. She hadn't run operations in the U.S., and she hadn't run operations internationally.
>
> There were some internal candidates, and there were some external candidates. But by the time that we brought Charlotte in, we'd had disappointing results with, I suppose, the two previous people [both insiders]. And Charlotte represented a very different approach. She was a woman, so that was what made it different. As I said, she was very bright and very sparky.
>
> So it was a bit of a jump into the wild blue yonder from that point of view. But I think Charlotte was spectacular. In fact, Charlotte declined an opportunity with Saatchi, funnily enough, which was much more aligned with her two biggest clients where she had big relationships . . . which were P&G and . . . Mars. So the natural place for her to go, in a way, was Saatchi, but she didn't. She came with us, and she did very well.[8]

But past success was no guarantee of future triumphs for Beers. In the words of Shelly Lazarus—by then a twenty-year veteran of Ogilvy & Mather, who would ultimately succeed Beers as a brilliant CEO—the agency that Beers took over on April 9, 1992, was not really being run as a business:

> The goal was great work; the belief was that financial reward and commercial success would certainly follow. And, in fact, the growth in the industry was so remarkable you couldn't help but get more successful. It was a very strong culture that reflected David Ogilvy. It was all about decent people with strong beliefs who approach advertising as both art and science. Extraordinary integrity and commitment to clients. David ran this place as a true meritocracy. I mean when he stood up and said we abhor toadies and politicians, it was true. I actually think that one of the reasons that Ogilvy sometimes gets killed inside client organizations is that we have a very underdeveloped sense of politics.[9]

For her part, Beers was astonished at the informality of the organization and its near-total disregard for the chain of command. "It's an amazing thing to walk in an office," she later recalled, "and have the current CEO not even quite sure that you are coming that day, and having none of the secretaries know who you are, and have to introduce yourself."

But the far more troubling problem that Beers perceived was a dearth of leadership. "It was alarming," she admitted. "The head of International had been fired the previous year. The current CEO had resigned. He had lost his own CFO. I then did fire the head of North America, so the top four were gone."

Beers knew she had to operate on several fronts simultaneously. One of the more important fronts, she decided—one that needed immediate attention—was morale. Sagging morale was having a direct and negative impact on the agency's performance. "The morale of the company," she later explained, "was so bad because this is a proud company and very intellectually sophisticated. [Executives] came across as arrogant and distant because they were so embarrassed."

Beers's response was both novel and courageous: she decided to spend six months visiting the agency's remaining major clients and learn firsthand how they viewed Ogilvy's output. She was looking for a "highly accelerated learning curve," she later recalled, and she got it: "I went to most places on my own. The feudal lords in the offices worked hard to brief this woman about what they thought they were doing, so that I wouldn't get them in trouble. If anything, they were too severe on themselves. Because of all the hoopla about my appointment, I got in every client office I needed to get to, and they told me what they thought about that work. I would say, when they got to the criticism, 'Those days are gone, we're not going to do that any more. The important part of this meeting is what you and I are going to do together to solve it.'"

On her return, Beers would write long, blunt, critical notes to her colleagues. "I was so well briefed," she recalls matter-of-factly, "that I could speak without a single note on the state of the company. I was a mirror for the agency to look at itself. I absolutely pulled no punches."

Meanwhile, not surprisingly, she also paid a lot of attention to costs and revenues, which required making some tough choices:

There was financial pressure of an unexpected, unprecedented kind, because they had never performed so poorly. Then they had an overseer in the holding company who said, "This is completely unacceptable." In fact, the financial performance of the agency was really dismal. We weren't getting our share of multinational business, but we had all the cost.

We had to retrieve the business we had lost. I called that Operation Win Back, because that was the shortest distance between where we were and new profits. I also made clear that new business was not a priority.

"Win-backs" included Jaguar's entire $12 million U.S. account and—with great fanfare—American Express's $60 million book of business. As Beers later recalled, it was both an unlikely outcome and a natural fit: "The O&M team worked to help

American Express through their crisis only to lose the account. Yet they had talent and knew the brand better than anyone. They really won back the business by sheer brand sophistication, which was one of the first times I began to recognize the power of a long lived brand owner. The core group did the work. My job was to make somebody rethink the option of Ogilvy again."

Even as this critical firefighting was going on, Beers encouraged her colleagues to think about the Ogilvy brand. She led an ad hoc group of company leaders in an effort "to re-invent our beloved agency," with an eye firmly fixed on the future. The group reviewed the firm's options and soon decided to focus on multinational clients. To this end, a new organization was created—worldwide client service—that would provide line responsibility for its accounts with a group called "worldwide client supervisors."

Then, at the end of 1992, Beers introduced the concept of brand stewardship. Based on an audit of clients' brands, rather than an agency-derived creative strategy, Ogilvy sought to uncover the emotional subtleties and nuances by which brands live. The results were the company's first BrandPrints, a trademarked process that focused on four key questions:

- How does the brand make you feel about yourself?

- How do you feel when others see you use this brand?

- What memories or associations does the brand bring to mind?

- What is the significance of this product in the user's life?

Clients—who, not coincidentally, tended to think this way themselves—quickly bought into the BrandPrint concept. The biggest win came in May 1994, when Ogilvy landed the entirety of IBM's worldwide business—an account worth between $400 million and $500 million annually. And in 1995, Ogilvy won the Kodak account in a creative shoot-out, beating archrival BBDO after the latter had resigned its Polaroid account specifically to pitch Kodak.

So what, exactly, did Charlotte Beers do at Ogilvy? It's a fairly astounding list of accomplishments. In a relatively short period of time, she acquired a detailed knowledge of the firm's major client relationships. She developed positive personal relationships with those clients, which, in the short term, provided the foundation for a holding action pattern and some early win-backs. She engaged the firm's leaders in a collective process of developing strategy and then provided energy to drive its implementation.

In short, she accomplished the tasks laid out by Andrews: *6 M* ·

responsibilities

- Owned results ✓

- Built organizational capacities ✓

- Defined near-term objectives and secured commitment to ✓ those objectives

- Defined strategies and (along with her successor, Shelley ✓ Lazarus) defended those strategies against erosion

In fact, Beers turned a headless organization that was hemorrhaging business into a jewel in WPP's crown. The agency reestablished its reputation for excellence, regained its confidence, and at the same time, greatly improved its economics.

And how did Beers pull it off? She had a real command of the substance of the advertising business, an understanding of what it meant to run such a firm, and the toughness to set priorities and follow through.

As noted at the outset of this chapter, just because it's an impossible job doesn't mean that *some* people can't succeed at it.

Outside/Bad:
John Sculley at Apple Computer

Now let's look at another case—a very different kind of story, with very different results.

In 1983, PepsiCo executive John Sculley was lured to Apple Computer by Steve Jobs. His challenge was to bring organization and marketing discipline to complement the skills of Jobs, who, along with Steve Wozniak, had founded the offbeat computer company in the 1970s. Jobs had deep industry knowledge and was considered to be (at least by his admirers within the company) a charismatic leader. But he was young, volatile, and inexperienced, and he clearly lacked the marketing and administrative skills that were needed to take Apple to its next stage of development. Sculley, by contrast, had built a considerable reputation for himself as a hardworking, creative, and highly professional senior manager at Pepsi. To many, including Sculley himself, it appeared that he had been brought in as a sort of regent who would school Jobs in the ways of corporate leadership until Jobs had matured into the CEO position.

It was not to be. Two years later, Jobs and Sculley clashed, and Sculley was made CEO. Jobs departed in a huff, taking several key Apple lieutenants with him.

Sculley knew enough about Apple to understand that he faced a formidable challenge. The IT industry was beginning to experience a fundamental change, which some commentators have called an "ecological shift." In the past, great profits were reaped by companies that could bring to market reliable "closed systems" of hardware and software, such as IBM had made nearly universal in the 1970s. Now, building on Apple's early successes, Intel and Microsoft were in the process of creating a desktop computer market, based on so-called open-source solutions that used their products—that is, Intel microprocessors and Microsoft operating systems—as core modular components of systems that would be assembled by firms as varied as giant IBM and start-up Packard Bell. While the resulting desktops were not as easy to use as the Apple II (or the soon-to-be-introduced Macintosh), Microsoft's DOS and the follow-on Windows operating system proved good enough for the vast majority of consumers—and were produced on a scale that soon made them affordable to vast new legions of users.

Like Beers, Sculley reorganized Apple and improved its products in the first five years of taking over the CEO position. With his prodding, manufacturing became an asset, rather than a bottleneck. Sculley explicitly chose to "preserve the best parts of the unique Apple culture," taking full advantage of his customers' fa-

natical commitment to the Mac.[10] He kept his gross margins high—
in fact, the highest in an industry that was quickly becoming characterized by plunging margins. The results were nothing less than
phenomenal: between 1983 and 1990, Apple's sales and profits went
up by a factor of six.

But behind these seeming triumphs lurked potential disaster.
For all his marketing prowess and careful cultivation of Apple's
bottom line, Sculley never understood the strategic upheaval in
his industry. Apple was an increasingly precious niche product—an
isolated engineering marvel—in an exploding market for "Wintel
PCs" (personal computers based on Windows operating systems
and Intel processors). Eight years after his arrival, Sculley was gone,
and the firm was on the ropes.

Given this outcome, it is easy to criticize Sculley. But the challenge that overwhelmed him was simply an extreme example of
the challenge that often faces CEOs: they have to change the way
their companies create value. Sculley failed to accomplish that at
Apple, and so he had to go.

The metaphor of an ecological shift is a very useful one in
Apple's case. The world in which Sculley was operating was changing radically as changing technology and the evolving strategies of
industry participants dramatically altered the value of company-
specific capabilities. Apple sold an integrated system—all the hardware and all the software—and emphasized the user experience
(elegant, but expensive) that resulted.

Intel and Microsoft took very different paths. Under Andy
Grove's leadership, Intel sold the guts of the computer—"Intel inside," as the clever slogan later phrased it. Grove and his colleagues
were quick to perceive that all the other stuff surrounding the pro-
cessor—the box, keyboard, mouse, printer, and so on—had little
distinctive value and was rapidly being transformed into commodi-
ties. So Intel focused on constantly improving the microprocessor
and then on making and selling it efficiently, performing those
specific tasks with spectacular success.

There was one other notable exception to the commoditi-
zation of high tech: the operating and application systems that

made the hardware useful. Here's where Microsoft came in. Bill Gates understood his ecosystem and sought to co-opt or capture the other participants within it. He kept improving his klunky operating system and provided the necessary tools so that the most creative software designers outside the company could write powerful programs to run on top of Windows. And the advantages of scale proved overwhelming here: developers quickly learned that writing for Windows' installed base—forty times bigger than Apple's installed base—was far more lucrative.

For Apple, higher prices (needed, in part, to sustain R&D over a low sales volume), poor distribution, and minimal third-party development combined to spell huge trouble. Soon even many of the people who loved Apple had to abandon the odd-duck computer maker from Cupertino. (The downward spiral was self-reinforcing, of course.) And in the midst of all this turmoil, John Sculley—a marketer most famous for mounting the "Pepsi generation" campaign for his former employer—was ill prepared to form an independent strategic view about what had to be done at Apple.

In 1992, during a visit to Harvard Business School, Sculley told an audience of MBA students that Apple's board had made a mistake in choosing him. Why? Because, he explained, he did not have the technical background necessary to take a position on the fundamental strategic question right from the start. This illustrates one of the most central problems to solve during succession: most of what a board or an incumbent CEO has available as evidence for assessing a potential new CEO is that individual's track record. But will skill at dealing with the world of the past match up to the challenges of the world that lies ahead? Does experience in one sector have relevance to the demands of another, very different sector?

In retrospect, we can see that Charlotte Beers had the skills needed to help Ogilvy. She had two great advantages: (1) she knew her industry, and (2) her industry still required the same basic set of skills that she had developed over decades of work within it. Neither was true for John Sculley: he was from a different industry, and his new industry was undergoing radical, wrenching changes.

How Sculley might have done better—how he might have succeeded at Apple—is the subject of many a Harvard Business School class. In theory, at least, he might have been able to tap into what Apple's potential markets may have wanted in the future. He had developed highly regarded marketing skills at Pepsi, and these might have served him in the strategic planning and visioning aspects of his new job. Indeed, he did foresee the importance of networking personal computers, the advent of the personal digital assistant, and the lure of Internet-based games.

But to take full advantage of this personal capability, he would have had to engage the talent of technologists who understood and shared his vision as well as the great Apple cult, and who would, in turn, embody both in products that would engage the masses. Impossible? No, just hard. There are compelling examples of nontechnical executives who have done it: Joseph Wilson, the guiding genius behind Xerox, is a leading example; Lou Gerstner, mentioned earlier, is another.

Sadly, however, wooing and winning technologists over to his vision was not one of Sculley's skills. He got better at it, over time, but he didn't get good enough fast enough to save himself. After his departure, Apple continued on its path of strategic irrelevance and chewed its way through two more short-lived CEOs until it was rescued in the mid-1990s by a returning Steve Jobs.

Sculley's case raises important questions about the challenge of engaging a company's talent. The kinds of people who rise to the top ranks of organizations almost always enjoy the use of power. Somewhere in their minds—maybe the back, maybe the front—they entertain the possibility that they might someday be sitting in that corner office, doing the very job that the incumbent CEO is doing today. (Generally, they imagine themselves doing it better, of course.) With the corner-office prospect in mind, they carry out their current responsibilities while also competing with peers—and sometimes even with their leader—for advantage in the battle for succession.

We don't have to look too far back in history to get to a point where political succession was often accomplished through murder, including patricide. Even after succession-by-violence receded from the political stage, sage political leaders acknowledged and played on the siblinglike rivalry among their top lieutenants. Abraham Lincoln, for example, put his most talented rivals in his cabinet—where he could keep an eye on them—and worked diligently to keep them happy while they served him. Nor was he above manipulating their mutual jealousies to serve his own ends.[11]

Similar sorts of intrigue often surround modern corporate succession. Several of the executives close to the throne want the king's job. They live in a state of low-level anxiety, looking for signs that either they or their fellow princes have risen in stature or fallen out of favor.

This, of course, puts another kind of pressure on the CEO/king. Building and managing a team that includes at least some individuals who are (1) aggressive, (2) accomplished, and (3) waiting to take your place requires a Lincolnesque juggling act. Defer too much to the team, and you lose your ability to lead. Demand too much deference from subordinates or dominate them too much, and the best of them are likely to leave, disengage, or develop overly deferential habits. In the end, Sculley was replaced by a number two, Michael Spindler, who was better able to capture the confidence of the Apple organization and the company's board.[12]

Sculley embodies the challenge facing a board that must search for a successor to the CEO in the absence of an articulated succession plan. The new CEO must either have an instinctive understanding of the threats and opportunities posed by developing markets, technology, and competition—or be very, very good at working with the people in the company who do. He or she must have (or quickly develop!) a plan for dealing with the immediate future and for harnessing the talent of the company that is relevant to that envisioned future. Finally, he or she must be prepared to deal with the more distant future, drawing on those inside or outside the company who can help craft and implement a new strategy.

This is what the task of picking leaders is all about. It has a lot to do with judging where the world is headed and, therefore, what will have to be done. And it has everything to do with the ability to identify and engage the talent of those in the company who can see what is truly happening in markets and technology. They are the ones who can think out of the box and work to devise programs of action—building capabilities—that can support strategies that are appropriate for a new time.

There are three elements in this description that deserve our attention. The first is judging where the world is headed. My phrasing here is intentionally vague. I'm *not* talking about forecasting. Gordon Moore, Intel's past chairman and CEO, once told me that he could see three or four generations ahead in the technology of semiconductors. Based on high-tech time, that is a remarkable six years into the future, and it is a rare executive indeed who has that talent. But even that degree of clairvoyance didn't help Moore fully anticipate the impact that the Internet would have on the demand for digital communication and the associated chip technology. Of course, Intel has since responded to the emergence of the Web and has developed a position in the Internet ecosystem, but it enjoys nothing like the dominance it has in desktop computing. "Where the world is headed" has to include judging how demand for capability will develop and how that demand will be met.

Identifying the talent in the company is the second major task. It is not unusual to find the people who understand how the future will likely be different in secondary positions in a company. They are often viewed as lone wolves: derided as mavericks or Pollyannas if they are optimistic, or condemned as Cassandras if they are pessimistic.

Why this skepticism? Healthy organizations (and even some unhealthy ones) have all sorts of reasons to continue to commit resources to programs and activities that profitably serve current customers. Therefore, opportunities that will disrupt those arrangements look very unattractive, and the champions of those new opportunities are met with skepticism. In addition, my own research has led me to realize that operating managers are reluctant to exit from activities that they understand and think of as being part of the franchise. They believe, in their hearts, that a certain product or service is at the very core of their company and, therefore, must be considered sacrosanct.

For these and other reasons, when a CEO sees the need to re-deploy assets to attack new opportunities, there generally are very few managers who leap forward to show how it can be done; there are few who are willing to say what can be cut in order to allow something new to be built. Identifying "the few, the proud, and the brave," as the U.S. Marines used to put it, is critical.

Engaging that talent is the third critical task. An incoming leader who seeks to drive an agenda of change needs plenty of active support, especially from those who are knowledgeable and capable in the new arenas. If the agenda is new, it involves risk. Managers do not readily put their careers on the line unless they respect and like the leader who is making the call. If told that they must participate, they "suck it up" and take directions, but that is not what is needed to embrace and help drive a major change.

These elements of a new CEO's job constitute three key reasons that managers chosen from outside the organization tend to have a hard time with succession. Like Sculley, they may not fully understand where their new world is headed. Also like Sculley, they are very unlikely to know where in the company they can find the talent that shares their vision of what might be. And, finally, if they are able to engage the talent, it is because they have the unusual ability to quickly get strangers to help them develop programs of change.

This line of argument helps explain why those outsiders who *do* succeed often play the role of turnaround artist. It's usually a multistep process that follows one of a small number of pre-dictable patterns. First, the turnaround artist identifies those individuals and activities that don't seem to be part of the future of the company and gets rid of them. Second, he or she then leaves the company, so that an insider can get on with the business of building the future. Alternatively, he or she sells the company to a buyer that has a vision about how the company can grow and the capabilities to achieve it.

It is extremely difficult to point to examples of companies in trouble that are saved as independent entities by turnaround artists—outside CEOs or otherwise—who then go on to grow the company. That is why Lou Gerstner's achievement at IBM is so remarkable. He was able to translate an understanding of what IBM's customers wanted into a program for growth by identifying and engaging those who could make a reality of his vision.

That's all too rare. Much more typical is the work of James Kilts at Gillette. He straightened out the company and then sold it to Procter & Gamble. (This might be described, unkindly, as the "take the money and run" approach.) At the other end of the spectrum—but also typical, unfortunately—is James McNerney at 3M. McNerney was recruited from GE to jump-start 3M. During his tenure, sales were flat, and profits increased only because costs were controlled more stringently. This was a sad fate for a company that was once viewed as one of America's most innovative firms. What is really fascinating is how well McNerney appears to have fit into the CEO job at Boeing—whose industry he knew intimately, having led GE's aircraft engine business before losing the race for succession at that company to Jeff Immelt.

For many observers of business management, myself included, a successful CEO transition is the ultimate test of a CEO's tenure. High grades go to the CEO who leaves the company a better place than he or she found it and then puts it in the hands of an insider who has a good chance of doing the same. With understandable exceptions—exceptions that may have to do with the transition from family ownership, the privatization by a government, or a radical shift in the environment—transition to an outside CEO involves such high risks that it can be thought of as a failure to manage succession. The CEO who presides over such a process, or lack of a process, deserves failing grades.

True, the stock market doesn't always price companies that way. Indeed, the arrival of a well-known outsider, fresh from victories on some other corporate battlefield, may be the occasion for a price surge. But my conclusion remains the same. And if we look at the record of companies that choose outsiders to succeed their CEOs, the data supports my argument: it is risky business.[13]

I discussed these issues with Jack Welch, the celebrated former CEO of GE, who wrote the best-selling memoir *Jack: Straight from the Gut*. Here's how Welch looked at the inside-outside phenomenon: "First of all, if they're coming from outside, the situation is probably pretty bad. And then they don't know the people. Everyone gives me lots of credit, but you can't do this alone. When I took over GE, one-third of the company would do anything for me. They'd climb a mountain. And then there's [the issue of] time. I had twenty years!"[14]

That's how he saw himself. Others in GE were stunned that he was selected. One old hand described him as "young, brash, and the least traditional of the GE executives in the race" for the top job.[15] My late colleague Richard Vancil invited Welch to visit his class each year. As the race for succession at GE developed, the students would discuss whether Welch might become CEO. They always thought he was too young, too candid, and too abrasive. But this unusual man was chosen.

GE is one of the world's most respected companies in part because it invests so heavily in executive development and succession planning. (Many other companies have benefited from those investments; some of GE's ambitious leaders who don't move up move out.) Unfortunately, this intensive focus on inside succession is relatively rare—and it's one of the reasons why I decided to write this book. If outside succession is risky and often fails, and if that failure tends to be very costly, then it makes good sense for us to learn as much as we can about the successful management of succession to an inside candidate.

Inside/Good:
Ron Fromm at Brown Shoe

At this point, it's tempting to devote a few pages to Jack Welch as an illustration of the third category on our typology: an inside candidate who made good. But since most people know at least the fundamentals of Welch's story by now—and many, apparently, are buying his book to learn the details—I'll focus instead on a less-prominent but equally good story: the story of the accession of Ron Fromm to the leadership of the Brown Group in

1999. For me, it holds a special interest because, as chair of the compensation committee, I managed the process for the board and because the story so far has a happy ending.

Brown Shoe was founded in St. Louis in 1878 by George Warren Brown. It rose to be the most powerful force in the U.S. shoe industry, functioning as a vertically integrated firm with tanneries, shoe factories, Kinney Shoes (a powerful retail chain), and more than a thousand independent stores grouped under Wohl Shoe. An antitrust case interrupted this growth, forcing Brown to divest Kinney in 1963 and engage in an unsuccessful attempt to transform itself into a diversified manufacturer of consumer goods and a specialty retailer of shoes and apparel. Recruited to Brown because of the board's experience with him as a McKinsey consultant, Dolph Bridgewater took over the company in 1982. A lawyer with a Harvard Business School MBA, he discovered that a changed world required a new strategy. Remarkably, he liquidated the diversification efforts, dismantled the domestic shoe-manufacturing capability, and sold off the Wohl-branded independent shoe retailers. At the same time, he acquired and developed an overseas sourcing capability and a mass discount retailer of fashion footwear.

While these efforts were ultimately successful and the company remained independent, profitable, and dividend paying, the stock slowly declined from the high thirties to the low teens. At first, I watched the difficult work from the vantage point of a seat on the board, but gradually my own involvement increased. In 1996, I became the chair of the compensation committee and began to discuss succession with Bridgewater, since he would turn sixty-five in 1999.

We began by considering the possible internal candidates. One executive seemed particularly talented. He had joined the company as part of the team that managed the overseas sourcing business that was acquired in the mid-1980s. On more than one occasion, I met with him between board meetings and soon developed an appreciation for his talents.

Because the board was small—only nine members, including the chief executive and chief financial officer—discussions of the compensation committee often were conducted with the full board present. This was always the case in matters pertaining to succession. At a 1998 meeting, we concluded that the man we thought ought to be the successor should be made president so that he could begin the process of being groomed for the job and so that the board could make a better assessment of his capabilities.

During the same period, at dinners the night before board meetings and on-site visits, the board continued its practices of meeting two or three times a year with other executives. I remember in particular meeting Ron Fromm when we visited the Famous Footwear offices in Madison, Wisconsin. Fromm was then the division's chief operating officer. He spoke about the business with a fine-grained, data-based precision that struck me as totally different from almost all the other executives whom I had met in the company.

In early 1998, just as we were organizing the details of the accession of the chosen successor, a series of inventory problems in the international division raised serious questions about our choice. The final resolution of the problems uncovered involved the resignation of that executive.

When we discussed the matter as a board, it seemed clear that we needed to accomplish two objectives. First, we concluded that we did not have an internal candidate ready to take on the job of president, so we would turn to a search firm to develop a list of candidates and help us choose a successor. Second, we needed to put in place an acting president who would be able to provide an understanding of the business for the newcomer and continuity for the rest of the organization. (There was always the chance that our internal choice might develop into an internal candidate.) It turned out that the rest of the board held Ron Fromm in the same high regard as I did, and we brought him down from the Famous Footwear division, where his boss remained the division head, to St. Louis, to take on the presidency of the company.

I was asked by the CEO and the board to chair the external search process and was given a budget. After some discussions outside the company, we settled on a smaller search consultant firm that had special knowledge of the shoe industry. We worked with the owner-president of that firm. The consultant knew the candidates. The CEO knew the company. And the representative of the board worked diligently to keep the process as effective as possible, as we moved from a long list to a shorter one that we discussed with the board, and then to a "short list" list that would, at first, be interviewed by me alone. Working with my reports, the board eventually agreed that we should pursue one very attractive candidate who was serving as a group executive in a company that made unrelated consumer products. I began negotiating the terms of the offer with him, and he began interviewing with board members in St. Louis.

Although Fromm's work as acting president proceeded famously, the process with the external candidate went off the rails. The company offered a package of compensation and bonus that would more than match the candidate's current compensation, as well as stock and retirement credits that would make up for the loss of the executive's holdings at his present employer. But a bitter dispute arose over future long-term incentives. The company was willing to offer what it believed was an excessively rich package that was contingent on performance. The candidate finally accepted that package but insisted that he receive the package if he was asked to leave the company because of inadequate performance.[16] After months of negotiations—made longer by lawyers who billed by the hour—we terminated discussions.

In the fall of 1998, as the smoke cleared in the wake of the negotiation crash, we were pleased to see that Ron Fromm, the acting president, was doing a good job managing those parts of the business with which he had not been familiar. Confronted with the choice of returning to the external search or helping Fromm succeed, we embraced Fromm and the opportunity he presented.

Fromm was elected chairman and CEO of the Brown Group in 1999. From the board's perspective, we went from one superintelligent man of high integrity to another. Whereas the original CEO dressed like a Wall Street patrician, his successor was, heart and soul, from the Upper Midwest. Whereas the original CEO was a director of FMC and Boeing and a member of numerous social clubs, his successor was a "shoe dog" who knew everyone of importance in the industry.

What followed was a remarkable renovation of Brown's core shoe business. Its most well-known brand, Naturalizer, was given a successful face-lift, making it possible to address a younger audience. Other brands were energized, and share improved in department stores. The name of the company was changed from Brown Group back to Brown Shoe. New leadership was recruited for Famous Footwear. In 2003, *Footwear News* named Brown the "Company of the Year." In the following years, new brands were introduced, new management talent recruited into many key positions, and two major acquisitions completed to grow the company's brand position in higher-priced segments of the market.

Operating efficiencies dramatically improved, resulting in higher margins, lower inventories, and much-faster times to market. Fromm recruited an outsider and made her chief operating officer—the first woman executive in a company whose core business was selling shoes to women. The personnel activity was transformed so that it began to look like a talent machine. Fromm and his chief talent officer encouraged the executive leadership team to adopt Jim Collins's *Good to Great* as a template for transforming Brown into a great company.

Brown Shoe has since begun to recapture its position in the market. Wall Street has welcomed the change, and Brown's stock has appreciated more than five times since Fromm became CEO.

We can use Fromm's accomplishments to help emphasize our main points. To begin with, Fromm fulfilled the functions set forth by Ken Andrews, as introduced earlier in this chapter:

- He accepted his inheritance and delivered in the near term on plans made before his own ascension to power.

- He rebuilt his organization, upgrading the organizational capabilities that would make achievement possible in the future.

- He integrated the management team and secured a corporatewide embrace of the organizational vision.

- He began the work of developing a strategy that would ensure the company's profitable future.

To do all this, he drew on his industry knowledge—an intimate understanding of where his world was and where it is headed. He recruited extensively to improve the talent of his management team (most notably, the chief talent officer). And he engaged his organization in the very difficult task of renovating a tired company in a hypercompetitive industry.

Inside/Bad:
Peter Salsbury at Marks & Spencer

Let's look at the final scenario in the inside-outside/good-bad matrix: an inside succession that failed.

The case involves U.K.-based Marks & Spencer. This leading British clothing and food retailer began as a stall operated by a Polish Jewish refugee, Michael Marks, at the Kirkgate Market in the city of Leeds in 1884. The company today comprises some 400 stores throughout the British Isles and another 150 stores worldwide, including 130 franchise stores operating in thirty countries.[17]

Like the three cases we've already looked at in this chapter, this is one that we'll return to at regular intervals throughout the book. But it is worth taking a first look at Marks & Spencer (M&S) now for two reasons. First, the M&S story underscores the importance of the three elements we have begun to focus on—judging where the world is headed, identifying talent, and engaging talent—in the context of an internal search at a company that was once regarded as one of the world's best managed retailers. And, second, its insider clearly lacked the outside perspective that success required.

Sir Richard Greenbury, the chairman and chief executive of M&S, told me that he had begun to seriously consider the challenge of succession in 1992, eight to ten years before he was informally scheduled to retire. The company was managed by a board consisting of twelve inside executives and five nonexecutives. This governing board was established back in 1917 by the Marks and Sieff families. Michael Marks's successors symbolize the tight control once exercised by the founding families over the affairs of the company: the chairmanship passed from Michael Marks to his son Simon Marks (Lord Marks), to Simon's brother-in-law Israel Sieff (Lord Sieff), to Israel's brother Teddy Sieff, to Israel's son Marcus Sieff (Lord Sieff), then to nonfamily member Derek Raynor, and finally, in 1991, to Greenbury.

In our conversation, Greenbury described to me the state of the company at that time:

> As I became chairman, this country was heading toward (or already in) the worst recession for 60 years. That was my priority. I had no illusion. The U.S. economy on which we also depend was also in trouble. But the U.K. was the worst. We didn't know then that Europe would follow into the recession.
>
> Alongside that, we had a credibility problem overseas. Canada was disastrous, and the U.S. was perceived as a mistake . . . The problem posed by Canada and the U.S. was that they cast a cloud in shareholders' eyes on our ability to develop business overseas. Still, the M&S stores and the M&S labels everywhere in the world were very successful except for Canada.
>
> The third problem I considered was at home. The potential in the U.K. to drive the business forward was still there. We were undervaluing that potential. Related to that, our cost base had gotten a bit fat and comfortable. We had put our margins up to cover the cost of new IT systems, and other overheads. I wanted to see if we could bring our costs down so that we could then bring our margins down, and pass the benefit on to our customers.
>
> On top of that, we were not a "turn-around" with a low base. So, the ability to make 10, 12, or 15 percent improvement each year was gone.[18]

Despite these early challenges, Greenbury acquitted himself well in his new role. By 1995, Marks & Spencer was the United Kingdom's most profitable retailer, with profits of £1 billion on sales of £10 billion. In a *Financial Times* poll, M&S's European peers chose M&S as the best managed company in Europe.

But the biggest challenge lay ahead. As Greenbury contemplated succession, he noted that half the executive members of the board were men of his age or very close to it. They, therefore, were not logical candidates to succeed him. His two vice chairmen also presented some succession challenges. Clinton Silver, generally considered to be a brilliant merchant, was retiring that year, at sixty-five. The other, Keith Oates, recently appointed vice chairman and managing director, was the company's CFO. Then fifty-six years old, he had held posts at IBM, Black & Decker, and the Thyssen Bornemisza Museum, and had spent the past twelve years at M&S running the finance group and later, international activities.

Oates evidently saw himself as heir apparent, but Greenbury concluded that it made sense to mount an informal competition to see whether some of the younger merchants might also meet the test of leadership. With that end in mind, he asked the older cohort of the board to retire and moved three other executives up to the rank of managing director along with Oates.

Greenbury believed that Andrew Stone—then fifty-six and the very successful director of women's wear—might be a plausible alternative to Oates. Looking across the remainder of the board, the two outstanding members appeared to be Guy McCracken in food and Peter Salsbury from operations. Both were forty-seven, and Greenbury believed that they would inevitably become managing directors. "So why not elevate them now and give them the pressure that comes from having no one else to turn to when there is a problem?"[19] Several years later, he rotated all but Oates in their assignments so that they would have a broader view of the business. Not long after that, Andrew Stone, by then elevated by Tony Blair to Lord Stone and an active Labor Party peer, clarified the picture somewhat by tendering his resignation.

Then, in the summer and fall of 1999, everything fell apart at once. First, business results turned down for the first time in memory. The Asian financial crisis hurt sales in Hong Kong, and the strong pound turned their European business from a profitable adjunct of the United Kingdom to a losing operation. Operating expenses soared as a consequence of costs associated with a major modernization of the cash-register system. Investment capital became constrained as the result of the acquisition of ten large department stores that had come on the market. (M&S might have bypassed these acquisitions, except that they involved excellent locations.) Finally, sales across the U.K. retail system turned downward.

As the poor results piled up, the London financial markets were further stunned by a leaked letter from Keith Oates to M&S's nonexecutive board members. The letter called for Greenbury's replacement as chief executive by Oates, with Greenbury to remain on as chairman.

In the ensuing months of crisis, Oates resigned, Salsbury was appointed chief executive, and, after it became clear to Greenbury that he could not work with Salsbury, Greenbury resigned. After a search, Luc Vandevelde, a Belgian food retailer, was appointed nonexecutive chairman in February 2000. After seven more months, Salsbury departed, and Vandevelde assumed the chief executive's role as well. While Vandevelde was able to stabilize the turbulent situation, his tenure was not destined to be long. His own choice to succeed him as chief executive was asked to leave, at which point Vandevelde resigned as chairman, and a new team was installed by the spring of 2004. Vandevelde was succeeded by Stuart Rose, who returned to M&S after a significant absence to lead a dramatic recovery.

How could this happen to a company with iconic status and a rock-solid balance sheet, which had just turned in record results? How could this happen when a talented chairman began working on the succession challenge at least eight years in advance of the event?

Obviously, a case this dramatic has many contributing factors. But the mismanagement of succession was central. Let's look at that process through the three lenses described earlier:

- *Judging where the world was headed.* To begin with, the JD5
world of retailing was changing in ways that challenged
the core advantages that M&S enjoyed as the preeminent
provider of high-value clothing and food to a large fraction
of U.K. customers. In clothing, the rise of high-quality
factories in the Far East, principally China, permitted new
competitors to challenge M&S, which moved only slowly
to abandon its U.K. sources. In food, Tesco emerged as a
well-run, vigorous competitor, which lured in customers
with modern stores, low prices, and quality that nearly
matched that of M&S. In the face of stronger competition and slowly rising sales, M&S fought to increase its
earnings by cutting back on features, thereby jeopardizing
its clear position as the leading provider of value in the
market. The vaunted M&S process of incremental improvement could not cope with this fundamental change
in sourcing.

- *Identifying talent.* With the partial exception of Keith   J2a
Oates, every M&S executive director on the board was a
white male who had taken his board seat following a
lifetime career at M&S. (Oates, as noted, had previous
experience elsewhere.) None had more than a limited
exposure overseas (the leader of overseas development had
been one of those asked to retire because he was in Greenbury's cohort). As the succession horse race developed, it
was far from obvious that an executive with the perspective to see where the world was headed and the talent
required to drive M&S into a new market space had a seat
at that table. And whether or not Salsbury was the best of
the candidates, he clearly lacked a sense of what was
needed for M&S to again deliver on its value premise—
the premise that justified its premium place in the market. J2b

- *Engaging talent.* When Peter Salsbury assumed the job of
chief executive, he hired legions of consultants to help him
change the strategy of M&S and modernize its processes.
But it became clear to Vandevelde—after two major

inventory crises—that Salsbury could not engage the talented managers of the organization in implementing his programs. Indeed, close observers believe that many of the most talented midlevel executives of M&S left during Salsbury's tenure as CEO.

bm?

JD 6

Oaks, Acorns, and Succession

So now we arrive at still another set of conclusions. Somehow, a company must be managed so that at least some of the executives who are building and sustaining its current success are also developing the talent needed to lead change, if and when he or she takes on the leadership role. One of the CEOs with whom I discussed this problem put it this way: "Succession is not a phase that you get to late in the game. Management of succession must be at the core of how you manage the company."

I agree. But this is far easier said than done. Sir Martin Jacomb, former chairman of Barclays Bank and a key nonexecutive director of Marks & Spencer during the period just described, provided a trenchant commentary for a BBC story on the crisis. He observed, "Acorns seldom grow in the shadow of great oaks."[20] This crisp assessment of the talent problem points to a more general observation. As noted earlier, a critical challenge facing the leader is the maintenance of a loyal team during periods of prosperity and adversity. But the energy levels, breadth of vision, and raw ambition necessary for success as a leader are not necessarily found in the ranks of those who work closely at the top with a "great oak."

Why did Brown's Fromm succeed when M&S's Salsbury failed? It was helpful that Fromm had worked in Madison, Wisconsin—far from St. Louis, Missouri—running the retail operations of the business. There was no shadow. He could then focus on the core of the business—branded shoes—with a fresh perspective, an outsider's perspective. He concluded that the business was broken and began to fix it. His knowledge of branded shoes permitted him to focus his considerable energy and intellect on the details of how the business was being conducted.

And he brought to that detail his high performance standards. Jack Welch would say that Fromm "raised the bar." Fromm was able to do this because, in addition to his knowledge, he communicated competence and commitment. He met with his people and engaged them in the process of winning. (Reading and discussing *Good to Great* was part of that.) He was everywhere: talking with CEOs of customers and competitors, visiting stores, meeting vendors in China, and, in general, talking with people. Finally, in the past three years he has worked closely with the board building the strategy for the company's longer-term future.

If there was a single weakness that Fromm needed to overcome, it was that his energy, intelligence, and desire to take his message everywhere meant that sometimes he failed to find the time for listening. But here he adopted another interesting tactic. From the start, on the basis of advice from two of his local board members, he began working with a psychological consulting firm based in St. Louis. That firm helped him become a better listener, but it also helped him with his team, providing them with 360 analysis and other tools that let them manage the human side of their business better.

I want to suggest that these are not just stories. There is a strong pattern from which we can learn.

Let's take a closer look at the executives we've discussed in this chapter and compare their attributes along the Inside Outsider lines we have discussed. As suggested in chapter 1, Jack Welch is perhaps the prototypical Inside Outsider. In a book published after most of this one was drafted, ex-GE strategist William Rothschild describes the selection of Welch "as a surprise to many both inside and outside the company."[21] Welch's predecessor, Reg Jones, had the intellectual inclination to take on and change the GE portfolio, but Jones was a gentleman with many connections to old "GE components." "Welch was not part of this culture. He prided himself on being an 'outsider,' even though GE was the only company he had ever worked for."[22]

How can you be an outsider in a place you've always worked for? Consider the CEO profiles we've examined thus far. Welch's education was not traditional for GE—he was a chemical engineer in a company of mechanical and electrical engineers. He worked in the plastics business selling polycarbonate plastic under the brands Lexan and Norell, not turbines or toasters under the GE monogram. He had a Boston accent and stuttered. Rothschild describes Welch as "willing to challenge almost everything, and he made clear that nothing was sacrosanct."[23]

Immelt
also
default
outsider

Welch's successor, Jeff Immelt, has doubled the earnings of GE in his first five years on the job, so even though the stock has not performed, I classify him as a winner. Again, Immelt is a GE lifer. But his defining experience was in medical systems, *not* GE's core, and he is the first CEO in GE's history to come from the sales side of the business. And he is moving the company away from its focus on financial services toward products and services demanded by huge sectors of the twenty-first-century economy.

Ron Fromm and Stuart Rose illustrate the same pattern. They have long experience with the company, but the business experience that made their reputation was not at the core (in Rose's case, it wasn't even in the company). On the other hand, they have deep knowledge of the core—enough to know how to radically change it and lead twenty-first-century markets.

Gerstner and Beers look similar in this light. Of course, they were outsiders. But they had a strategic substantive understanding of what the business needed. From the start, they began to rebuild the core of their companies—even though they were facing financial crises. In other words, they didn't just cut and sell off things or just operate efficiently. They knew enough about what was needed to build and innovate while they were getting finances under control.

What about the insider information that is integral to effecting change? To gain insider knowledge, both Gerstner and Beers took strong remedial action. As I will discuss later in the book, Gerstner brought back a key insider to help him sort out the vast central kingdom of corporate IBM. In a business that is the sum of client relationships, Beers drew on her knowledge and notoriety as a woman to go out and shore up those relationships herself while she was learning about the people and saving "our beloved company." Her power inside came from the outside accomplishments that are prized most highly in her industry.

The contrast with Sculley is instructive. Sculley, by all accounts, was a good manager and a brilliant marketer of Pepsi. He could even see where the personal computer industry was headed in terms of the uses to which machines would be put. Those skills were enough to provide five brilliant years of rapid growth in sales and earnings at Apple. But what Sculley couldn't do was understand the strategy in terms that linked up with the leaders of technology development. He didn't understand until much too late the mortal threat of open architecture. And he never found a capable, trusted insider to guide him through the interstices of the Apple organization.

Luc Vandevelde's problems were very similar to Sculley when viewed this way. He had the generalist retail skills appropriate to the turnaround but lacked a strategic understanding of the M&S value proposition and a knowledge of product that was adequate to judge whether, on a day-by-day basis, the company was delivering on that proposition. Women's clothing isn't high tech, but it's just as strategic.

That brings us to Salsbury. His misfortune was to inherit the M&S CEO mantle at a moment in time when tough, intelligent, inspired leadership blessed by product knowledge was needed. His background provided none of these and, in particular, none of the experience with finance and the media that were necessary at that moment. Nor was he a strategist. I was surprised when he was picked because it seemed to me that while he might be a capable manager, he had none of what was needed. One might say he was a pale version of Greenbury, an acorn that failed to flourish in the shadow of the great oak.

That brings me to a central question, which I'll pick up again in chapter 4: in a company that is doing well, how do you foster Inside Outsiders? Are Welch, Immelt, and Fromm accidents?

inside/outsider

Well, let's look at <u>Sam Palmisano,</u> Lou Gerstner's choice from inside IBM to succeed him. In every one of Palmisano's defining assignments, he was on the side of revolution—personal systems rather than mainframe computers; outsourcing rather than vertical integration; and Linux, the open system, in IBM, the temple of closed systems. So he was an insider, but he made his reputation in those realms of the company that were strategically outside.

Table 2-1 summarizes elements from the biographies of the four executives in our inside-outside/good-bad matrix. (Other

TABLE 2-1

Insider versus outsider attributes: Executives from the main case studies

Name	Insider attributes	Outsider attributes
Charlotte Beers— Ogilvy & Mather*	• Deep knowledge of the advertising business as well as key clients • Took 6 months to learn about Ogilvy through the eyes of its clients	• Successful early career at an industry leader, followed by success as CEO of a regional player • First woman to head the industry's association • First woman CEO of major agency
John Sculley— Apple	• No technical knowledge of key IT question (i.e., closed systems) • An easterner with no relationships with key Silicon Valley engineers	• Outsider with no industry knowledge • Success at Pepsi with aggressive marketing • Strong general management skills
Ron Fromm— Brown Shoe*	• Successful career leading to COO role at Famous Footwear division of Brown • Good operating skills as a retailer, which was known to the CEO, CFO, and board	• Experienced extensive friction between the retailer Famous Footwear (in Madison, WI) and the wholesale and sourcing divisions (in St. Louis, MO) • No experience with manufacturing or corporate finance
Peter Salsbury— M&S	• An M&S lifer • Long career in the company's U.K. store operations • Strong, solid performance	• Limited and unsuccessful experience on the product and merchandising side of the business during the succession process • No overseas assignments

outside leader - good results

outside - was often good

inside - good results

(continued)

TABLE 2-1 *(continued)*

Insider versus outsider attributes: Executives from the main case studies

Name	Insider attributes	Outsider attributes
Luc Vandevelde—M&S	• Inherited an organization that had lost many top insiders during succession • Brought in a strong general manager of branded hard goods as head of operations • Brought in other outsiders for key product roles (many from branded hard goods and electronics)	• Success as CEO of Promode, a French food retailer, which he turned around and sold to Carrefour • A Belgian in the ultimate U.K. company • Brought in an outsider for a key operations role and later promoted him to CEO • Good relations with the City of London (finance)
Stuart Rose—M&S*	• Began his career with M&S • Moved up over 17 years before leaving in frustration • Upon return, had a clear understanding of the value premise and deep product knowledge (especially in apparel) as well as a vigorous understanding of finance	• Left M&S to become CEO of the Burton Group, an apparel company • Joined Argos as CEO, defended it, and then sold it to a raider • Joined Arcadia, turned around the operations, and sold it, becoming wealthy • Brought his CFO and COO with him to M&S

*Strong performer.

(handwritten annotations: "outside — less", "good results")

names we have discussed fit this pattern, as demonstrated in table 2-2).

The success stories are Inside Outsiders or outsiders with a strong understanding of the strategic heart of the business. Problems happen when insiders lack an outside perspective and when outsiders lack critical industry knowledge or the ability to engage those within the company who have it.

While the sample is small, it may well be that the best successor—like the best source of ideas for the future direction of the company—is found on the periphery of the organization or in the cohort a generation below the group that has worked closely with the incumbent.[24] This frames a new challenge: we want an oak to choose something other than a nearby acorn, perhaps

TABLE 2-2

Insider versus outsider attributes: Other key examples

Name*	Insider attributes	Outsider attributes
Jack Welch— GE	• Lifetime GE manager • Very strong track record building the plastics business into a world-class industry leader • Strong record when moved as general manager to other businesses	• Chemical engineer by education in a mechanical/electrical engineering company • Development as a manager in the plastics business (not GE's core) • An abrasive style for a young man in a patrician's company
Jeff Immelt— GE	• Lifetime GE manager • Recruited and recognized as having high potential from the start • Success in a series of increasingly demanding assignments • Tremendous achievement managing rapid and global growth to establish company as a leader	• Defining experience in medical systems (not GE's core) • Strong agenda for change • Growth based on technology and acquisitions during an era of productivity improvement and cost cutting at GE • Sales and marketing skills in a financially oriented company
Lou Gerstner— IBM	• Brought back ex–vice chairman for insider knowledge	• Outsider with deep knowledge as general manager of IBM's largest private IT customer • Experience as CEO of American Express Travel and RJR Nabisco
Sam Palmisano— IBM	• Lifetime IBM manager • Gerstner's choice to restore the inside line of succession	• Came up through personal systems, global services (where he led outsourcing), and enterprise systems (where he led the adoption of Linux)

*All four of these men were strong performers.

even an elm from another part of the forest. That requires a strong understanding of the traits of leadership and a willingness to embrace that Inside Outsider when he or she is found.

In the next chapter, I focus on exactly what the Inside Outsider looks like.

Churchill

THREE

Inside Outsiders

[I was] conscious of a profound source of relief.
I felt as if I was walking with destiny and that
all my past life had been but a preparation
for this hour and this trial.

— WINSTON CHURCHILL, ON BEING NAMED
PRIME MINISTER IN MAY 1940[1]

WINSTON CHURCHILL was the ultimate Inside Outsider. This chapter opens with a brief survey of his life. I've chosen Churchill despite his being a politician because his success as a leader is widely acknowledged and he exemplifies the attributes of an Inside Outsider.

Born into the Marlborough family, he was descended from a long and noble line. His family lived at the center of British life. His father was in Parliament; his mother was a prominent socialite.

He was not an especially good student, and although he went to good schools, he didn't go to the best—Eton, Oxford, Cambridge. He joined the cavalry, got bored, began to study with an energy he had never exhibited at school, and then was off to Cuba to observe the Spanish troops engaged against the Cuban rebels (with a visit to New York along the way).

In Cuba Churchill began the practice of sending dispatches to London newspapers. Later, when he was posted in India and sent to deal with the Afghan revolt, his mother persuaded the *Daily Telegraph* to publish his letters. His bravery, exploits, and connections resulted in prominent assignments to important generals. Eventually, he served as a cavalry officer in Sudan under Lord Kitchener. Returning to London, he ran for Parliament and nearly won. After another exciting tour as soldier-journalist in South Africa, he succeeded in winning a Conservative seat. Four years later, he walked across the aisle to sit with the Liberals.

By 1910, he was home secretary dealing with emergent unions, and by 1911, he was first lord of the admiralty. In that capacity, he oversaw the disastrous Gallipoli operation of World War I and was blamed for the catastrophe.

The defeat led to Churchill's eventual departure from the War Office and the temporary end of his career in Parliament. To finance his activities and his lifestyle, he authored books and articles on the geopolitical state of the world. These publications gave him a voice that was known, if not always appreciated, in the halls of power. By all accounts, however, he was a leader in the key debates of the day, and he had a substantial following. In the early 1920s, Churchill returned to the House of Commons and served as chancellor of the exchequer in the Conservative government that held sway in the postwar years. His conservative economic policies contributed to a painful general strike in 1926 and persuaded many in England (especially those in the labor movement) that he was not to be trusted. Though he kept his seat in Parliament, he left the government in 1929 and was officially out of power for the next decade.

But he continued to write and speak publicly on current issues. In the early 1930s, he proposed remedies to counter the general economic collapse. He decried the rise of fascism, especially in Hitler's Germany. He spoke ever more urgently about the need for Britain to rearm—calls that largely went unheeded, in part because of Churchill's earlier perceived political and military misjudgments. The government of Neville Chamberlain, appalled by the cost of rearming and unimpressed with the threat of Hitler, favored appeasement.

Let me resort for a moment to the language used by Jim Collins in *Good to Great*: Churchill was urging the British people and leaders to "face the brutal facts." They refused to do so. Eventually, after Germany's invasion of Poland, Churchill was named first lord of the admiralty; after Belgium and Holland fell, he was named prime minister.

The rest, as they say, is history—except that we tend to forget what happened right after victory was won. As Churchill put it: "At the outset of this mighty battle, I acquired the chief power of the state, which henceforth I wielded in ever-growing measure for five years and three months of world war, at the end of which time, all our enemies having surrendered unconditionally or being about to do so, I was immediately dismissed by the British electorate from all further conduct of their affairs."[2]

Churchill was "fired" in July 1945, when the British electorate came to believe that his skill set was no longer needed. Churchill—now seen as the embodiment of Tory arrogance—was unseated by Clement Attlee and the Labour Party, who pledged to address the economic concerns of the British people.

This simplified and compressed version of Churchill's life through the end of World War II highlights several important characteristics of the Inside Outsider as a leader.

First, Churchill had a view of what had to be done with the situation he inherited—a view that had been formed from the periphery of power but was informed by considerable knowledge of the inside. Churchill's arguments concerning rearmament were informed by his intimate involvement with the geopolitics of Britain, France, Germany, and the rest of Europe during his childhood, his time in school, and his military service.[3] Beyond his personal experience, he was able to stay informed in the decade when he was out of power because deeply concerned insiders provided him with intelligence. Finally, as one who traveled, read, and gathered intelligence, he took Hitler's autobiographical tract, *Mein Kampf*, seriously and also tracked the German military buildup. Churchill was an outsider, but he was just as well informed as all but one or two insiders.

Second, Churchill's long experience gave him a good understanding of electoral politics, parliamentary maneuverings, and the workings of the government bureaucracy with which he would have to deal. When in power, it didn't take him years, or even months, to learn how the government worked. He knew who had information. He knew what sorts of skills potential appointees possessed. He knew a great deal about the strengths and weaknesses of specific military leaders, even those whom he didn't know personally.

Third, and perhaps most important, Churchill had always wanted to lead. He had studied leaders and honed the skills that he believed were important. He was a master of spoken English. This gave him power in the cabinet, in Parliament, and in his addresses to the people. He could lead. He understood how bureaucracies worked and could bend them to his will without destroying them. He was a masterful diplomat, able to work well with personalities as different as Roosevelt and Stalin. He viewed his ascension as destiny fulfilled—and was thrilled by it.

To reiterate, Churchill possessed four virtues of the great Inside Outsider. When translated into business terms, these are virtues that we should look for in prospective CEOs:

- An extensive, critical understanding of the substantive and political problems facing the company and the consequences of ignoring them

- An equally deep understanding of how the business actually works, including an awareness of the people who, if appropriately motivated, could help change things

- The skill set needed to lead change

- The desire to drive that process

You might well ask, "If Churchill was so good, why did they throw him out so quickly—in fact, immediately after his sweeping victory?"

I'll propose three answers and leave the details to the historians. First, Churchill was bossy, noisy, and in your face, and the terrible struggles of the war made the British people long for both peace and quiet. Second, Churchill stayed focused on foreign policy (the Soviets were establishing the Iron Curtain) while the populace was, literally, hungry and wanted jobs. And finally, he could lead, but his sense of how to get things done was more suited to wartime than peace. Churchill's biographers—even the adulatory ones—do not describe him as a great manager. And, somehow, the voters understood it was time for a manager.

So perhaps instead of the third point in the previous bulleted list (the "skill set needed to lead change"), we should say the "managerial skill set needed to lead change." In other words, the ideal Inside Outsider should be a capable manager in addition to being substantively grounded and plugged in.

Let's look at these last two points—being substantively grounded and plugged in—in greater depth.

Why "Substantively Grounded"? *Chm. 1*

Good leaders don't actually operate their businesses; they delegate the operation to their skilled lieutenants. So why do I argue for an in-depth substantive knowledge? Doesn't knowing the substance of a business prompt leaders to second-guess their lieutenants?

In some cases, unfortunately, the answer is yes. When I was studying resource allocation in a huge diversified petrochemical company, I kept hearing operating managers saying the same thing, almost in identical language: "All the capital budgeting committee wants to know about is whether the tubing will fit under the pipe rack."

This was code, of course, for a bigger problem. The operating managers believed that rather than examining the strategic characteristics of the business for which capital was being requested, members of the board committee responsible for reviewing projects tended to focus on details with which they were familiar from their own years of running operations, now many years in the past. That kind of substantive knowledge—often outdated, by the way—was leading them to review and second-guess detailed decisions, rather than to focus on the strategic and economic premises of the project proposals.

This critique is fair. On occasion, top management may choose to make a point by taking what Jack Welch has called a "deep dive" and pursue a problem all the way down to its roots in operating units. But, in fact, you'll never find that task written up in a CEO's job description. CEOs may want to drill down deep to take a core sample of how their company is running, but they have to be very careful to avoid interfering in operations. And it's worth noting that by Welch's own account, he really did very little deep diving until his major transformation of GE was accomplished.

What's involved in substantive grounding? First is a basic grasp of the company's financials. Reported earnings aside, is the company really making money? Are the earnings commensurate with the capital invested and the risk involved? This may sound elementary, but all the evidence suggests that at many companies, the leaders either (a) are content with mediocre performance or (b) don't know exactly what's going on. Look at table 3-1, which shows that many companies destroy value over significant periods of time.

The second meaning of substantive grounding has to do with the strategic prospects of the business. If the company is growing 20 percent a year but the market is growing 35 percent, then the company is losing share—clearly, a problem for the future. Tracking market share, especially unit market share, is a good way of taking a business's strategic temperature. Knowing why things are the way they are and what can be done to fix them distinguishes the Inside Outsider from the outsider.

This is not necessarily subtle stuff. Consider foreign sourcing. I remember accompanying the CEO of a large domestic company on a visit to assess the work of a small competitor that was importing product from China. The year was 1990. The CEO liked

TABLE 3-1

S&P value destroyers: Loss in market value, 1996–2006

Company	Change (in billions)	Change (%)
Dana Corporation	−2.7	−87
Parametric Technology Corporation	−4.1	−74
Eastman Kodak	−19.4	−74
Goodyear	−5.5	−74
Gateway	−1.9	−73
Hercules Inc.	−4.1	−70
Ford	−25.8	−67
Cooper Tire & Rubber Company	−1.2	−63
General Motors	−22.8	−57
Andrew Corporation	−1.8	−56
Lucent	−13.3	−55
Novell	−2.6	−54
Electronic Data Systems Corporation	−13.7	−52
CenterPoint Energy	−2.5	−40
International Flavors & Fragrances	−2.1	−39
Dillard's	−1.6	−39
Radioshack	−1.0	−33
ADC Telecommunications	−0.9	−31
CA Inc.	−5.4	−31
Tenet Healthcare	−1.3	−29
Dow Jones & Company	−1.2	−29
HCA Inc.	−6.4	−27
Xerox	−4.5	−26
Sara Lee	−3.6	−23
Mattel	−1.4	−18
Coca-Cola	−20.9	−17
AutoNation Inc.	−0.8	−15
DuPont	−6.1	−14
Campbell Soup	−2.2	−13
CMS Energy Corporation	−0.2	−7
Eastman Chemical Company	−0.3	−7
Interpublic Group	−0.2	−4
Tyson Foods	−0.2	−4
Louisiana-Pacific Corporation	−0.1	−3

Source: Standard & Poor's Compustat data, www.standardandpoors.com.

the product he saw but concluded that Chinese factories could never produce fast-moving designed goods in the volume and mix, and within the short time cycles, that he believed were necessary. That judgment was just plain wrong, and it had strategic consequences. As an outside hire, that CEO was blessed with powerful analytic skills, but he knew neither the product nor the sources. Nor did he develop any trusted allies who did understand the lay of the land from an insider's point of view.

Ungrounded at Marks & Spencer and Hewlett-Packard

Another telling example can be found at Marks & Spencer. As noted in chapter 2, an inadequate process of internal succession led the board to appoint Luc Vandevelde CEO in 2001. His background was in food retailing in Belgium and France. It was an odd choice: yes, Marks & Spencer had an important food business, but its most pressing problems at the time were in clothing. While Vandevelde and the team he recruited had experience in retail, most had no experience with clothing. In a company where the value proposition of the brand was all about product, Vandevelde and his team were lacking the essential substantive knowledge.

To be sure, they stopped the financial bleeding. They made a number of very interesting moves and effected a turnaround of sorts. But they failed to solve the company's basic strategic dilemma: customers who came into the stores did not find the clothing particularly compelling. To grow, Marks & Spencer needed a management team that understood both the company and the intricate mechanics of selling clothes at the retail level. Nothing less would turn the tide.

Belatedly arriving at this understanding, the board asked Vandevelde's chosen successor to step down and, in 2004, brought in new management: Stuart Rose. Rose had a management career at Marks & Spencer but had left ten years earlier. After a decade in various leadership roles in the apparel business, he was brought back—an Inside Outsider. He focused on the core business, improved values, and sales began to move. In the two years after his arrival, sales (of clothing, in particular) and profits were up, the share price more than doubled, and Rose was chosen by the *Financial Times* as 2006 "Manager of the Year."

Another example of the outsider who didn't "get it" is Carly Fiorina at Hewlett-Packard. My executive education students from HP have mostly conceded that over the years, the company had developed a kind of corporate sclerosis that needed attention. But what HP really needed, they believed, was pruning—not the spin-off of its instruments business and especially not the acquisition of Compaq. A bit like Apple's John Sculley, Fiorina simply did not have a deep enough grounding in the company's products and their uses to make the strategic decisions she did.

The Manager as Musician

Managers are like musicians. How so? Musicians have a standard repertoire. They can learn new pieces and even new instruments, but it's difficult for them to perform the new pieces as well as the old standards that they have practiced for decades. Managers too have a standard repertoire. In addition, they have a way of getting their arms around the unknown. So if they are smart enough—and if they are given enough time by shareholders and Wall Street—they can figure out how to do new things.

But, as any CEO will tell you, those are a couple of big ifs.

A CEO may grasp that China is important and point his team in that direction. But if the company has never operated in China, the CEO's understanding is intellectual—that is, not grounded in the intimate knowledge of consumer and competitive behavior. Unilever entered China long before its rival Procter & Gamble (P&G), giving it a substantial head start over P&G. But after the death of Mao Tse-tung, P&G reestablished itself under the leadership of a dynamic marketer, in partnership with a leading Chinese partner. Over time, they devoted talent and money to studying the market and developing a strategy that leveraged P&G's capabilities to provide real competitive advantage. The results have been brilliant.

Meanwhile, Unilever made a series of mistakes that sent the company in the other direction. Most significantly, it installed in

China an individual who had made a great success in India. He drew on his repertoire and re-created what had worked in India—which was *not* what was needed to succeed in China.

Think back to the Marks & Spencer example. Vandevelde's team was experienced with the mass retailing of manufacturer-branded goods. They really did not know what was needed to reestablish the Marks & Spencer brand. So they started with improving the core clothing business but quickly added subbrands and other departments. This helped somewhat, but it didn't fix the basic problem. Their repertoire didn't include an appreciation for the power of a great store brand which depended critically on product.

A final example may help make the point. In 2002, the Block-buster division of Viacom was facing serious problems. On a visit to Blockbuster's Dallas headquarters to explore the problem, Viacom CEO Sumner Redstone was told that a fundamental difficulty was keeping the latest movies in stock in the stores. When he inquired why such a basic problem was tolerated, he was told that the stores could not afford to carry enough copies of the new releases because the studios charged too much.

Based on his experience as an owner of one of the largest movie theater chains in the United States, Redstone concluded that this was nonsense. Theaters shared movie revenue with the studios; why shouldn't Blockbuster stores share video revenues instead of buying tapes? The tapes or DVDs cost literally pennies; the stores should have as many as they thought they needed. Redstone went to Hollywood and renegotiated the deal by which stores obtained new releases, and the problem disappeared. What appeared to be an insurmountable obstacle to those without the knowledge—without the relevant repertoire—turned out to be a simple task of negotiation for Redstone.

INSEAD Professor Yves Doz and Mikko Kosonen, who was a senior vice president at Nokia at the time, have studied this phenomenon. Their research in ten high-tech companies focused on the characteristics that enable a company to transform itself as technology changes.[4] On the basis of their extensive interviews, they reached some conclusions that are relevant to our Inside

Outsider discussions. A CEO, Doz and Kosonen concluded, can turn around a floundering company based on professional executive skills, but he or she cannot lead growth without understanding the product.

In some instances—apparel, for example—that means understanding how the product is made, sold, and used. In other instances, including cell phones, the relevant knowledge extends to component technologies. In still other instances, process is key. At Dell, for example, the indispensable knowledge concerns purchasing, assembly, and logistics.[5]

A study of twenty star GE executives who were recruited to be the CEO of other companies has underscored the critical importance of industry or product knowledge.[6] If anyone understands generic business processes, it's probably a senior GE executive, trained for decades at one of the world's great people factories. Nevertheless, the authors of this study concluded, that knowledge is relevant only if it maps to the new environment. If it doesn't, you aren't likely to cut it in your new assignment.

The authors provide several examples that illustrate the point. John Trani moved from GE Medical Systems and GE Plastics—two GE businesses where he enjoyed remarkable success—to the Stanley Works, where he turned in a dismal performance. The evidence suggests that Trani was hired simply because he was one of the best managers at GE.[7] But nothing in his experience prepared him for the challenges of a branded tool business.

The same proved true for Larry Johnston, who moved from GE's home appliance business to Albertson's, the giant food retailer, with poor results. By all accounts, Trani and Johnston are first-class managers, but their knowledge and repertoire just didn't fit the demands of their new situations. This is a brutal challenge for the outsider: their repertoire doesn't fit.

chap 2

Why "Plugged In"?

The second requirement for the ideal Inside Outsider is being plugged in.

Every organization has what I call an "administrative inheritance." Especially in organizations with some scale and history—say, a thousand or more people, a decade or more of operations—there is knowledge that is important to anyone seeking to manage change. At its simplest, administrative inheritance refers to the way things are done: how plans and budgets are prepared and reviewed, how performance is assessed and promotions made, and how compensation and incentives are awarded. Just as important, the administrative inheritance shapes how these things are discussed or not discussed.

The administrative inheritance also comprises relationships, both interpersonal and organizational. Sometimes there are long-standing rivalries between units or their managers. Especially when units are the remnant of an acquisition, these residual frictions can hold great meaning for the managers.

Logically, the administrative inheritance also extends to the reputations of individuals and units. Successes and failures may be alive and well long after their economic consequences have passed. The research department may be regarded—correctly or otherwise—as being committed to a particular technology. As a consequence, its leaders are biased (or are *perceived* to be biased) in favor of anything that advances that technology and opposed to anything that might undercut or replace it. A previous manager may have unsuccessfully used very expensive consultants to introduce a set of processes. Obviously, an individual taking over the helm needs to understand this background before engaging the same consultants or introducing the same set of processes.

More deeply submerged, but still a key part of the administrative inheritance, are factors like family and tribal relationships. Especially in regions outside the United States where family business is still the pervasive form of ownership, familial relationships are critical. Vendor relationships, for example, may be forged or reinforced by marriage. It is worth knowing these things before proposing change.

All these factors contribute to being plugged in—or not plugged in. Of course, they can be learned. But that takes time.

As John Sculley discovered at Apple when he tried to find insiders who could help him make his vision concrete, time is the commodity that you don't always have.

The Plugged-in Insider

An insider who is promoted has an established reputation. She is likely to have a wide constituency of friends and acquaintances that trust and respect her. They will go to considerable lengths to help her succeed because they believe that she's competent, knows what the situation requires, and knows how to get things done. In an HBS case study of her accession to the CEO job, Ann Mulcahy describes how colleagues helped at critical moments after she had taken the helm of Xerox.[8] They provided moral support when times were tough and substantive support in areas where Mulcahy's background was weak. This isn't simply altruistic behavior, of course: these friends and acquaintances have a vested interest in their organization's success. When a talented colleague is promoted, their collective chances of success go up. They expect that the new CEO will continue to manage well, thereby creating a self-fulfilling prophecy—a honeymoon period—as she begins to lead.

The plugged-in insider knows how to work with and through the organization—talents that are critically important when the organization needs to change. The plugged-in insider knows which functional specialists to put on the task force. She knows whose views must be solicited. She knows how to share her own views. She knows how to get help. She can get help even from people who may not agree with the direction in which she's heading because she knows how to make them feel a part of the team.

The Unplugged Outsider

Outsiders start with none of these advantages. Whether or not they have substantive knowledge, they lack knowledge of the administrative inheritance. Especially when they have previously worked in only one company and that company had a strong culture—think IBM or GE, for example—they are likely to assume that this new place will operate somewhat as their old place did. ("After all," they think, "aren't most businesses trying to emulate the best practices of my outstanding former employer?")

But it's not true. The unplugged outsider can't *imagine* how much he or she doesn't know. It's all too easy to miss the subtle clues about what's important here. It's all too easy to discount elements of this new culture that would have been truly unimportant in the organization where the newcomer built their reputation.

A sad perspective on the damage an unplugged outsider can do is provided by the story of the DaimlerChrysler merger. The two companies' administrative practices could not have been more different. Daimler was heavily staffed and relied on position papers; Chrysler, by contrast, tended toward direct communication and more delegation. The Germans took long lunches and worked late. The Americans sometimes pulled all-nighters but generally worked shorter days. The fundamentally conservative Chrysler management took offense when Jürgen Schrempp, Daimler's CEO, drank wine and smoked cigars in his Detroit office.

Some of these differences may appear to be only cosmetic—but, in fact, they led to misunderstandings and failed communication with profound consequences. For years, Daimler has failed to reap the benefits it sought in the Chrysler acquisition, in large part because the two divisions don't trust each other.

Let's conclude this section on a happier note, by looking at the story of Phil Casey, who took over the CEO job at Ameristeel. Recruited away from his position as COO of Birmingham Steel by Ameristeel's Japanese owners, Casey's substantive knowledge was nearly complete. Almost immediately, he made an unplugged mistake—but it turned out to be a mistake that served him well. Upon arriving at Ameristeel's Tampa headquarters, he announced that for health reasons, smoking would no longer be permitted in Ameristeel's offices. What he hadn't thought through, he later confessed, was that the heaviest smokers in the office were the Japanese managers who represented the owners. "Fortunately for me," Casey told me in an interview, "the organization drew the conclusion that control of the company had shifted from Osaka to Tampa."[9] CEO's are on stage with bright lights on. Everything they do is interpreted as having a message. It helps to know the language that will determine the interpretation. This is what I mean by "grounded" and "plugged in."

Have Leadership Skills, Want to Lead

Let's digress briefly to dig a little deeper into the qualities of leaders and leadership.

"It is one thing to feel confident," Winston Churchill once observed, "and it is another to impart that confidence to people who do not like your plan, and who feel the same confidence in their knowledge as you do in yours."[10]

In other words, leadership involves getting people to develop and implement a successful plan, even when they are not sure that your choice is the best. They will act because they are persuaded that working as a group toward your objective is better than continuing to debate.

Note that Churchill does not talk about telling others what to do. He emphasizes the activity of imparting confidence to people who are not sure that your plan is the right one—people who, in fact, have more confidence in their *own* worldview. By the time Churchill took power, the validity of his persistent warnings about Hitler overcame his track record (forged during World War I and the immediate postwar years) of getting things wrong in a big way. True, he still had enemies in many powerful camps—but he was able to impart confidence.

In the military, the chain of command compels soldiers to obey (lawful) orders without question. That's the point of basic training: to break down recruits' innate resistance to the voice of authority. But even in a military organization, persuasion is of paramount importance. Generals persuade privates to put themselves at risk by imparting confidence through the articulation of a compelling vision. When troops have confidence in their leaders' vision, they fight well. When they cease to believe in their leaders, they decline as a fighting force.

Business is different from the military, of course, but some of the key motivators are similar. The business leader, first, must have a vision and, second, must be able to articulate that vision in a compelling way. The leader makes a choice about what is important and communicates it succinctly enough, and with sufficient passion, that others sign on.

Leaders remove clutter and background noise. They highlight what is essential—what needs to come to the foreground—when there are lots of distracting forces at play.

This almost always requires a choice. Choosing what is essential does not mean ignoring complicated information. It does not mean avoiding conflicting counsel. Great leaders are famous for the range of views they consider and the extent to which they engage with and listen to all kinds of people.[11] But at the appropriate time, they choose and then speak with passion. "Diversity in counsel," ancient Persia's Cyrus the Great advised, "and unity in command."

Having made their choice, leaders are tireless in telling their story. They seek out the people who can turn their vision to a reality with plans and programs for concrete action. They talk to them relentlessly, face-to-face, whenever possible. They model the behaviors they seek to instill. In one of my favorite examples of this behavior, a chairman of Marks & Spencer, Marcus Sieff, explained to his board in 1975 why he was spending more time getting to and from the office: he had publicly embraced energy conservation. "It wouldn't do," he told his board, "for the archangel of energy conservation to be pinched for speeding."[12] In the American vernacular, good leaders "walk the talk."

Vision and Translation

Vision helps provide focus for the plans made by operating mangers who understand the substance of product and process. The experience of John Sculley at Apple, described in chapter 2, captures the problems of a leader who could not get his organization to make his vision concrete. Yes, he made a huge success producing and marketing Steve Jobs's Macintosh computer. But he could not devise a clear response to the company's strategic challenges. It took him years to understand that as long as the Apple system was closed, his cost structure would be too high and the menu of application programs too limited.

But there was a deeper problem at work: a failure to connect vision with implementation. Sculley had a compelling vision of networked computers that were wonderfully easy for home and school use. But according to the Apple managers I've interviewed, Sculley never understood how to translate his vision effectively. He made powerful speeches to vast audiences, but he couldn't provide the necessary direction when somebody had to choose which team of engineers got funded. Meanwhile, the outsiders he brought in to help manage the unruly Apple team had trouble disguising their contempt for the long-haired geeks around them.

Having communicated a vision, leaders must hold their direct subordinates accountable, even if accountability means firing key executives. When a CEO chooses to implement a new strategy, he or she may be surprised by the changes in the top management team that flow naturally from that decision. In several instances in which I have served as a consultant, I have asked the CEO whether he understood that the new strategy would require a change in his team. People would leave. Without exception, these have been good teams, so the universal response from the CEOs involved has been polite skepticism.

But people left, nonetheless. In one instance, the leader of a division that had to serve as the key building block for a more in-tegrated approach to the market would not take part in work that would blur or erase the boundaries of his division. (He had to go.) In another instance, a strategy workshop revealed that only one of seven key executives would actually work on the de-velopment of the new strategy. (The other six had to go.)

You Have to Want It

Obviously, then, you have to want to lead. If you're going to let go executives who've become close to you—and who've carried your standard into battle in the past—you have to want to lead. You have to believe passionately in the importance of the challenge. You have to be willing to make sacrifices—and impose sacrifices on others.

Great leaders do just that. Vittorio Merloni relied on a small group of executives who worked with him for two decades to build Merloni Elettrodomestici, from scratch, into a European leader. But once he determined that new leadership was required, he gave up the job of chief executive, and, as chairman, chose a professional CEO who proceeded to eliminate most of that small group of veterans. After what had been several years of slow and unprofitable growth, the firm surged forward, earning record profits in extraordinarily difficult markets. In earlier chapters, I referred to the intellect and passion of business. Great leaders are aggressive. They want it. Baseball managers speak approvingly of the pitcher who wants the ball in tough situations. Great leaders want the ball.

Seeing the Need for Change

Although I have left this attribute of the Inside Outsider—seeing the need for change—for last, it is arguably the most important of all.

Many inside candidates for CEO possess substantive knowledge, are administratively grounded, and want to lead. The problem is that they do not see how much needs to change. That, ironically, is where outsiders have an advantage—although as noted, their ability to turn vision into plans, and plans into outcomes, is constrained by their lack of local knowledge.

Why can't great insiders see what is needed? Part of the answer lies in what they know, the data they gather, and the things that occupy their calendar. To begin with, they are obsessed with execution. There are numerous commitments on which the performance of their organization depends, and, as Ken Andrews points out in one of the passages I quoted in chapter 2, these insiders are responsible for the outcomes, not for the plans. So they use a lot of their time to see how things are doing and to make sure help is there when it is needed.

Because they are focused on execution, they spend a lot of time talking to the people responsible for results: the key managers, suppliers, and customers. That means they are likely to know where things could be done better at the margins—lower costs, improved quality, higher sales. They are very good at calibrating the capabilities of their organization, so they know what kinds of undertakings are likely to be successful. They know how hard it is to do new things: why new technologies aren't likely to be as simple as described; why substituting plastic for glass in an application may take a year, rather than a month; and why the Argentine market is different from the Mexican market, even though Spanish is spoken in both countries. They know why *not* to do a lot of things, and as a result, they have a stellar track record of delivering on their plans.

Let's look again at Vittorio Merloni. When the Berlin Wall came down, he announced to his organization that Europe now stretched from Lisbon to Moscow. Whereas the company had previously sought to build a pan-European company exploiting the rapidly integrating market of the EEC, it would now have to address a more variegated market that was almost twice the size—and it would have to do so quickly.

Whereas most business leaders in the West looked at the nations of the former Soviet Union and saw chaos, Merloni saw customers who had been deprived of good home appliances for their entire lives. Where others saw only crime and corruption, Merloni saw opportunity and could draw on the work that one of his subsidiaries had done in selling factories to the Soviets. Despite all these advantages, it took Merloni nearly a decade to enter the former Soviet bloc as a manufacturer. (It's not that being an insider is easy; it's only easier than being an outsider.) Today, his company commands market shares of over 40 percent in Russia and neighboring countries, and makes good profits.

I have observed Merloni closely over three decades. He sees changes in technology and markets as a mandate to take action.

Sometimes, the process of exploring the new opportunity is costly, and once in a while, it ends in failure. But he learns and almost always gets things right in the end. So today he is the number two appliance manufacturer in Europe, having started dead last in 1975.

5a   *Misunderstanding Drivers of Change*

Another example of a leader who saw the need for change is Alex d'Arbeloff, the founder and former CEO of Teradyne, which is a leading manufacturer of semiconductor test equipment. In 1998, shortly before he gave up the CEO job to an insider, he reached the conclusion that an increasing portion of the innards of the IT industry's products was software. In other words, the beating heart of future technologies would be operating and applications software systems, rather than microprocessors. He thought this trend would limit Teradyne's growth.

To explore this notion, he acquired five small leaders in the emerging field of automatic software testing. He integrated them into a single company called Empirix, recruited a CEO, provided funding, and formed a board to nurture the new venture.

So far, so good. But as the idea took root and Empirix grew and profited, the new leaders of Teradyne concluded that Empirix was a distraction to their business and asked d'Arbeloff to lead a spin-off of the company. Today, Empirix continues its growth and makes its profits as a private company, while Teradyne has struggled on in its highly competitive markets—just as d'Arbeloff predicted it would.

Of course, we can't yet predict the long-term fortunes of Empirix. But note that the insiders who were promoted to take over Teradyne focused on the premise that Empirix "did not fit." Stuck in their existing mind-set, they declined to heed the warnings of the entrepreneur who had built their company in the first place. (Alex d'Arbeloff had a pretty good track record up to that point.) They effectively discounted a radical view of the future, based on a commitment to the present. Being an insider can be difficult, too.

In the past, one way of dealing with a critical or contrarian view was to categorize it as "entrepreneurial." By labeling it this way, you could define it as a set of psychological attributes managers should not reasonably be expected to possess. True entrepreneurs would have it—because they were born that way—and those favored individuals would succeed if they were also good managers.

Well, if that proposition was ever true, today's world has turned it on its head. Great leaders are necessarily critics and contrarians—and if they are good managers, or have the support of good managers, they will succeed. But the world is moving too fast for incremental improvements to sustain success. The chances are that you will have to embrace the equivalent of Empirix in your own context, rather than banish it from the corporate family.

Fear of (or Lack of Interest in) the Unknown 5 b

There is a second reason why leaders sometimes don't see the need for change: they are afraid.

Often they can see ahead well enough to assess the cost of change, but they can't see the benefits. If they ask their colleagues or customers for thoughts on the situation, they are likely to have their negative assessment of net costs and benefits confirmed.

The research of Clark Gilbert on the strategic response to disruptive technology illustrates the point nicely.[13] Gilbert worked with leaders of newspaper groups as they tried to respond to the challenges posed by the Internet. In the United States, 70 percent of revenues generated by newspapers comes from advertising. Half of that comes from classifieds, mostly ads for jobs and cars. But new technologies threatened to change all that.

Initially, some publishing groups saw text over video as an opportunity. They invested some modest resources and discovered that very few people wanted to get their news that way.

What newspaper publishers saw next—the Internet—was a direct threat to their lifeblood. Once they decided the threat of the Internet was real, their reaction was to invest major resources under the leadership of their best people. And what those people did, unfortunately, was to put the newspaper on the Internet. Bob Ingle, publisher of the *San Jose Mercury News*, recalls the sequence: "We lost over $60 million on videotex. We recognized the potential threat in 1978, launched, and didn't change strategy once until 1986 when we shut it down. We learned from the videotex experiment that there really wasn't much of an appetite among readers for an 'electronic' newspaper. But when we launched our websites, we quickly forget the lesson from the first go around."[14]

Even when some of the insiders saw more promising opportunities, their visions were often overwhelmed by the status quo. As Martin Nisenholtz, CEO of the *New York Times'* Internet division, put it: "The month prior to my arrival, I was thinking quite radically about my notions of what this could become . . . I had the notion that the paper could be more than a newspaper on the web. Remember that I had said to the CEO at the time that it made absolutely no sense to replicate the newspaper on the internet. Then I saw the prototype and it was just that."[15]

For a long time, in other words, the operating managers at leading newspapers continued to behave as if the challenge had something to do with news being delivered over the Internet, rather than a total transformation in the way they conducted their business.

Gilbert's findings about company leadership reinforce what psychologists have known about individuals for some time. When we humans perceive an opportunity to do something new, we may well try that new thing out—but in a particular way. We experiment, rather than committing wholeheartedly to the new thing. Not surprisingly, the result of the halfhearted experiment tends to be uninteresting, and we ignore the resulting stimulus. "Every once in a while we may stumble across the truth," Mark Twain observed, "but usually we pick ourselves up and go on as if nothing had happened."

But if we are threatened, psychologists tell us, we react very differently. We really focus, and we use our core repertoire of behaviors to defend ourselves. (If the occasion is vital, a musician does not fool with a new piece.) The challenge, then, is to channel this defensive reaction into a creative experiment. This is our best chance of developing an effective new approach.

As suggested earlier, this goes against human nature, and it is far from easy. But some leaders pull it off. Take Gilbert's example: eventually, some in the newspaper industry saw their situation clearly and began to explore the real opportunity. They turned their online Web sites into fascinating portals that customers began to use in all sorts of ways. While they're still not as aggressive as leading portals they are making progress. Some 45 percent of the revenue growth of the *New York Times* between 2001 and 2005 came from its online operations. Case studies reveal the central role played by *Times* publisher Arthur Sulzberger and Nathan Taylor at the *Boston Globe* in effecting this critical transition. These leaders bypassed their organizations to find new people who could develop the online operation as an opportunity.

In short, if leaders let fear direct their behavior, they can't act forcefully to explore the need for change that they perceive. Not knowing how to proceed can paralyze a manager—but it can also provide a mandate for a leader with a willingness to learn by doing.

The afternoon that I finished writing those preceding paragraphs, I picked up the latest issue of the *Economist* and read a short essay on Procter & Gamble's CEO, A. G. Lafley, whom the magazine described as a "post-modern proctoid."[16] The essay provides a perfect example of the Inside Outsider that I have been describing. The *Economist* noted that Lafley was appointed as CEO after P&G had experienced a particularly disappointing run of years:

> It was a surprising appointment for a company that was a
> byword for conformity . . . Mr. Lafley has been employed by
> P&G for almost all his working life. Such people used to be
> referred to as "proctoids" in a derogatory swipe at the sort
> of organization man that would choose to work for life for a
> large company based in Cincinnati, in the Midwest. But Mr.
> Lafley, if a proctoid, is a different breed from his predecessors.

He was educated at Hamilton College, a liberal arts school in upstate New York. Some time later he got an MBA from Harvard Business School . . . It was all a little too east coast for Cincinnati.

Neither has Mr. Lafley's career at P&G been the traditional one knee-deep in fats and soaps. (The company invented Camay and Pringles and "soap operas.") In the early 1990s he ran P&G's then very limited Asian operation out of Kobe in Japan . . . After that he was put in charge of the worldwide beauty business, and Asia and beauty have since been his cornerstones of his strategy for growth . . .

Perhaps it was Mr. Lafley's unconventional inner proctoid that helped him take the culture of the place in new directions as P&G's business shifted in both products and geography.[17]

From the perspective of 2006, it seems pretty obvious that China and beauty were good directions in which to take a company like P&G at the end of the 1990s. The commoditylike characteristics of laundry detergent are also apparent. But Unilever—a very comparable company—stumbled badly in China, even though it had a head start. And until Dove's recent surge, Unilever had been outdistanced globally in beauty. Lafley's perspective and his substantive expertise, together with his managerial skill and his desire to lead, make him the right example with which to end this chapter.

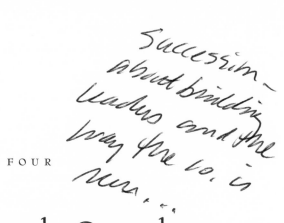

Succession — about building leaders and the way the Co. is run...

FOUR

Building Inside Outsiders

> *Very few organizations have more than one legitimate inside candidate, and an increasing number are caught without anyone properly groomed to take over.*
>
> —TOM NEFF, SPENCER STUART[1]

TOM NEFF IS the top CEO scout at one of the leading American search firms—that is, the consultants to whom the most important U.S. companies turn for help in picking their next CEO. I begin this chapter with Neff's appalling indictment because most people don't understand the scope of the succession problem we face. People tend to assume that most companies have a CEO succession plan in place—whereas, as indicated in chapter 1, something like 60 percent do not.

I also like Neff's quote because it begins to focus us on a process—which he refers to as grooming—that is the necessary preamble to good succession.

Yes, grooming the next generation of leaders is about nuts and bolts. Yes, it sounds a lot like Management 101. But as Neff suggests, these are basics that are all too often ignored.

Why is this happening?

One reason is that in today's hypercompetitive markets, the emphasis in management is on performance. By "performance," of course, management and Wall Street mean "creating shareholder value," which in turn means "pumping the stock price up." There is a pervasive tendency to focus on this particular kind of performance and to link that performance to the performance of the manager. Eighty percent of the human resource managers polled in a recent survey—the same ones who confessed that their company had no CEO succession plans—say that pay is tied to performance in their company.[2]

This isn't exactly misguided—accountability is good—but there's an insidious corollary to this performance emphasis. We "pay for performance." If the person we're paying can't perform, we get rid of him or her and get someone else who can. Dan Ciampa, an author and adviser to executives, says that two out of every five new CEOs are relieved of their jobs within eighteen months.[3]

Inevitably, in this environment, the grooming process gets downplayed, distorted, or thwarted. For many performance-oriented companies, executive development means scrambling to find the managers who can run today's businesses. Many companies count themselves blessed if results are simply "good enough"—and if they are able to keep people in positions to maintain those results. Talent is so scarce that people are used wherever the business needs them, rather than where those people might grow the most and serve the company the best in the future. It is less a process of identifying and developing a cadre of individuals who can lead the company in the future and more a process of throwing logs on the fire. *Keep the numbers respectable!*

Building Inside Outsiders requires far more. It's a little bit like raising children: a complex, frustrating, rewarding process that can only unfold over the long term. It requires enormous investments of money, management time, and patience.

I was told by one of the senior faculty at Harvard Business School in the late 1950s about a research assistant who had attended a meeting at General Motors (GM) chaired by the legendary Alfred P. Sloan Jr. (At that time, GM was far and away the most formidable car company in the world.) In the meeting, the committee approved one executive's proposal for a $10 million plant, which at that time was a huge amount of money.

"Mr. Sloan," observed the researcher, "you must have thought that proposal to be a very good idea."

"No, young man," Sloan reportedly replied. "In fact, I have grave reservations."

"But then why did you approve it?"

"Young man," Sloan said, "you have no idea how expensive it is to develop good general managers."

Building leaders is at the very heart of managing succession; it is part and parcel of how the company is run. How talent is recruited, how the company is organized, how business is planned and measured, how resources are allocated, how managers are evaluated and feedback given: these are the core elements of any management system, and they are the critical activities that build leaders. You can't just outsource the process to HR. Helping great insiders develop an outside perspective is especially hard, and it is necessarily unique to each leader. It requires differentiation, which is usually anathema to HR staffs. In fact, it is a task for general managers that cannot be delegated. General managers can get help, but they can't give up the responsibility.

When I was the faculty head of one of Harvard Business School's general management programs for executives, I would occasionally put my sales hat on and talk to senior executives and their human resource managers about executive development. The specifics of those conversations would vary, but the refrain I'd regularly hear was amazing. It would go something like this: "Oh, yes, Professor Bower; we know Harvard has very good general management programs. But frankly, they take too long, and they only help one person at a time. And anyway, our CEO has close ties to Old State. So we generally run courses there for about forty of our people every year. We're well aware that they're not very good—in fact, Professor Glotz seems to read the same lecture he's read every year for the past ten years running— but they only take two weeks, and we can get a lot of people through them at once." Sure, I'm biased toward Harvard, and I never liked to hear that Old State was winning this particular competition, but what a way to think about this critical task!

Oftentimes, it is these same companies that despair when the time comes for management succession and there are no obvious candidates. "Alex would be great," they say (sometimes with someone like me in the room),"but we never developed his financial and strategic skills."

Quite typical is a succession process that identifies Alex as the best candidate, tests him against an outside candidate, finds him wanting in some significant way, and yet decides to let Alex learn on the job anyway. I call this "blindfolded parking." You back into the space until you hit the car behind you, then you go forward until you hit the car in front of you, and you repeat the process until you're close enough to the curb. It is almost always costly to both the company and the candidate.

Doing a good job of managing succession means managing your company in such a way that people moving up the organization are learning to lead at every step along their way. Obviously, they're being helped to learn different things at different stages in their career. But it's a consistent process of grooming.

Once again we return to a central theme of this book: the way you manage the company is the way you manage succession. That includes how the company deals with independent thinkers. The trick (if that is the appropriate word here) is to recruit a diverse group of talented men and women and then to develop their talents without destroying the creative potential of that diversity. Over time, they will learn to manage effectively in the context of the company's strategy, systems, and culture—in other words, they will become good insiders. But the best of them will also see the potential for radical improvement, and that vision may synch up with a sense among the departing leadership and the board of where the world is headed. Grooming that kind of insider—the one who is blessed with an outside view—should be the fundamental goal of the executive development process.

Framed another way, the goal of a well-managed succession process is to groom Winston Churchill on purpose. That's what GE did when it developed Jack Welch.

The next two chapters work through this idea, but let me go over it once in advance to make it clear where we are headed.

By definition, Inside Outsiders are not run of the mill. But whether a particular skill set is important at the time of succession will have a lot to do with technology, markets, and the world at that time. Had the 1930s developed as a period of peaceful global economic progress, Churchill's talents might well have been irrelevant. So if you are to have *appropriate* Inside Outsiders at the time of succession, you have to have recruited a diverse group of executives.

For Inside Outsiders to develop, those with the intelligence and critical perspective that makes them potentials must be nurtured, not ground down. That means these acorns need to be planted away from the great oaks. And they must get water—they need mentoring.

A key task of the mentor is to recognize when a young executive has the perspective of an outsider. This is precious and needs to be encouraged in constructive ways such as task forces or overseas assignments. When he or she has a difficult boss, the resulting frustrations may have to be "metamanaged" from the sidelines. It's important to learn to work with difficult people, but a company doesn't want to lose its potential stars.

That's very different from sink or swim. In the story I was told about Alfred P. Sloan Jr., he thought the new factory might not do so well. In fact, if he cared for the executive involved, he would have to monitor developments carefully and intervene if necessary, so that the result was problems overcome and lessons learned, not a career ruined.

Coaching can make all the difference in developing Inside Outsiders by helping them think through how to succeed in meeting their targets. If they've got new ideas, they are buying extra chances to fail.

In other words, the uncertainties associated with plans for new ventures are opportunities for teaching; those teaching moments can be destroyed by turning them into negotiations over short-term targets. The heat of budgeting battles is where future leaders develop their essential traits. It is learning how to drive new initiatives forward so that they can amount to quantum change and not merely targets met that makes experience a graduate school of management.

What these simple propositions imply is that if you first start thinking about succession when the time comes to make a move, it's too late. You're stuck with what you've got—or with what you can find outside. Henry Schacht, past CEO of Cummins and chairman of Lucent, noted, "Succession itself is a process—even though a lot of people don't think of it as a process; they think of it as a point in time. But all the successions I have been involved in and have observed over time essentially are processes, and they take place over a much-longer period (if done successfully) than one generally thinks or than external observers might conclude."[4]

The task of this chapter is to describe how the systems of a company can be managed to build leaders, especially leaders with an outside view. With that in mind, we start at the beginning—looking at the nuts and bolts, hopefully without diving too deeply into Management 101.

Who can run our company? How do we use our organization to recruit, develop, evaluate, train, and reevaluate great people? And when we see that independent streak in a manager, how do we help them develop it so that they can sustain what I am calling the outsider perspective?

Recruiting

Building leaders begins with the people you hire. In most cases, people are hired to fill a particular role: sweeping the floor, moving the mail, maintaining the Web site, keeping the books, supervising product design, or whatever. While some of the people hired to fill an open position may eventually rise to important leadership positions, companies don't usually run their recruiting processes with that in mind.

Instead, recruiting typically begins with an analysis of what kinds of capabilities the business needs to fill certain slots. This analysis generally leads to very specific kinds of "content" answers: General Mills needs food chemists; DuPont needs polymer scientists; Nucor needs metallurgical engineers.

But what if at the same time, these companies recruited with long-term leadership in mind? What would they look for in addition to specific technical training?

Several important characteristics need to be considered. These include things like intelligence, originality, perseverance, energy, ability to produce, and integrity. (I leave *charisma* off this list because it's overrated and it's usually associated only with recruitment at the most senior levels.) When your company screens for a food chemist—or your corporate equivalent—do you also screen for these qualities, which are likely to serve your company better over the long run? If not, why not? How do you know such people are not out there if you're not looking for them?

Let's look at two very different examples of companies that have accepted this responsibility: Kenan Systems and GE.

Kenan Sahin, an MIT-trained engineer and teacher, founded a very successful software company, Kenan Systems, in 1982. He insisted that his company recruit for AAWE, which stood for *aptitude, attitude, willingness to learn, and experience* (although the *E* also stood for *extra*, at times). As Sahin saw it, AAWE was the exact reverse of the traditional hiring model: "The traditional employment advertisement starts with experience—'Wanted, individual with ten years' technical experience.' I put experience *last* for technical positions, because the 1980s were technically turbulent years, and knowing something for ten years was irrelevant."[5]

Aptitude came first because Sahin wanted the very smartest people. In his classes at MIT, Sahin saw that the very best students would begin a course knowing very little yet, within a few short months, would be challenging the professor. This helped convince Sahin that, with technology rapidly advancing, aptitude was far more important over the long term than knowledge or experience. To get high-aptitude people, Kenan Systems recruited only at the top-ranked universities and interviewed only students with a 3.5 grade point average or higher.

Attitude was the second criterion. The company sought out individuals with positive can-do attitudes who believed in teamwork and constructive collaboration, while trying to avoid cynics and skeptics. *Willingness to learn* was also key, in part because Sahin knew too many very bright people—even young people—who had lost their curiosity. Finally, *experience*—or something beyond aptitude, attitude, and a willingness to learn—was a bonus, although not necessarily the deciding factor.

A very different view is provided by GE under Jack Welch. Among GE's recruiting mechanisms were long-standing relationships with many U.S. schools, overseen by line managers who usually were alumni themselves. In the 1980s, realizing that it got better results from a particular candidate profile, GE began to reconsider the allocation of its recruiting resources. The company resisted competing against recruiters from Wall Street and consulting firms for the most hunted college and business school graduates, figuring that those interested in a management career would be available to GE later.[6]

Instead, GE drew heavily from state universities and engineering schools located in the Midwest and Southeast. These graduates were bright, well trained, and ambitious, and GE could attract many of the best. In fact, GE believed that the students at the top of these classes were as good as their peers at East Coast schools. They fit well into GE's results-driven culture. GE was able to pick up the talent it had skipped by creating "an elite group responsible for internal consulting projects and corporate initiatives staffed by ex-consultants in transition into management roles."[7]

The Kenan and GE approaches could not be more different, but each represents a careful effort to match recruiting to the need for great people who can manage the company in a way that fits the culture and objectives. What is particularly instructive is that as Jeff Immelt has refocused GE on growth in nonfinancial businesses, the need for innovation has emerged clearly, and recruiting practices have shifted in part to include the sort of talent Kenan Sahin sought when he was active in management. The link between strategy and people could not be closer.

Note that Sahin was seeking brilliant generalists. His head of software development had an MBA rather than a technical degree but grew up in a circle where everyone programmed—much the way guys play football in Texas or Ohio. Sahin had a very diverse team. Welch's GE, in contrast, was looking for a specific type, which I'll sum up as "midwestern engineers."

The comparison of Kenan Systems and GE illustrates the range of issues that need to be considered when designing a recruiting system. For example:

- What kinds of people do we want?

- How much are we willing to pay them?

- How do we think today about tomorrow's needs?

Let's look at each of these questions in some depth.

What Kinds of People Do We Want?

In thinking about the kinds of people wanted, the criteria can vary widely, but they still have some common touchstones. Education is perhaps the most obvious, and easiest, because it involves focusing on certain schools and/or degrees. Educational background reveals not only a candidate's performance at that level but also suggests the kinds of socialization that the candidate will have experienced. How rigorous is the program that this candidate has taken, and how challenging/diverse/stimulating an environment has this candidate been living in for the past several years?

The more you know about the target schools, the better. St. John's College in Maryland has a four-year, all-required curriculum focused on the great books of the Western tradition. And, accord- ing to St. John's Web site, the social life at that college is also dis- tinctive: "Students pursue life outside the classroom with the same passion and intensity that they bring to their studies. Extracurric- ular activities include those found at most colleges: student news- paper, political forum, drama club, and intramural sports; those that reflect the intellectual interests of the students: Hegel reading group, Latin study group, and Plato in April; and special St. John's traditions: the waltz committee, croquet in Annapolis, and a search- and-rescue team in Santa Fe."[8]

An extreme example, perhaps, but an interesting one. A re- cruiter stopping at St. John's expects (or *should* expect) something different than he or she would find at the nearby University of Maryland or the U.S. Naval Academy (down the street).

But the school and the degree tell only a part of the story. There is likely to be a big difference between the top student in the graduating class at an Ivy League school and the valedicto- rian at the City College of New York. If the latter has fought her way up from an underprivileged family situation, she may have more grit, guts, and talent than her more fortunate counterpart. Extracurricular activities may also be telling: experience as the starting quarterback on the football team may imply more entre- preneurial ability than being the right tackle, and we could make similar distinctions in student government, the drama society, and so on.

Outside the United States, other factors may come to bear. There are a number of countries, for example, where despite some degree of democratization, the educational system still serves as a sorting system. In other words, social class and wealth are often associated with entry into the schools that produce a dispropor- tionate percentage of business and government leaders. This is true in France, where the École Polytechnique and École Nationale d'Administration still produce a high percentage of the country's leadership. It is true in the United Kingdom, where Oxford and Cambridge graduates remain dominant. In Japan, many decisions are still made in the "Todai" (University of Tokyo) Club, and the graduates of that University's law school populate the peaks of the national ministries, from which they descend to the tops of many companies.

In countries where the school system has been designed to sort capabilities, these schools represent important passkeys to networks of power and influence. In some countries, private high schools perform this function. The United Kingdom's Eton may be the most obvious, but Groton, Exeter, Andover, and St. Albans in the United States play similar roles.[9]

It is not that a company *must* hire from those pools. They must simply be aware that those pools exist—and that in some countries, in some roles, entrée into those networks is important.

Beyond education—formal and informal—companies have to seek evidence of integrity, intelligence, energy, persistence, and a sense of humor. Sometimes, one can see these qualities in a job application, but usually it takes interviews to reveal them. Many companies are now asking candidates to take psychological tests as part of the entry process, to obtain a more systematic assessment of personality. I confess to having been skeptical of the practice, but there is mounting anecdotal evidence that such tests can be a very useful part of the selection process. Not only that, there's a surprising benefit when you hire for attitude: it's associated with low turnover.

Substantive knowledge and experience may be harder to establish. What does the candidate actually know about products, processes, an industry's practices, or customer behavior? And how much of the performance revealed on a résumé is a product of the team or company in which that individual was embedded, as opposed to the individual's own qualities?

Boris Groysberg has conducted a number of fascinating studies that suggest that the performance of individual stars suffers when they move from a home of stars to a barren organization.[10] The support systems that helped those stars develop turn out to be crutches—admittedly, *wonderful* crutches—on which the stars have come to depend. Similarly, we have also seen top managers move from people factories such as GE to situations where their talents ought to be appropriate, but where the managerial infra-structure is far less developed. Neither their line subordinates nor their staff have the skill sets that they are used to. They find that they literally lack the information and the systems that they have come to regard as necessary for managing.

I liken these frustrated stars to 747 pilots who find themselves in single-engine prop planes without instrumentation and realize that they can't remember how to fly the plane—especially in the tumultuous circumstances that have led them to be hired in that company.

Of course, these observations don't add up to a system for re-cruiting talent. (Every smart company develops its own system.) But I hope that at the very least, they highlight the astounding va-riety that is to be found in the pools in which corporate recruiters fish. A logical starting point is to (1) know what you want and (2) know what kind of place is most likely to provide that resource.

How Much Are We Willing to Pay Them?

What you are willing to pay for recruits must be considered a function of the company strategy, the job, and the market. Large companies build personnel systems based on the markets in which they compete. In effect, if you want to hire a CPA from one of the top three accounting schools, or a master's in electrical engineer-ing from Stanford or Caltech, then you should expect to pay the going rate for an individual in the top, middle, or bottom of the class. (The same is true at other schools, of course.)

Certainly, there are other sources of talent. A security com-pany I know of built its cadres by hiring noncommissioned offi-cers who were retiring from the U.S. Marine Corps. Again, the decision to choose one source of talent over another is largely sit-uation specific. But in the professional world, firms tend to build their company on a foundation of talent that has proved its abil-ity to perform at an outstanding level in the context of a top aca-demic institution. And those firms that are willing to pay top dollar generally get their pick of the litter.

The decision of how much you pay a new hire is more than an issue of money. There are other rewards. The location of the job, the reputation the company has for training and development, and other benefits all factor into the equation. In markets where recruits are free to move toward what seems to be the best opportunity, it is hard to argue with the proposition offered to me by a banker friend: "If you are in a business that depends upon talent and you want to win in that business, then pay the price for the talent or get out of the business."

All this must be cross-correlated with what a company does after the recruit is on board—the subject of our next section. But consider a provocative example of a very specific recruitment and development approach, provided in the *New Yorker*'s July 2005 account of New York's counterterrorism task force under Police Commissioner Raymond W. Kelly.[11] Kelly hired the best talent that had been let go by the returning Bush administration. He took advantage of the city's diversity—and hence the diversity in its police force—to build teams with extensive language skills and cultural diversity. He helped his people build relationships with their peers from around the world—including London, Moscow, Tel Aviv, and Jakarta—so that New York could learn instantly from events everywhere. Compare this with the efforts at the FBI, where language skills are still so inadequate that translation of intercepts languishes and agents often must ask the New York City Police Department for help.

A much-older example comes from the glory days of IBM's dominance in the computer industry. Women were beginning to make their appearance in the company's management and scientific ranks, and a flurry of complaints from women about discriminatory and hostile actions arose. CEO Thomas Watson Jr. sent a sharp letter to his organization in which he explained that the challenges facing IBM were great and that competitive success could only come from the talent of the organization. There was no excuse for not recruiting and promoting the best talent possible, without respect to race or gender. He would personally chase down alleged violations of company policy.

Surely, this forceful stance became known out in the world and made the recruitment of qualified women and minorities easier—and perhaps less expensive, as well. People may not demand top dollar if they are convinced that the work environment that you're providing will be especially congenial.

How Do We Think Today About Tomorrow's Needs?

Let's pause and take stock of where we are in this chapter. We are still at the very front end of the succession process, thinking about the people who may turn up twenty years from now as part of the pool we are considering for the next CEO. What do we know today about the kinds of talent that will be needed tomorrow?

In truth, except for the personal attributes listed earlier, we know very little about what tomorrow will demand from us. What we do know is that it's certain to be something unanticipated. Logically, then, if you want to be prepared for the unexpected, you'd better hedge your bets and have a range of different sorts of people on board. It is at this early stage that you may be hiring the insider who will develop the all-important outsider's perspective.

As suggested by the example of the New York City Police Department, a critical aspect of effective recruiting is respect for diversity. Talent and the ability and willingness to use it come in all shapes and sizes. Organizations that cannot work with all sorts of people simply lose out.

There are two important principles working here. One is scale, pure and simple. Insist on recruiting from a narrow pool, and your odds of finding the smartest and hardest-working folk plummet. Tom Watson made the point forcefully: white males in white shirts were no longer good enough. Companies whose leaders fail to recognize this are less like competitive organizations and more like social clubs.

But there's a second principle at work here that's equally important. It has to do with the impact of heterogeneity on the behavior of groups. Groups where everyone is the same can perform routine operations at a very high standard, especially if the people involved are all brilliant. But research continually reveals that when creativity is required of the group, that group benefits greatly from what one of my colleagues calls "creative abrasion."[12] The members of diverse groups learn from the very different reactions that their colleagues have to the same events. Because they are seeing such events through different lenses, they can come up with new interpretations. Those different lenses increase the odds that someone seeing what everyone else has seen will think what no one else has thought.[13]

In other words, a certain level of discomfort is important if people are going to develop truly new approaches to problems. One of the great teachers at Harvard Business School, C. Roland Christensen, always preached the beneficial effects of what sociologists call "status incongruity" in a group. For Christensen, it was the mixing of the young, the old, and different backgrounds that led to the formation and sustenance of a powerful team. The team members, of course, experienced huge personal growth.

By logical extension, when you're looking for talent, you need to make sure that today's team doesn't frame the recruiting policy so that it selects for team personality, rather than tomorrow's talent. No, you can't ignore the question of fit, but you also have to guard against inbreeding.

And once you've hired all these different kinds of people, you have to ensure that they are given the chance to grow and are evaluated fairly. You may have hired someone with truly original views, but let's face it: organizations have a way of getting people to conform. They exert pressures that can snuff out the spark in a young person. How? Demanding conformity. Giving enough resources to try an idea, but too few for success (enough rope for a hanging). Passive aggression—"great idea"—followed by nothing. Every book about change devotes chapters to these sorts of barriers. A future Inside Outsider has to be nurtured—which sometimes means protected from the wise old hands of the organization. These are the subjects of subsequent sections in this chapter.

Using the Opportunities of Organization

More than a half century ago, Peter Drucker made a series of amazing assertions about managers and management—amazing both for their audacity and prescience. Here's one of my favorites: "An organization's structure must make possible the *training and testing of tomorrow's top managers*. It must give people actual management responsibility in an autonomous position while they are still young enough to acquire new experience. Work as a lieutenant or assistant does not prepare a man for the pressures of making his own decisions . . . Training is not enough. A man must also be tested in his capacity to manage a whole business responsibly."[14]

As usual, Drucker got it right, although today we would broaden the gender base of his assertions. Once you've hired the right people, the next step is placing them in a series of jobs that will help them develop. A company's job assignments, and how planning and budgeting systems cause roles to interact with each other, are the schoolroom in which managers learn. (That's what Sloan was talking about.)

Let's look first at coordination across functions and then at coordination across levels—and explore how each contributes to developing a pool of potential leaders. Then, in a subsequent section, we'll look at planning and budgeting systems: the other half of the schoolroom.

Lateral

Coordination Across Functions   *Org design + not*

Organization is usually discussed as a problem of design: how should analysis of the tasks to be performed by a company lead us to allocate responsibilities, authority, and reporting relationships among a set of jobs?

Organizational specialists provide advice such as "authority should match responsibility" or "decision rights should be aligned with incentives." These writers see organization as architecture that can be used to shape the way managers behave, so that at any point in time, it will add up to coherent activity. Good organization, in this worldview, involves carving up the work of the company so that everything gets done and there is no duplication.

Would that life were this easy! But it isn't, of course. Let's imagine that you could accomplish the impossible and take a perfect snapshot of your organization at a particular instant in time. You then set about assigning bodies to slots in such a way that everything coheres and no one is redundant. Even as you're making those assignments, the organization is changing—as is the context within which it is operating. As every practicing manager knows, nothing is static. Coherence is a chimera. (And, by the way, you'll never get that perfect snapshot in the first place.)

When recruits join an organization, they are given a role to play—salesperson, engineer, financial analyst, and so on. As they master their role, they are given larger responsibilities, usually as functional managers. In some companies, they keep rising up a functional "chimney" until they reach the top—as, for example, when a salesperson becomes the vice president of sales and reports directly to the president. But such a person, as talented as he or she may be, is likely to be peculiarly unprepared for general management responsibilities.

Organizations that care about developing their people move those people laterally, as well as vertically. Thus, a sales manager will work with different products and in different geographic regions. One might start as a salesperson for a product line in a U.S. territory, become sales manager of that territory, then sales manager in a large region in a different part of the country, then vice president sales in a small foreign organization, and only then general manager of that product group. After that, the person might move to other general management positions.

But it is important, in this process of moving around, that a person stay in a position long enough to be held accountable for the results of his or her decisions—whatever that length of time might be in those particular circumstances. As a rule, it's also important to stay with a business for perhaps five to ten years, so that you can develop true substantive expertise—that is, real mastery. The domain knowledge may or may not be valuable. What is valuable is knowing the difference between resolving a problem and surfing over it, between managing when you understand the substance and when you don't.

The basic general management problem of organization is captured by an adage from political science known as Myles's Law: "Where you stand depends on where you sit." In other words, as soon as individuals are given a task and know how they will be measured, they come to see the world through that lens. That means that as you change the way the company is organized, you change the information you have, as well as the way people think.

The first lesson is that Myles's Law applies to the people you are managing. The second lesson is that it applies to you.

To illustrate the point, let's look at a business that's very simple but complex enough to have both manufacturing and sales organizations. I once worked with a company that had a factory in the hills of North Carolina that manufactured garments for fashion-conscious consumers in New York City, where the company's sales force resided. In the factory, workers and managers were well aware that long runs made for lower costs and higher quality. (Quick changeovers cost setup time and increased the risk of mistakes.)

Meanwhile, the market for particular items in particular colors was extremely short—often no more than a few weeks. The sales force in Manhattan needed to give their customers product when those customers wanted it, not when it was convenient for North Carolina to make it.

As it stood, there was no organizational design to link the two groups. Each knew a different set of facts to be true, and both were right. Not only that, the manufacturing personnel and the sales force were from different cultures.

An organizational economist might have argued that the right payment system—say, linking the compensation of both the factory and the sales organization to the profit on their lines—would have helped integrate the two arms of the business. Clearly, that sort of adjustment can start to move things in the right direction. But what one savvy general manager chose to do was have a key set of workers from North Carolina spend a week in Manhattan, watching the frenetic activity in the sales room, and learning in rich detail what happened when an important customer needed to respond to a shift in fashion and the factory couldn't—or wouldn't—help them.

In turn, salespeople were sent to North Carolina to experience what happened when the factory was "jerked around" by wildly shifting orders. Armed with that information, the groups worked out a flexible system for communicating priorities and problems that allowed some kind of cooperative trading of costs and benefits, which, in turn, improved profitability dramatically. How they were paid could have been a barrier to that solution, but removing that barrier would not have provided the understanding that was gained from reciprocal visits.

This solution was based on the general manager's understanding that sales and manufacturing would inevitably see the same set of facts differently. A new organizational design wasn't needed and, in fact, might have been very counterproductive. The trick was to get each group to understand that there was another perspective and that both groups would have to participate to really resolve the problem.

Future leaders need to learn that each of the operations that contribute to the business they run has a perspective. If run with skill, each has a repertoire of specialized practices that are constantly under review and being upgraded.

And they need to learn that just doing well today and improving tomorrow is hard work. Organization is all about getting those specialists to do their job well, and learning how to coordinate and integrate their activities with other specialists, so that the business runs smoothly and can respond and improve as the environment shifts. That requires acknowledging and respecting other perspectives and trusting those who hold them to do their jobs. Building those relationships is what is meant by "team building," and general managers earn their keep by doing it well.

Learning the need for teams and their value is part of developing as a general manager. Learning that the team will only really function if its members understand the reality of their counterpart's world is another crucial lesson. "Developing the leadership pool" means giving managers assignments through which they can learn and then helping to make sure (often through coaching) that they make the best they can of the opportunity—and giving them resources to do what they think is needed, even if you are not sure they are right.

A word should be said here for mentoring. A lot of the learning described in the previous paragraphs is situational. A problem arises in a particular situation; you try to solve it; you don't do it very well. A mentor observes the failure and provides immediate, specific, constructive advice—or responds with advice when you call to describe the screw-up. One-on-one, informal discussion that provides useful feedback is invaluable to the development of leaders.

Coaching / Mentoring

Coordination Across Levels   *vertical*

An equally important organizational lesson, and one that usually comes later in a career, has to do with coordination across levels—from functions, to business units, to the company. In the following example of Myles's Law—also from the apparel industry—a business unit and corporate clearly sit and stand in different places.

The manager of Marks & Spencer's Per Una joint venture, which sold up-to-date fashion to young women, knew that some customers might try to return items after wearing them once or twice. Ethics aside, returns are a problem because fashion goods quickly become obsolete. To avoid unacceptable markdowns, a strict policy on returns would have to be enforced.

On the other hand, all Marks & Spencer store employees knew that allowing unrestricted returns was a core operating principle of the larger company. Marks & Spencer had a decades-long tradition of trusting their customers—a tradition that had come to be part of the store brand. Was the brand to be put at risk because of a peripheral new venture?

Both groups—the parent company and the joint venture—were correct in their respective viewpoints. But Per Una and the store managers needed to learn that there are always at least two logics: organization and strategy. Each would imply a different solution. Reconciling those two logics would be a huge development experience. Only a corporate decision could balance the competing costs and benefits against long-term strategic objectives.

The same kind of problem developed at medical-device maker Medtronic, when Asian country managers asked for a low-cost "basic" pacemaker. The pacemaker division's engineers refused to develop a pacemaker that they considered to be inferior by definition. ("Would you want one in *your* chest?" was the unspoken question.) This sequence is almost universal when country units based in developing markets seek what they consider to be appropriate innovation from laboratories based in the United States and Europe. A now-significant body of research has documented the need for companies to innovate in ways that their operating units believe involves producing inferior products.[15] Once again, for better or worse, there is no organizational design—no magic bullet—that avoids the problem.

In these early leadership assignments, you can begin to observe how the individual approaches the role. Some young leaders will produce excellent results but will do so by really beating up on people. Yes, they use the talent they have been given, but they squander it, rather than helping it develop. Others, by contrast, produce excellent results and even do something extra—for example, new products or programs begin to emerge. The business unit strategy is transformed, so that there are broader opportunities than were previously imagined. The people in the unit become energized and demonstrate new skills. Wherever that kind of leader emerges, he or she needs to be flagged for special investment. Why? Because these rare abilities—to make new things happen and help people grow—are at the heart of the CEO's job. Finding them in a young person is like finding a gifted pitcher on a high school baseball team: it's a rare commodity and one worth taking note of.

Mentors can do something here that is critical for nurturing the outsider dimension. When a mentor hears or sees something new—something that doesn't fit within the normal confines of the organization, but that for some reason really engages the interest of a young manager—the mentor should encourage some exploration: Why don't you study that? Why don't you see if Sue in Division X, or John at Customer Y, has thought about that? If you think that is really going to happen, why don't you see if there's a seminar at MIT or an academic conference that explores that idea? In fact, the ability to turn out-of-the-box ideas into new businesses can be learned, and the right mentor can make a huge difference in that learning process.

Learning how to manage so that a company operates and innovates well is another lesson at the core of career development. Managers learn first how to operate within the confines of an organization but then must learn how to fine-tune an organization so that it functions better in a particular business context. And they have to learn when a context must simply be abandoned because it is obsolete. Their superiors, who are responsible for their development, must look beyond the results—which, of course, are a vital indication of capability—to see whether these managers have the instinct for how things can be changed in ways that improve operations and enable growth.

One executive who worked at Kenan Systems in the midst of the technology boom and stock frenzy of the 1990s explained why he chose to be there, despite the fact that this particular high-tech firm handed out no stock options: "Working here gave me a fantastic opportunity to learn and grow. Where else could I be VP of marketing of a firm this big and successful? The company constantly asked me to do new things that made me develop new capabilities that were of great value to me as a manager. And [CEO Kenan Sahin] would always take time to talk with me about my work and help me to do it better."[16]

Firms that use job assignments as a way of helping their executives grow often gain a reputation that attracts talented young managers. As long as their compensation is not unreasonably low, they choose to join because they know that their value in the market for executive talent will grow in ways that provide them more long-term value than stock options. And it's fun!

These companies become known as "people factories." They do better at recruiting. And, ultimately, they do better at managing succession.

Getting Development into Your Processes

We've seen how important roles are to development, both across functions and across organizational levels. Now let's look at the processes that connect those roles, especially the planning and budgeting processes that link individual units with corporate, and see why and how these processes are crucial. If managed well, they provide wonderful opportunities for learning. They are at the heart of the resource allocation process because they involve trade-offs between the short and the long term and require managers to back judgment with commitment.

These are critical lessons for a future leader. But in order for them to take place, two prerequisites must be met.

Two Prerequisites

First, the processes by which the business is studied, problems are shared, uncomfortable solutions are considered, and targets are agreed on all must be open. This sounds like a naive proposition, but I have become persuaded that in business much less needs to be confidential than general practice would imply. Secret deliberations are not very instructive. Worse, the results of those deliberations are inevitably given political interpretations by the troops. And worse yet, secrecy very often is a convenient mask for sloppy process and sloppy thinking.

Second, the planning process has to be seen explicitly through the developmental lens. The managers reviewing plans have to ask, "Can we make this plan work not just for the company but also for the individuals involved?" If these two criteria are met, then the succession process—and the company—are greatly improved.

Making Planning a Developmental Experience

At the risk of dipping down into Management 101, let's look at the planning process in a little more depth.

In many companies—I'm tempted to say *most* companies—business unit plans that are submitted to corporate for approval represent little more than an expression of the reasonable hopes of those who prepared them. For all the studies that are conducted, these plans are one-year extensions of what happened the previous year, modified to take account of what managers think might actually happen in the marketplace. Because business unit leaders are well aware that actual results will be compared to the plans, both revenue estimates and costs include some wiggle room to accommodate for things that might go wrong.

Now, unless something very unusual is going on, the sum of business unit projections are very likely to be lower than the sales and earning expectations of the company's leaders (and, by extension, its shareholders). As a result, there is a negotiation over "the numbers," with corporate pushing for more and the business unit pushing for less.

Not infrequently, the outcome falls halfway in between. Jack Welch once described this process to me: "There are a bunch of people with suits in the room. One group says two; the other says four. The outcome is three. None of the people who have to make the numbers happen are in the room. They may not even know about the meeting."[17]

What happens at the end of the year depends on the company. In one version, the managers who make their numbers get a bonus. Those who do not may get a lesser bonus, reflecting their excellent work under difficult conditions.

This may seem like unprofessional management, but it's actually quite benign compared to other patterns of planning that I have observed. For example, there are companies in which planning begins with the establishment of earnings targets at the corporate level. Corporate management then parcels out fractions of these targets to serve as objectives for the business units. These are what the business managers are asked to achieve through their plans—no matter whether the targets represent easily achievable goals or virtual impossibilities. Again, the consequences of meeting or missing targets can be benign or severe.

This kind of behavior poses several problems. First, the communication is dishonest. Managers are not sharing what they really believe about the business. And rewards are not really tied to management performance. Instead, they reflect the outcome of the business, which, in fact, may have performed either well above or well below its true capabilities.

Second, this variety of managing for performance breeds the worst sort of cynicism. At Enron, management performance was assessed in a forum consisting of top executives from the company's several business units. Incentive compensation amounting to as much as 200 percent of base salary was awarded based on a forced ranking across units. On an individual level, millions of dollars could be at stake. Because performance was measured on the present value of deals stretching many years into the future, there was a huge incentive to be optimistic in the forecasts of future revenues that provided the basis for current reported earnings, as well as for current incentive compensation.[18]

It is not surprising that this turbocharged atmosphere led to optimistic projections of earnings! And since your ranking depended in part on how hard your boss fought for your ranking in these cross-unit sessions, it is not surprising that individuals were willing to project whatever their bosses requested.

Using and Abusing Strategy

Bad communication and rampant cynicism won't help you grow leaders. The problem is greatly compounded when strategic issues arise in discussions between business units and corporate managers. In one scenario, corporate asks the business unit to accept risk inappropriately. In another, corporate imposes its timetable and wishes in place of the business judgments of unit managers.

In one instance that I observed decades ago, a senior executive at Xerox was discussing with a group manager the prospects for developing a small copier, code-named Project Alpha. He asked what the manager thought should be done. The manager said the payoff was high and important, but the risks were also great.

"What are the odds that Alpha will succeed?"

"Fifty-fifty."

"It's your decision. What do you recommend?"

The *gulp* was almost audible. "I think we should try it."

When Project Alpha failed, the group manager was fired. Why? He told me to go ahead," explained the senior executive in a later interview, "and he was wrong." It was not too long before the pace of innovation in the copier business slowed to a crawl.[19]

In another instance—this time at Hewlett Packard—a new product was proposed by a business unit. HP's top management embraced it passionately, seeing it as the answer to slow growth and declining market share in that business. In the planning process, the unit was asked to substantially raise its business forecasts so that success would also represent a quick strategic turnaround of the business. The steps taken to enlarge the market for the product involved establishing a much-expanded set of product specifications—which ultimately doomed the project.[20]

Line managers will readily recognize these two stories as all too typical. In the first, the risk of an important project is imposed on a lonely manager who, in fact, is really *not* recommending that the company take the risk. He is trying to communicate uncertainty. But when business risk and career risk are tied together—one to one—companies often find that they are taking only very small risks, or no risks at all.

In the second, the imposition of corporate hopes for a large business on a truly new product can doom the project by denying it the time to find an appropriate market where it can grow and develop.[21]

So why this detour into planning and strategy issues? Because from the point of view of management development, these are all examples of decision making where planning took the form of a negotiation about targeted outcomes, rather than a discussion of what the business might be. The development dimension was ignored.

For the latter to happen, the superior who is dealing with a subordinate manager about a budget or plan needs to think about both that manager and his or her business. It's not a question of letting the manager off the hook. Ultimately, a commitment must be extracted. But it is a question of using that moment to do some teaching. And to teach, you have to prepare. Is this the individual's first general management assignment? If so, then the odds are good that the manager will not have been careful enough in calibrating the judgments of those functional managers and specialists who contributed to the plan and whose expertise lies outside that manager's competence. You can imagine the questions you could ask that would illuminate that set of possible problems for the manager.

If the manager is new to the business, it is unlikely that he or she will know the rules of the market, the peculiarities of customers, or the competitive precedents that guide behavior. How this situation is handled determines how the organization works, not the lines on the chart or the "decision rights." Again, this is a developmental opportunity—a "teachable moment," in the jargon.

These moments are critical for the future of Inside Outsiders. If they are trying something new, for their reputation to blossom they need to succeed. For success to happen, they need to manage expectations and the nature of their commitment. They have to avoid over-promising while still fighting for the resources they need. Again, this is a teachable moment. And, again, they may need help—or even direct intervention—to overcome the natural resistance of the organization or the politically motivated obstacles of individuals.

Executives up the ladder have a terrible tendency to think that newly installed general managers ought to have the capabilities necessary for the job, regardless of their background. They have the title, right? But what would happen if a violinist were asked to play the clarinetist's part? What would happen if the tenor who prepared *Rigoletto* were asked to perform *Tosca* instead? Maybe moving from one division to head up another doesn't seem quite that bad, but it can be a baffling and frustrating experience. It is amazing the things a person may not know about a business. The general manager's superiors need to understand that individual's weaknesses and design a series of interactions that will help him or her succeed.

Imagine a manager whose first leadership assignments come in the context of a rapidly growing division. This manager succeeds at every step and shows signs of being a true leader. But how much of that individual success grows out of the division's success? Can this manager deal with a turnaround situation?

Sink or Swim?

Let's put our imaginary hot prospect in a new job: as head of a struggling division. Here, he or she faces totally new problems: a large customer making unreasonable demands, a competitor initiating a price war, or whatever. Not surprisingly, our up-and-coming manager starts to flounder.

What's the responsibility of senior management in this case? One approach is the sink-or-swim model: sit back and let the manager attempt to deal with the problems on his or her own. And, in some cases, this may make sense. But in other cases—I'd say *many more cases*—it makes more sense to lend a hand. For example, is some sort of mentoring or coaching appropriate? Analogies between business and sports are always risky, but is this young star only a tweak or two away from having the perfect swing or the overpowering fastball? Is it a matter of pushing them to reach deep inside, so that they'll work harder than they could imagine? Most young managers with innate talents can be helped to manage a new set of challenges; senior management simply has to acknowledge that it has a supporting role to play, and then it must play that role.

And, of course, none of this happens in a vacuum. Companies that want to be people factories need to think about the assignments that are opening and the managers who are developing across the entire company. What kind of talent does this business need? What kind of assignment does Sally or Bill need? At any given moment in time, the needs of the business will probably take priority. But, over time, the development needs of the talent must also be met, or the business will run down. A. G. Lafley summarizes the thinking at Procter & Gamble:

> Every step of the way, P&G works a disciplined talent growth and development process. We are constantly seeking leaders. We hire individuals on the basis of their leadership. We give them assignments to develop and grow as leaders. We assess their leadership in annual performance reviews. Leadership is a critical criterion for top development talent.
>
> The process of identifying top development talent waterfalls all the way down in the company. At every level, we are continuously identifying top development potential. We are looking for the top 10–20 percent in every business and in every function.
>
> I have three global leadership council meetings per year, and leadership is one of the most important agenda items at every meeting. The talent review is as important as the business review and the review of critical strategic issues. All P&G top leaders are involved in the discussion. In those top development reviews, we look at top development managers all the way down to middle-management levels. We include presidents and general managers who run businesses, the director level of management, and emerging top talent that feeds the director level. In total, this includes the top three thousand people in the company.[22]

And this is not just a process for megafirms with tens of billions in revenue. At one $2 billion company on whose board I sit, we have a room configured so that the management organization of each of our businesses can be arrayed around the walls. The potential and performance of each manager is on a card attached to the wall with magnets so it can be moved around. Rankings are color coded to identify those people who are ready to move and those who are not performing. Where business units have large numbers of people who are ready to move, the fact is immediately visible. Conversely, an abundance of a certain color in one division highlights that business as a problem area.

The room provides the venue for extensive reviews of the talent that is available and the talent that is still needed—reviews that have played a critical part in improving the performance of the company along standard business metrics. But there has been an ancillary benefit of this talent war room, as well. A group of businesses that in the past has been seen as quite separate is now understood to be part of one management organization. It's not just dollars that have to be deployed most effectively and efficiently for the good of the organization; it's also leaders.

Evaluation and Feedback

The ways in which companies evaluate the candidates for succession is at the heart of chapter 5, but we discuss evaluation and feedback here briefly because a firm's reputation for providing useful feedback for its executives helps materially in recruiting the kinds of executives that might one day be effective leaders. It is also the heart of the process of differentiating between those who will do a good job managing the business and those who have the potential to become senior executives.

Consider what Harvard MBAs are encouraged to reflect on when they begin to plan their job search. First, they're asked to think about what job will help them successfully fulfill their vision for their career:

- What do you need to learn and experience to be the person selected to fill the work role at the heart of your five- to seven-year vision?

- Where will you best learn and experience these things?

Then they're asked to contemplate how they'll learn from their experiences at their first post-MBA job, considering questions like these:

- How does a pro handle the day-to-day reality of making business happen?

- How are business objectives actually accomplished within the context of a larger organization?

- How do you work successfully with a wide variety of people with varying motivations?

The advice focuses on what these students will be able to learn from the jobs in order to progress toward their career objectives. In other words, the career counselor is helping them understand that their learning is going to have to continue if they will achieve the kinds of ambitious goals they have and that it is vital to consider how their first job will help them learn.

To put the point in the extreme—and as I noted at the beginning of the chapter—there are firms that boast that they pay for performance. Meet your bottom-line objectives, and you will be rewarded and promoted. Fail to meet those objectives, and you're gone. And, by the way, next year's objectives will be more demanding.

You could summarize this approach as "test tube development." Put a manager in a test tube, turn up the heat, and see what you get. If you don't get what you want, get another manager, and heat up another test tube.

In contrast are the firms that work hard to train their executives so that they will be effective—first as doers, salespersons, engineers, or controllers; then as functional managers; and then as general managers leading businesses. To accomplish this training, they usually make use of company and outside programs.

As I write this chapter, GE is the people factory par excellence. Not only does GE use its extensive program to develop managers and leaders, but it also uses the availability of these resources as a recruiting tool. It's illuminating to wander through the GE Web site and look at the range of functional, business-oriented, and corporate-level offerings that GE makes available.[22] "Part of GE's appeal," begins one page, "is the attraction of lifelong learning. We invest nearly $1 billion a year in career

Feedback + evaluation

development for our employees at every level of professional growth."[24]

GE is hardly alone. All the great people factories train for the functional and management skills they need. But they also invest heavily in individual feedback as part of an annual process of planning and evaluation, and, even more important, they provide hands-on coaching in response to observation of day-to-day activity. It is one thing to learn at the end of the year that your colleagues think that you're an unpleasant person to work with. That helps a little bit (and probably hurts a lot). But it's far more helpful to be asked immediately after a meeting if you've thought about the consequences of the aggressive way that you've just presented your idea. And it is still more helpful if the question is followed with discussion of other more effective ways of introducing ideas. Of course, not all managers can provide skillful coaching—even in the people factories—but many do, and they are valued for that skill. They are builders.

I want to close this section with one more observation from the recruit's point of view: potential recruits may make more money at the first sort of firm—that is, the one that puts heat under test tubes. But in the longer term, even if that person stays for years and rises high in the hierarchy, the chances of getting the feedback needed to develop the mix of skills and attitudes that make him or her a great leader are slight.

Training

For someone who has been teaching at Harvard Business School for more than forty years, training is a dangerous subject—rife with strongly held personal opinions—so I'll keep it short and sweet. We can help people succeed—in part, by giving them concepts and tools that are relevant to their jobs and values that help them lead.

If they are selling, for example, we can video them and show them how they are presenting themselves to the world. We can teach them to listen to what the customer wants to buy before trying to sell them what they have to offer. If they are managing, we can teach them to plan, prioritize, budget, and listen to and observe their people.

When they get to the general management level, we can help them to see that their job is not telling people what to do but instead setting objectives, raising the bar, and providing the necessary information and resources (human, material, financial, etc.). We can have them meet as a group in order to learn about the talent in their sister divisions.

Even CEOs can learn—any evidence to the contrary notwithstanding! They can rethink the way they're managing their board and contemplate how they might recast their relations with government and the media. They can focus on succession!

At each of these stages of development, moreover, there is technical information that can serve as useful inspiration, backgrounding or backstopping.

The larger the company, the more sense it makes to consider investing in company-specific training. Company courses provide common language and frameworks for working problems. They are a virtual necessity when significant shifts in organization and systems take place. They provide a context within which executives can meet to discuss something other than the most pressing day-to-day issues. They are a place where trust can be developed and sensitive company problems can be discussed in an informal setting. They also provide a wonderful venue for senior management to interact with the cohort that includes their successors. Companies can design and manage such courses for themselves, or business schools can do it for them. (In the latter case, companies need to guard against being sold a canned product with only minimal customization.)

Probably more important for those executives who are possible candidates for the most senior jobs are longer external courses focused on general management. The best of these courses convey multiple benefits. First, they assemble an outstanding and highly diverse group of peers. (To take just one example, the program I headed at Harvard Business School had between seventy and eighty participants from fifty companies, and there were always at least twenty-five nationalities represented in the room.) Everyone already has a big job and is headed for a bigger one. In contrast to company-sponsored courses—where, by definition, everyone sings from the same hymnal—you learn that other companies may have much the same problems as yours but take a very different approach. Nothing helps more in getting rid of internally focused blinders than sitting for a few weeks with people with very similar problems who see things very differently—at least in part because they bring different perspectives on the world.

One theme that emerged constantly over the run of the course that I developed and supervised was how much of a leader's job consists of the topics covered in this chapter: finding great people, helping them grow by giving them a sequence of developmentally oriented jobs, and managing the commitment of resources through planning and budgeting so that the company moves forward.

Finally, longer external management courses give participants a chance to think about themselves and compare their skill set with those of other talented peers. They can explore their life objectives and decide how exercising leadership can help them achieve those objectives. They can ponder powerful forces that are reshaping the markets. Again, assuming that it's a high-quality course, the participants return to their respective companies with the skill and the will to drive change.

Differentiating

At several points in this chapter, I have pointed out that the leadership of a firm needs to treat those who may be the future CEO differently from other managers. The obvious ways of doing this are compensation and assignments, as well as in the nature of discussion during regular reviews.

But I have also tried to emphasize the importance of coaching. The kinds of people who strive to be leaders need feedback.

They want praise, but if they get helpful criticism, they tend to value that even more—in part because it is so rare. If you think again about how hard the job that they are preparing for truly is, you can immediately see how valuable personal attention can be. Yes, on a day-to-day basis, leadership requires what might be called "inner-dependence," but it is always wonderful to know, as a young leader, that you have been noticed and can get help.

At most companies, the time of skilled and sensitive senior coaches is necessarily limited. That means you have to differentiate and allocate your mentoring and coaching resources to the young men and women who seem most likely to lead the company some day.

Performance

Several years back, I was talking with the founding CEO of a great computer company. Discussing the talents of his executive group, he said, a little wistfully, "I wish just *one* of them had made money running a pizza parlor."

I knew what he meant. These were all very talented individuals, of course, but they were all completely absorbed by the process of managing a highly successful company. In their early years, they were wonderful sales managers, marketers, engineers, and financiers. Now they were executives, brilliantly running their function or business—but not building the company. They'd become "suits." The CEO wanted people who knew how to make money the way the owner of a pizza parlor would—making customers happy every day, pizza by pizza.

In the business world, we talk a great deal about the importance of managing for the long term. By that, we mean making the investments that will enable the firm to grow and prosper year after year. But the economics of the long term are cruel. Compound interest means that every year that profits are postponed, the next year's profits must be even higher for the return on capital to be adequate. The easiest way to make a good return is to earn profits on a regular basis—steadily, reliably, increasing step-by-step.

But as we've seen, the world is not steady or reliable. Think of the impact that Hurricane Katrina had on businesses along the Gulf Coast of the United States. Managers of those companies first abandoned their carefully thought-out plans in the interest of saving lives. Then, as best they could, they moved to protect their property. In the wake of the storm, they picked themselves up, assessed the damage, worked out arrangements to get power and supplies, took steps to make sure that customers knew they were back in business, and went back to producing the good or service that they had produced before chaos struck.

An extreme case, to be sure, but representative of the whole universe of chaos-inducing factors that wreck plans and whack performance. As plans go awry, managers stay current with the situation and respond. If possible, they find a way to cut costs. They find new customers to make up for lost ones. They scramble without panicking. They improvise without undercutting the stature of plans and planning, and thereby without harming their enterprise.

This involves two kinds of activities. The first is looking ahead. What could go wrong? If my business is dependent on sales from a country with a volatile currency, can I plan the year so that costs can be cut dramatically if the currency weakens? Can I plan so that my costs fall faster than my sales? Can I hedge the currency?

The second is responding fast. If a customer is failing, are the lawyers on top of the situation? Are there salespeople moving fast to develop the customers this year that we had planned to sell next year? Are people committed to doing their personal best—within ethical and legal bounds—to perform the way they said they would? If they are, that is a performance culture, and that is what you want your managers to express in the way they go about their business. Effective leaders don't just see what is happening; they act and engage others.

Becoming a manager is not going to school. It is learning to get others to plan and deliver results. School can help, but there is no experience like delivering on the job when the going is tough. It can be tough because the business is growing so fast, because it is so uneven, or because it is so depressed. But the people factories have found a way to use powerful people-development processes to turn in a winning performance—and I believe that every company can aspire to do as well.

FIVE

The Succession Process

THE CENTRAL PREMISE of this book is that a certain kind of person—an Inside Outsider—is usually best qualified to lead a company.

This argues that attention to the succession process—how a company identifies, grooms, and installs its leaders—is critically important. In other words, if you know what kind of leader you want, you must ensure that the processes you put in place will deliver that kind of leader, according to your schedule.

But there's a catch: absent a deliberate intervention, the way you manage succession is likely to mirror the way you manage the rest of your company. For the best-managed companies, of course, this isn't a problem: as we've seen, they tend to have outstanding succession programs and a great track record of strong leadership. But if your company is only an average performer, it's likely to have only an average succession plan—if it has one at all.

In this chapter, I look at best practices in the area of succession. For reasons of space, I will keep a fairly tight focus on succession, rather than broadening out to the multitude of organizational issues that tend to lie behind succession, as we did in chapter 4.

Here, I'll focus on succession as a developmental process that often involves a number of standard building blocks. A key question, of course, is this: what are you looking for? Every company answers this question differently, but, I maintain, every company wants a small number of all-important things in its successful candidates—including, for example, integrity and a clear sense of where the world is headed. I'll also look at techniques for growing and pruning the pool, at the transition process, and at the role of the board in these critical activities.

Let's begin with two contrasting views of the succession process, first laid out in the book *Passing the Baton: Managing the Process of CEO Succession* by a former colleague of mine on the Harvard faculty, the late Richard Vancil.[1]

Passing the Baton Versus the Horse Race

Vancil's book used two metaphors to analyze the succession process: passing the baton (as in a relay race) and a horse race. When the baton is passed, a candidate is identified well in advance, and responsibility is steadily shifted onto his or her shoulders. In a horse race, two or more candidates are identified as competing for the CEO job, the starter's gun goes off, and the race is on (although the candidates may or may not know formally with whom they are competing). Ever since the publication of *Passing the Baton*, Vancil's study has encouraged people to dichotomize the succession process in this way.

I don't think it's an especially useful dichotomy.

Baton Passing: Rare, Risky, and Difficult

For one thing, examples of pure baton passing are extremely rare. Usually, when the baton is passed, it is two or three years— or even more—before succession, which tends to break down the analogy of a relay-race handoff. In addition, in most cases, baton passing has already been preceded by a horse race. Either the race had a victor and the baton was passed to that person, or it failed, in the sense that the incumbent CEO—with or without the help of the board and a search consultant—concluded that an outsider should be brought in and groomed for the job.

A relatively pure case of baton passing can be found at Cummins—the diesel maker based in Columbus, Indiana—at least in its successions through the early 1990s. There, the late Irwin Miller, whose family helped found Cummins just after World War I, hired a recent Harvard Business School graduate named Henry Schacht as part of a long-term recruiting effort aimed at upgrading the company's management talent. In fact, for more than a decade, Miller hired one or two people from the top of the graduating classes at both the Harvard and Stanford business schools.[2] Then the company groomed a subset of these talented young people for leadership positions.

As Schacht describes it, the company developed a small group of people who, in effect, took turns leading the company over two decades:

> In essence, I was president for four years. Then I was president and CEO for four years, and then I was chairman and CEO eight years after I'd been chosen to be the leader of the next generation at Cummins. And we ended up with three of us, essentially—Jim Henderson, John Hackett, and myself. John left to do other things, and Jim eventually succeeded me . . .
>
> At Cummins, the succession process was decided by Irwin Miller and his then most senior colleague, Don Tull. I went through the presidency and CEO, chairman and CEO. I immediately picked Jim as a partner, and we built a partnership, and that lasted for twenty-some years, which is very unusual in the U.S. corporate culture.[3]

Another (and more typical) place to find a relatively pure case of baton passing is in family businesses. Thomas Watson Jr. succeeded his father at IBM in that manner, and Brian Roberts Jr. has done it at Comcast. The baton was passed at Loews from Larry Tisch to his son Jim. In each of these examples, a son was identified early on as the one who would run the company after the father, and the company took the necessary steps to make it happen.

The common characteristic in all these cases, including Cummins, is that a founder with effective control of the company chose his successor in a very traditional fashion. Irwin Miller, notably, did not turn to family; but sought to infuse the company with high-quality external talent.

The obvious caveat about baton passing is that the choice had better be a good one. Once the baton is passed, not only is the company's fate in that individual's hands, but those executives who were passed over and who have the itch to lead a company are very likely to leave—perhaps years before the transition. Phil Casey's description of how he left Birmingham Steel to take over Florida Steel is instructive:

> Early in '94, I was in Birmingham, and I went to a Rotary meeting downtown. Driving back to the office, I was checking my voice mail on the car phone, and there was a message there from Heidrick & Struggles in Los Angeles. So I punched in and called them back, and they said that they had been engaged by [the owners of Florida Steel] to find a new CEO.
>
> Well, I had been suffering from what I call the "Tonto syndrome" for a long time—eight or nine years, by then. It was just the chairman and myself, the Long Ranger and Tonto. And *I* wanted to ride the white horse and shoot silver bullets. I said, "I will listen to what you have to say."
>
> I went to the board and said, "Look, I have a tremendous opportunity." And they asked what would it take to keep me there. I said that it would take the assurance that I would be selected and appointed as chairman. Well, the chairman was then sixty-four or sixty-five, and they refused to make that commitment.[4]

For some people, frustration with the "Tonto syndrome" is a powerful force driving them to find a situation where they are no longer playing second fiddle to a healthy superior. From a company perspective, a drawn-out process of passing the baton can lead to the early loss of executives who might well have contributed great things to the progress of the company.

A related problem of passing the baton is that even where a commitment to succession exists, the candidate may not choose to wait. Jim Robinson, CEO of American Express in the 1980s, described his chagrin at losing Lou Gerstner, his designated candidate for succession. Faced with the opportunity to take over as CEO of RJR after the biggest leveraged buyout in U.S. history, Gerstner found the wait to succeed Robinson at American Express unattractive. During one of Robinson's visits to our Harvard Business School classes, he told us the lesson he drew from this experience: "Never get yourself in a position where you have only one candidate. It's too risky."[5]

In many cases of *apparent* baton passing, there's actually a de facto horse race involved. The CEO discusses her view of the candidates with her executive confidants who are not candidates, with the head of the compensation committee of the board, and with some mix of other board members. From that process, an individual emerges who appears to be superior to the other contenders. Jack Stafford describes the process of choosing his successor at American Home Products (now Wyeth): "It's performance. You just see how he's done. You see how his people react to him. At Wyeth, my successor is an unprepossessing, plump, bearded guy. But I saw him addressing his sales force. They really respected him and paid attention. He's very quiet and very intelligent. And his numbers were terrific. He's done a wonderful job."[6]

Another version of the same story is provided by Harvey Golub of American Express, describing how he chose—and then passed the baton to—Ken Chenault: "I don't want to be in a position where Ken steps up to CEO; I want to be in a position where Ken comfortably slides into it. I've done whatever I could, in concert with Ken, to change the nature and content of what he's been doing in the last couple of years, so that gradually he has absorbed more and more of what it takes to be a CEO. You can't actually be a CEO until you are, but you can do a lot of flight simulation, and that's what we've got. My objective is to make his first year as CEO better than my last year."[7]

And what about baton passing as seen from the vantage point of the would-be baton grabbers? Some number of your executives have it in their dreams to be CEO. They are competing for the job and watching the signals of their progress as closely as any suitor regards the object of his or her affection. Being grown-ups, they have usually learned to control their behavior, but—especially in decentralized organizations, where pay is for performance and performance is measured overwhelmingly on the basis of divisional profit—they can be remarkably aggressive in projecting their performance. It is not unheard of for executives to hire their own public relations consultants.

The Horse Race: Tough, Divisive, and Chancy

One of management guru Chester Barnard's wisest propositions is that the most important role of the executive is to manage the balance between competition and cooperation. Yes, competition is a phenomenal motivator, but it can also blow a company apart. Lew Glucksman competed ferociously with Pete Peterson for the leadership of Lehman Brothers, one of Wall Street's most prominent investment banks. The battle nearly destroyed the company, and ultimately it was sold to American Express.[8] The competition for the job of CEO is the ultimate motivator for some, but balance must be achieved.

Which brings us to the horse race metaphor for succession. To explore this metaphor, let's look at GE, which has provided us with two well-documented cases. The horses were identified, in the first case, by Reg Jones and, two decades later, by Jack Welch. In both cases, the horses were on the track for two or more years. At the end of both races, the winners were clear, and the losers left.

Let's compare the stories. Jones brought the candidates to headquarters, put them through their paces, and finally picked Welch. (In the process, he lost four talented executives.) Welch kept the candidates in the field running their separate groups, but with five months to go, he had the three finalists pick and announce a successor to run their business. Why? Because Welch had determined, in numerous one-on-one conversations, that all three were experiencing the Tonto syndrome: they would leave if they were not promoted.

Welch made sure that they would do so on *his* terms. The new CEO would stay; the others would go. (The two losers couldn't be allowed to spend the rest of their careers poisoning the atmosphere at the company, if they were so inclined.) Meanwhile, there was a hand on every tiller, and everyone—those inside GE, vendors, customers, and the financial markets—knew who was running the businesses.

Welch suggested to me that the key in the horse race was to have the candidates off on their own turf, running their businesses as well as they could and well exposed to the board through dinners and visits. In other words, there was no opportunity for the corridor politics that developed after Jones brought his candidates to headquarters. With the opportunities for politicking substantially eliminated, the candidates could compete through performance and still remain friends.

Procter & Gamble, another great people factory, is running a more informal kind of horse race. As CEO A. G. Lafley described it to me:

> My board of directors is involved extensively in managing succession and the top development program . . . At two board meetings every year—in February and in August— we review succession and the top development players in detail with the outside directors. This includes a review of geographic, racial, ethnic, and gender diversity, as well. At executive sessions of the board—at least four per year— we again update the progress of key top development players. I am frequently asked the question, "How is X doing?" Or a director may comment, "Y was great today, but Z wasn't on top of the questions the board asked yesterday."

At P&G, succession, strategy, governance, and risk management are the four key responsibilities of the board. Succession is every outside director's responsibility.

We try to create as many opportunities as possible for board members to get to know the company's top management and the top development talent. For example, we do one off-site board meeting per year that includes director visits to the markets to work with leaders in their businesses . . . At each of these off-site business presentations, we make sure there are active roles for the top development players. Another example: in December, there is a board and management holiday dinner. Again, many of the top development leaders interact with the board.[9]

That's a pretty good definition of a horse race. At the same time, isn't it also baton passing? P&G is cultivating a cohort of skilled leaders. At the time of succession, several years from now, one of that group—the one whose experiences and skills best fit the needs of the moment—will be elected CEO.

"I own the top three hundred people," says Lafley. "I rent them to the businesses."[10] In other words, if you're one of those three hundred, your career will get a lot of attention from the top. If that's considered a horse race, well, there's an awful lot of development going on as well.

Henry Schacht, who has thought a good deal about the Vancil-derived dichotomy, thinks the pure horse race is a bad idea:

If you're going to run a horse race, you have to then say, "I won't really be able to understand how these people are able to perform until I see them perform in a competitive environment where they are being judged in terms of whatever criteria you care to set up, one against the other, over a protracted period of time.

My main concern about that is that I don't think the world essentially runs as well in an adversarial set of environments as it does in a cooperative set of environments. And the horse race itself is adversarial, and it causes adversarial reactions—not only between people, but between organizations within the larger company.[11]

Schacht introduces another key point. If a company is managed as a horse race in which the most talented are always in a more or less explicit contest for the top job, then that pervasive competition will come to characterize how everything happens at the company. Yes, Schacht says—echoing Chester Barnard—competition is good, but it's the *balance* that counts: "I think the alternative is a more cooperative model that suggests we are going to think about a pool of candidates who could, in fact, run this firm one day. We're going to talk about what the criteria ought to be. We're going to be relatively clear, and we're going to choose relatively early. And we're going to choose at a time when we can build cooperative relationships among groups of people and hope that we can hang on to that pool of talent for a much-longer period of time than the horse race would suggest."[12]

It is clear that Welch and Schacht have very different views on the work environment they are seeking. It is also clear that how they manage succession is a direct reflection of their judgment.

Splitting the Difference: Helping the Company

To strike that balance the current CEO has to find a way of managing that is inclusive and that shares some of the fun and glory with talented subordinates—on whom, after all, the future of the company is likely to depend.

This is especially true after the race has ended and after the baton has been passed. In the months running up to succession in big companies, the business press often starts sniffing out horse races. They handicap the contenders and then publicize the winner and so-called losers—at which point keeping the losers in a company becomes a real problem.

GE's Jeff Immelt described his approach to this challenge a few months after taking over:

We have three hundred thousand people. I worry about *all* of them. But a particular emphasis you have, when you're taking over a company like this, is you want to keep the top thirty people.

So you have to have a certain style with how you interface with your top leaders. I knew I was going to have to run it like a partnership for a while, to make these guys feel like they had a bigger stake in the company than just the businesses that they're running. So you really reach out to the key leaders and wrap them into the company.[13]

Note that right after Immelt takes over, he is worrying about how to keep the great leaders working for him. He worked to build a partnership (which ultimately became his executive council). And he was working regularly with his senior vice president of executive development to begin sorting out which individuals among this talented group have the special attributes that would make them good candidates, down the road, to lead GE.

This brings us back to the point with which I opened the chapter. The succession process is very likely a reflection of the way the company is managed. At a great company, that process starts early. It is a developmental process, both for the company and for the individuals involved.

The Key Qualities

What are the key qualities that a company should look for in its CEO? The answer is, in part, driven by the specifics of that company in its industry. But there are also a number of characteristics that cut across almost all senior leadership positions.

A. G. Lafley described Procter & Gamble's approach, which involves developing criteria that seem broadly applicable:

We look at performance versus established criteria and performance over time for consistency and sustainability. We use scorecards to look at individuals' cumulative business, financial, and organizational results. We look at how the candidates' leadership and management skills are developing. We ask ourselves, "Do they put the greater good of the company and the longer-term health of the enterprise and the organization ahead of short-term financial and operational results?"

All of these assessments and data are important, but they are only a guide to what, in the end, is a judgment call. How in this process do you get at the real person? How do you make sure of the character of each of P&G's key managers?

To begin because we are primarily a build-from-within culture, we have worked very closely with each other for decades, so we know each other really well—almost as well as we know our families. We also use a very thorough 360-degree feedback process, starting when top development individuals are at the director level. We conduct 360-degree feedback on all hundred-plus general managers and all line presidents and functional leaders. We also get informal feedback from selected external consultants who have worked with us for decades, understand our company and culture, and have personal experience with most of our development managers. This helps get at the essence of the individual.[14]

It's a list both predictable and daunting. In other words, it's easy enough to identify these specs, but damnably difficult to know when you've found them all in the same package. In fact, this is one of the stronger arguments in favor of the Inside Outsider: you almost certainly know a lot more about the insider than the outsider. Again, Lafley: "And why are we concerned about understanding the 'real person'? It's because the selection of top development talent, including the CEO, is not just about financial integrity or business or organization results. It is because P&G is an institution, now 169 years old. We are interested in integrity and character in the broadest sense because at the end of the day, P&G suppliers and customers, P&G external stakeholders, and P&G employees all have to *trust* P&G leaders. This is the highest bar of all, and it is essential for sustaining P&G's growth for at least another 169 years."[15]

I'd like to pick up on the characteristic that Lafley summarizes in the word *integrity*. Note that it's the way he sums up his comments. As Lafley suggests, the issue isn't simply about seeking reassurance that this individual won't steal from the cookie jar. It's a far bigger domain. Read what Harvey Golub of American Express says about why he chose Ken Chenault:

> Why Ken? Often, CEOs pick people who are good number twos. But the attributes of being a good number two only incidentally overlap with being a CEO. The first conscious recognition I had that Ken was CEO material was when we were discussing the issues and problems we were facing and Ken was the only senior executive who stood up and said, "Here are the problems," in spite of the fact that his bosses didn't want that to happen. He had courage. Being CEO requires courage; that doesn't mean physical courage. But it requires courage of conviction and ability and willingness to make decisions when everyone else thinks you're wrong.[16]

So courage counts, too. But based on my own observations of succession in action, what many leaders are most concerned about is whether their potential successors are so driven to succeed that they will destroy others to realize their personal aspirations. This is another dimension of integrity. Research recently published by Scott Spreier, Mary Fontaine, and Ruth Malloy frames the problem sharply:

> The desire to achieve is a major source of strength in business, both for individual managers and for the organizations they lead. It generates passion and energy, which fuel growth and help companies sustain performance over the long term. And the achievement drive is on the rise. We've spent 35 years assessing executive motivation, and we've seen a steady increase during the past decade in the number of managers for whom achievement is the primary motive. Businesses have benefited from this trend: Productivity has risen, and

innovation, as measured by the number of patents issued per year, has soared . . .

[B]ut there's a dark side to the achievement motive. By relentlessly focusing on tasks and goals—revenue or sales targets, say—an executive or company can, over time, damage performance. Overachievers tend to command and coerce, rather than coach and collaborate, thus stifling subordinates. They take frequent shortcuts and forget to communicate crucial information, and they may be oblivious to the concerns of others. Their team's performance begins to suffer, and they risk missing the very goals that initially triggered the achievement-oriented behavior.[17]

Basically, this is the issue that leaders have in mind when they ask whether a manager has the integrity to be a good leader. Jim Collins raises the same issues when he describes "level 5 leaders," who "embody a paradoxical mixture of personal humility and professional will. They are ambitious, to be sure, but ambitious first and foremost for the company, not themselves."[18] Do these individuals think of the company first? Or are they driven—so personally ambitious—that they will take self-serving shortcuts? The question is vital, and to get at it, smart companies use many of the devices described by Lafley: 360-degree evaluations, psychological assessment by outside professional consultants, and months or years of simply listening to what others have to say about the candidates.

Again, all else being equal, this gives the edge to the Inside Outsider.

Multiple Challenges at Once

Let's look at one more trait on Lafley's list: the ability to anticipate change.

When I was in the MBA program at Harvard, my fellow students and I studied with a brilliant professor named John Lintner. As part of our work on business economics, we had to deal with

the problem of forecasting under uncertainty. To make the importance of uncertainty clearer, he would ask us how we would handle
a particular situation if we had "a telephone line to the Lord," who
would tell us what the world would be like, thereby removing all
uncertainty.

It was an interesting lens that allowed us to carry certain
kinds of academic discussions to the next level. But as every CEO
and his or her board of directors knows, there is no telephone
line to the Lord. Most of the time, the way ahead is murky.

This is especially true when the question under consideration
is succession. Almost all of us—*probably* all of us—do better in
some circumstances than others. If the challenge ahead is rapid
growth, the work of the leader will be quite different than if markets are stagnant and competition is intensifying. If the business
stays in the current model, one kind of leadership will be needed.
If an emergent situation requires a fundamental shift in the nature
of the business—for example, from being vertically integrated to
being focused on end consumers—another kind of leadership will
come into play.

The challenge for the leadership of a company in the run-up
to a CEO succession is twofold. First, those leaders—most likely,
the CEO and the board—have to come to an understanding of
what kinds of circumstances are likely to be facing the company
in the years that lurk out beyond the regular business-planning
horizon. For the purposes of succession, the planning that has
been done in the context of strategy development is likely to be
inadequate. They have to dig deeper and look farther out.

Second, the board has to find someone who seems to fit the
bill that results: "We've called the Lord on the phone, and he's
told us what kind of leader we need ten years hence."

But this in turn raises another kind of challenge. As an incumbent leadership group, we're only looking at our proven leaders,
right? We are assessing people who have developed an intellectual framework for thinking successfully about the company's
environment and dealing with that environment. Researchers some-
time refer to this framework as a "cognitive groove"—which
sounds pejorative, but is in fact a prerequisite for consistent and

effective action. Without such a set of premises in place, every situation would have to be thought out from scratch. The leader would be paralyzed, and his or her organization frustrated. And the first time the "from-scratch" thinking reached a conclusion that contradicted an earlier decision, that leader would be condemned as a flip-flopper.

Looking ahead with a set of premises is what all leaders do. When they see things coming that pose problems, they revise their plans, but rarely do they revise their premises.

So we're looking for a true rarity: an individual with firm convictions, who—in the face of a true discontinuity in the marketplace—can recast those convictions to fit into a new reality. It's not just the ability to anticipate change; it's the ability to change oneself. If you've "drunk the Kool-Aid," it's impossible. That's why the outside perspective is so vital. If you can't get outside the accepted rhetoric, you can't change your premises.

We all like to think that we're this flexible, but the truth is most of us aren't. Researchers who have focused on the way managers think when they make strategy have concluded that most managers simply can't make fundamental adjustments in their worldview. In my work with leaders who have successfully built large enterprises over decades—that is, highly accomplished leaders—they almost always talk about the periods when they have had to change as extremely hard and painful. The learning and changes in thinking that result from these periods are scarring experiences. And perhaps most telling, the changes that were required were unimaginable at earlier dates. The former regime couldn't have foreseen them when they were making their succession choices; neither could the successful candidate.

Vittorio Merloni, founder and chairman of Europe's second-largest producer of home appliances, Merloni Elettrodomestici (now Indesit), once talked to me about the changes in his company as it grew:

When you start, you have a limited vision, because you are not sure that you can succeed. Then there can be a second step as you understand your market. For us, the first step was to succeed in the market. The next was built in, a rapidly growing part of the market where we could make a bigger success than our other competitors. The next step was the Margherita washing machine, a completely different product in appearance with a woman's name—a marketing product, not an industrial product. It was extremely successful.

The next was to take over Indesit, one of our competitors. After the merger, we had significant market share in many countries, and we [became] a European company. Then, in '93—four years after the Berlin Wall came down— we entered the Eastern European markets and became number one in those markets. At the same time, we brought in a new CEO, a young man with skills to help make the company more professional. At each step, you have to deal with a new set of problems.[19]

The same theme emerges in the comments of Intel's Andy Grove:

[Our] objective changed roughly every five years. Five years after we started, the objective was to build an organization large enough to stand up to the other players in the memory business. Five years later, it was to make something out of the microprocessor. Five years later, it was to make winning microprocessors into a real business. Five years later, it was to become one of the leading forces in the PC industry.

The interesting thing is that if you take these objectives and think about what they would have been ten years earlier, they would have been meaningless.[20]

Keep in mind that these are comments from executives who have been leaders in their organization for decades They have the perspective to see the magnitude of change that their company experienced over long periods of time. But many leaders have shorter tenure. They see one or, at most, two periods. They are more likely to be thinking *inside* one of those periods of development, rather than across several. They have a commitment to present premises—both emotionally and structurally.

When the CEO and the board of a company consider succession, they too have a commitment to present premises—but they need to make every effort to break out of that trap. They need to think like well-informed outsiders. In preparing for succession at GE at the end of the 1970s, Reg Jones commissioned the preparation of extensive studies examining possible developments in the economic, political, and technological environment. The result of that study was a remarkably good view of the 1980s that lay ahead. As he later recalled:

> I lived in the decade where business and government had to establish some kind of dialogue, had to achieve some rapprochement that would get a better understanding from both sides. Jack [Welch] is going to be living in an environment where the economic growth rate is going to be much slower, where the international difficulties are going to be much greater, where demographic changes will alter a lot of our mores. So we needed somebody who was younger, therefore, to be better attuned to that environment.
>
> And I also feel that with the great change that General Electric Company is going to make in its technologies, you needed somebody that was really grounded in technology and that could not be fooled by some of the artists that you find on this front who are very glib but could also mislead you if you weren't that skilled yourself in understanding everything that they said. And I found these qualities in Jack.[21]

Now let's look at table 5-1. This is a set of criteria developed at another company—much smaller than GE, though still in the multibillion-dollar ranks of the New York Stock Exchange, and more narrowly focused on a set of consumer products. The criteria were developed by the board, working with an executive search consulting company.

At this company, there was no written statement about the environment in which the new CEO would operate. When discussed by the board, the premise was that things would be much the same, except more competitive.

TABLE 5-1

CEO search criteria for company X

Leadership skills	Visionary skills	Operating skills	Customer relations skills	Financial skills	Relationship-building skills
• Instinctive, aggressive leadership skills	• Strategic direction and business-building orientation	• Aggressive hands-on operating management capabilities	• Strong customer relations and sales capabilities	• Finance and deal savvy	• Board and investor relations skills
• High ethical standards	• Ability to conceive and implement a practical long-term vision for the company	• Ability to dig into products and distribution businesses	• Ability to work effectively with key customers	• Understanding of the balance sheet	• Ability to build external support for programs
• A real interest in people		• Willingness and ability to guide and develop the younger top managers	• Knowledge of how company's products are bought and sold and how money is made with them	• Understanding of the relation between operating and financial risk	
• Ability to listen					
• Ability to drive the organization					

Note that in the fourth column, "customer relations skills," the board appears to have a commitment to present premises—in other words, it is making an implicit choice to maintain its existing product/market focus. At the same time, it is looking for a CEO who will do the practical task of looking ahead (see the second column). This is very typical of circumstances in which the board does not believe a fundamental shift in outlook is required.

Contrast this worldview with that of Reg Jones, who, as we've seen, thought that the next CEO of GE would need a very different set of skills than he himself possessed. GE's study of the world ahead revealed an increasing importance of technology in a world of mature markets, and Jones, therefore, concluded that GE's leader should be (1) technologically sophisticated and (2) very aggressive. But if the conclusion is that the world will demand some version of "more of the same," then the search criteria in the table may be more appropriate—and will most likely call forth a leader with a hands-on style who can dig in and manage the marketing, financial, and people aspects of the existing business.

Most companies tend to believe that they have a good grasp on what their environment will be like, even if they do not know what to do about it. As discussed in chapter 1, they are more likely to go outside for their next CEO if performance has been poor than because their studies show that the environment will require a new skill set. Rakesh Khurana discusses this phenomenon in his book *Searching for a Corporate Savior*.[22] He found that when a company's board concluded that conditions were very tough, it tended to discount the talent of the inside candidates and look outside for a celebrity CEO who could produce a dramatic improvement in performance.

But this behavior is about as far from the analyses discussed in this chapter as you could imagine. It discounts the difficulty of learning a new situation, and it reflects a relatively low level of confidence in the company's own processes of executive development. Let me emphasize that looking outside for a high-profile CEO is entirely different from what companies do when they reach for a new skill set, although the results may look much the same.

When Nike asked William Perez—the CEO of S. C. Johnson & Son—to take over from founder Phil Knight, they sought to bring in an approach to brand building and marketing that would build on the success that Nike had already achieved in turning itself into the leading purveyor of footwear and sports apparel. They soon concluded that the skill set required for shoes and apparel was very different than that required for furniture wax.

When Home Depot hired Robert Nardelli after he lost out to Jeff Immelt in the race for succession at GE, the leaders of that founder-managed company were seeking a set of professional management skills of high order—skills that they were sure did not exist in their company. In this case, one of Home Depot's founders sat on the GE board, so he probably felt well informed about both Home Depot's needs and Nardelli's skills.[23] The board learned that whatever it was that seemed to work well at GE was not what was needed at Home Depot.

How to Look Ahead

Picking a leader really requires the CEO and those on the board involved in the process to step back and study some radical questions: If we were newcomers to this company, how would we think about its future? Where is there real potential for growth? Where are competitive conditions undermining our ability to create wealth? What part of our business would we want to keep? What would we want to discard? What would we like to acquire?

Getting a fresh look isn't easy. Why? For one thing, you're testing the thinking of the existing management team. Managers who are consumed with fighting the day-to-day battles with competitors and customers are rarely in a position to step back and look out ten years. Andy Grove and Vittorio Merloni, quoted earlier, suggest that it's simply impossible: they wonder how well you can see even five years ahead. Meanwhile, the incentives inside the organization are wrong. Managers who are battling for resources to support their current business plans are unlikely to endorse studies that suggest that the premises of those plans might be flawed. All in all, it is rare to find an operating manager with the detachment of a true strategist.

Bad incentives pertain to higher-ups, as well. If the findings of the study are dramatically different from what the company is currently planning on doing, they could be interpreted as being critical of the incumbent CEO, as well as being a prescription for the next leader.

For all these reasons and more, companies are susceptible to the trap of "grooved thinking." In other words, the current goals and policies of a company, and the plans to implement them, constitute a strategic context that shapes thinking.[24] A large body of research and cases reveals that this context for thinking is highly resistant to change. For one thing, the way a group of managers thinks about strategy is reflected in the way the company is organized, the company accounts are set up, that their talents have been recognized by promotions, and performance rewarded. After enough time goes by, the behaviors associated with the strategy are embedded in the culture of the company. It is the way the company does business.

Returning to Intel for an illustration: The organization continued to think of itself as the "memory company" even after memory products as a percentage of sales had declined to 4 percent. Grooved thinking prevailed.

If we agree that there is an inevitable inertia in the thinking about strategic matters among the leaders who have developed and are implementing a strategy, then we have to imagine an approach whereby, in considering the way ahead, a company can work independently of the premises of its being. That's the only way to value a perspective that looks very different. There are examples, so we know it can be done—but it is hard. It requires great discipline and seriousness of purpose. It is also one arena in which the board may well have an advantage over the CEO. Usually on matters brought for the board's consideration, the CEO has a tremendous advantage in the detailed knowledge that makes a difference to plans and policies. But in considering the way ahead, things may be different.

While a director may well choose to live with a strategy that has the clear support of the CEO and management team, he or she may be much more vocal when looking ahead to consider changes needed. Indeed, many of those who study the transition from Jones to Welch at GE are surprised that it could have happened. Welch reversed Jones's most dramatic acquisitions by selling Utah International and a large part of RCA. He dismantled a good portion of the elaborate organization and planning structure for which Jones's GE had become famous. In other words, Welch tore into his inheritance—and the evidence suggests that Jones knew that might happen. You can make the case that picking Welch was Jones's most remarkable and selfless achievement.

The company that does ask the "what's ahead?" question has to decide whether it has the people inside the organization to develop an answer. Almost inevitably, multiple consultants are needed. In large companies, this almost always means the retention of an executive search firm. Even companies that have great processes for the development and selection of talent find that they make mistakes that search firms or search consultants may help them avoid.[25]

Search firms can sometimes surface great Inside Outsiders simply because they themselves are outsiders. It is easy for insiders to undervalue the ability of the potential Inside Outsider because there may only be limited evidence that an insider can drive the kind of change that is needed. After all, if a radical thinker is lurking somewhere near the top of the organization, the chances are good that he or she has been flying under the radar—suppressing the evidence of his or her freethinking ways to remain in good standing among the more conventional thinkers in today's organization. A search firm may be able to smoke out such potential leaders.

Also, many companies are not sure that their internal candidates are right, and they therefore want to see what the outside candidates look like. Search consultants earn their keep by knowing which executives have the résumés that make for attractive candidates. Typically, these consultants will discuss a long list of ten to twenty candidates, talk to a shorter list that the company believes may be attractive, and then, after the company has identified a true short list, arrange for interviews.

The contributions here are quite important. The search firm knows who out there is capable and might want to move. The search consultants can approach individuals and protect the identity of the company. They can make the initial match and keep secret the fact that the company and the individual are talking. They can manage the interviews in their offices so that secrecy is preserved. And, of course, they can provide ongoing advice.

Another reason why a search firm may be used is that many companies fail to develop candidates whom the board believes are adequate for the job. Why? Often because there has been no development process. Sometimes, the CEO has interfered with the process and driven away logical successors. Sometimes, poor company performance has created a crisis that the board believes can only be resolved by an outsider. In these instances, a search firm is a necessity.

So executive search firms can play a key role in succession. Strategy consultants add another critical dimension—especially when it comes to generating forward-looking studies—but they usually require careful management by the incumbent leadership to obtain studies that are both objective and well grounded.

The problem of looking ahead several years to measure the candidates for the CEO job brings us back to the opening idea of this chapter: how succession is managed is part and parcel of how the company is managed. A company whose managers are in the habit of being tough-minded as they look at the environment may be capable of doing what Reg Jones did—that is, taking a look ahead that is independent of all investments in the status quo. But, in the real world, most managers have a hard enough time developing their own strategy. For them, second-guessing that strategy for purposes of managing succession would be a feat of magic.

Getting from Here to There

The impending retirement date of the CEO serves as a beacon, focusing the attention of board members and senior managers alike. Particularly in companies that take leadership development seriously, a great many people have that transition point riveted in their sights. It's worth keeping in mind that the planned retirement age has generally been set by the board, rather than the corporate charter; so it's always possible that the board will extend the tenure of a CEO, if that seems appropriate. But once that date starts to loom on the horizon, everything changes.

From the CEO's perspective, retirement takes on very different and personal perspectives. One founder with whom I sought to discuss the matter turned me down because, as he put it, "I don't want to talk about my death." Others—especially if they have been successful and are happy with their successor—see the event as a celebration. Chuck Knight, the former CEO of Emerson Electric, spoke of the nine trips to China that he no longer had to make every year. Walter Wriston, the legendary CEO of Citibank, told me that the only thing he really missed was the company airplane. (In today's environment, he might have negotiated access to the plane as part of his retirement package.) Some have no desire to leave and try to hang on, causing problems for management and the board. But no one wants to be a lame duck, and some actually leave early.

What are the organizational milestones along the way? The first is what is sometimes described as the "name in the envelope" discussion. The CEO discusses with an appropriate subset of the board, or with the entire board, the name of the executive who will take over if he or she "gets hit by a bus." That name—no matter whose it is—tends to trigger a lot of conversation.

If the CEO's retirement date is not imminent, the hit-by-a-bus candidate usually is *not* one of the eventual final candidates. Instead, that person tends to be a high-ranking executive who has a good knowledge of the entire company, has comfortable relations with sources of finance, and would represent a steady hand at the tiller should the captain be struck down. Given these criteria, this person is usually a member of the CEO's inner circle and is often older than the eventual successor.

As time passes and the bus doesn't strike, the situation usually changes. More work has been done on the planned succession, and new names emerge. The board may have become comfortable with one or more younger candidates, and the "name in the envelope" discussions may take on a different cast. In other words, they may evolve into becoming part of the next more formal phase of the succession process, perhaps even baton passing.

Normally, the chief executive and his or her confidants have been discussing the matter for several years before the date. Jack Welch says that he discussed succession with his senior vice president of HR all the time. I've had the same experience from the other side of the board table. As a board director chairing the compensation or nominating committee of several companies, I discuss some aspect of the matter almost every time I talk with the CEO. The committee discusses the question formally at least once a year, so the off-line conversations are more like "How is Laura doing?" or "How is Bill getting on with his new assignment?"

The point is that succession is on people's minds. In the five years or so in the run-up to the date, it is on the minds of all the top leadership. And there is the rub. As noted earlier, the kinds of people who might lead a major company are usually highly competitive. Managing the run-up to succession involves riding herd on a latent political race that can explode at any moment. How the candidates handle the pressure is telling; if they can't handle it, they could damage the company.

At Marks & Spencer, Sir Richard Greenbury, looking toward his retirement in 1998, established a succession process in 1994. Here's how he described what he was doing:

> I am heading towards fifty-eight, and [Deputy Chairman] Clinton Silver is retiring. And he, in my opinion, has been one of the really great merchant princes of this business.

And that leaves Keith Oates, who is fifty-one years of age, as the only managing director. Although he is not a lifelong retailer like every other member of the board and he's only been with us about ten years or so, he's a man of very, very considerable experience outside of Marks & Spencer, especially in the international sense. So I felt that, as a businessman and with mature judgment, he was the obvious replacement as deputy chairman.

And there was another reason in that thinking process. I felt that his skills were complementary to mine. So I took the view that, over these next four and a half years that I'm definitely here, we've got to put three or four horses in the traps and see how they run.

And then the age of those people becomes crucially important. So I had to say to all the directors who were within two or three years of my own age, "Sorry, boys. Even if you were geniuses, you can't succeed me. Because you're too close to me in age. And you're going to be retired either at the same time as me or within a year or so of me."

That focused my mind upon the next generation. So why not get them in the traps now and really start to put them under pressure? Because up to now, they've had Clinton to go to. And I thought it's about time for those younger people to start learning their trade not as directors of the company but as managing directors, autonomous in every way for their particular parts of the business, with the exception of myself as the chairman.

It took me eighteen months of thinking and thinking and thinking. Indeed, for the first year, I didn't discuss it with anybody outside of the nonexecutive directors.[26]

It is interesting to notice how central a role age plays in the process. In most cases, the amount of time that an executive might have in the CEO job, were he or she to be promoted, is critical. (Most companies believe—or at least *say* they believe—that a CEO needs to have a reasonably long period of time over which to manage an agenda of development and change.) Note that

Greenbury explains, first, that he had elevated one senior manager, Keith Oates, to deputy chairman. To avoid the obvious interpretation that he had passed the baton, he wanted to move up others—to put them "in the traps"—to see whether they had the capabilities to be CEO. In other words, he started a horse race.

To achieve a balanced competition, he picked a fifty-one-year-old to complement Oates and then two forty-six-year-olds. He also looked for complementary backgrounds: Oates was from finance, so the others were recruited from clothing, food, and store operations. Note that Oates was chosen because his skills complemented the chairman's, not because he was the one best equipped to serve as successor.

In effect, Oates was the hit-by-a-bus name in the envelope. Many of the problems that later plagued the process (as described in chapter 2) flowed from the widespread interpretation that Oates was the heir apparent. This perception was reinforced when Greenbury later shuffled the assignments of the other three. He did so to broaden their experience base, but it was interpreted as a vote of no confidence in them.

Note too how lonely a process this was. Greenbury spent eighteen months thinking until he discussed the matter with his four nonexecutive directors. This was four years before his planned succession in 1998 so the entire process began five and a half years before the date. Both aspects—long and lonely—are typical. As we shall see, most CEOs talk with more than their nonexecutive directors, but they manage the process in isolation to a considerable degree.

A remarkably different approach was taken by Reg Jones at GE in the late 1970s, as he worked his way toward selecting Jack Welch. The text that follows is an edited version of his remarks to an executive program class at Harvard Business School. I quote it at length because it provides a unique window into how Jones—and, by extension, GE—looked at the information-gathering challenge at a crucial juncture in the company's history:

> One technique that I used is what may be called the "airplane interview."

Jones

1st time

I sat down for a couple of hours, unannounced, with each of these seven or eight candidates. They didn't know the purpose of the meeting, and I made sure they didn't tell the others, so that everybody came in surprised. And they wouldn't tell, once they went through the experience, because they wouldn't want the other guy to have the advantage of knowing what this was all about.

You call a fellow in, close the door, get out your pipe, and try to get him relaxed. Then you say to him, "Well, look now, Bill, you and I are flying in one of the company planes, and this plane crashes . . . Who should be chairman of the General Electric Company?" "Well, some of them try to climb out of the wreckage." But you say, "No, no, you and I are killed . . . Who should be the chairman of General Electric Company?" And, boy, this really catches them cold. They fumble around for a while and fumble around some more, and you have a two-hour conversation. And you learn a great deal from that meeting.

When you've done that seven or eight times, once with each of the leading competitors to replace you, it's amazing what you learn about the chemistry among that group—who will work with whom, who just despises which other guy— and things come out, because this is a totally confidential session you're having with them, totally confidential.

2nd time

Now, having done that across the field of candidates, the next thing I did was to call them back three months later and do it all over again. This time they knew it was coming, and they had been through the experience. Now they came in with sheaves of notes, studied comments; there were states-men developing, you see, in this process. And we went through the whole thing again—it took a couple of hours.

While I was holding these interviews, I also did the same thing with those senior officers with whom I could talk. These were the ones who were not contenders, the ones who were going to retire before me or with me, whose opinions I valued. They were generally senior staff people.

And you get their reactions as to who should be running the company, what teams will work together, what individuals don't fit, and so on. I shared all this with the five members of the Management Development and Compensation Committee of the board in depth and, of course, with the senior vice president of executive manpower, who was intimately familiar with all these people.

Now, in the next series of interviews—again, two in number and, again, the first one unannounced—you call the fellow in and say, "Remember our airplane conversations?" "Oh yeah . . . ," and he starts to sweat a little bit. "Now," you say, "this time, we're out there together, we're flying in a plane, and the plane crashes. I'm done, but you live. Now who should be the chairman of General Electric?"

And again, you get a very interesting set of responses. Some don't want any part of it: "Here's the guy you should pick." Others: "I'm your man." And you say, "Okay, if you're the man, what do you see ahead as the major challenges facing GE, what sort of environment do you visualize, what programs would you mount, and who should be the other members of the corporate executive office?" Now you're getting very specific about the chemistry, about interpersonal relationships. And then you do that again on an announced basis, just as you did the first time; the second time they come in, they're really ready for you. They've got all their notes, and you have a very informed discussion.

Now, that was the way that we developed the information, which we shared again with the management development and compensation committee of the board and, finally, the full board. And the full board, having known these people intimately and been very much involved in the entire succession process, arrived at a set of conclusions as to the three candidates that we should move up to vice chairmen.

We then ran with a corporate executive office of myself and these three new vice chairmen for a period of about fifteen months, during which the board could look at these three in greater depth. Remember, they were attending every board meeting, and they were seeing board members in social as well as business situations. Only after that period of time did the board make the final selection as to the chairman.[27]

Again, it is noteworthy how long the pruning process takes. Jones began the first rounds of discussion in early 1978 and picked three candidates as vice chairmen in August 1979. Note that Jones explicitly asked the candidates what they thought the future environment would be like and what they would do about it. For the candidates, a visible pruning process was under way for eighteen months. The selection of Welch as CEO came in April 1981, almost two years later. It is not hard to imagine the extent of the politicking that went on, especially since six of the candidates were made sector executives and located at GE corporate headquarters. Twenty years later, in fact, Welch still spoke bitterly about the political aspects of the process.

It is also interesting how central a role Jones played. Although he shared information with the board's management development and compensation committee and later with the full board, *all* the information they received came from Jones. One can be impressed with the extensive information that he gathered and the openness of the process, but at the end of the day, Jones was the interpreter and reporter: the node through which information passed. Almost inevitably, the process had a high political content—a fact that evokes Stalin's comment on elections: "It doesn't matter who does the voting. What is important is who counts the votes." Jones maintained his control over the process by counting the votes.

The process by which Jack Welch chose Jeff Immelt, introduced earlier, provides a stark contrast. Welch described that process to me, and again, I'll quote his observations at length:

Beginning in 1994, Bill Conaty (the human resource leader), Paolo Fresco (who's a vice chairman), and I spent most of our time putting the pool together, with a fellow called Chuck Okosky from human resources. So there was a team of us who put the long list together.

Welch

In June 1994, twenty-three candidates were presented to the management development committee of the board. And then we put a path together for all the young people to get more experience, by putting them in different jobs, and to see if we could get an emerging candidate aside from the obvious senior people. We tried to give them different environments: a tough cost environment and a growth environment, [an] international assignment, turn-around situations, [and so on].

By 1998, Welch's team had settled on three candidates:

My board had been hanging around with everybody that we were talking about. And they had been hanging around with them privately by sending them out on their own and doing all these other things. So the familiarity of the board with the top candidates was quite intimate.

They would go out, go to a ballgame, stay late, have dinner. Guys would call me ahead of time and say, "What should I tell them?" I said, "Don't lie. It's up to you" . . . It varied. But what would come out of it was that the comp committee would send me notes.

It was their company. And a board member was coming to sit with them and talk about their company and its strategy and where it was going, and their boss wasn't there. Not bad.

In addition, we had a process in the last two years where I had private dinners with each of them. It was sort of like Reg's process, but handled outside the office. And each of them, more or less, to one extent or another, made it pretty clear that if they didn't get it, they were going to go.

I desperately did not want to make up my mind. I didn't want to get an early call. First of all, I liked all the people a lot. I thought they were all capable of doing the job, to one degree or another. I wanted them producing for the company and not thinking about the job, and that's what they were doing. They were really delivering *incredible* results. If I had picked one in my own mind, I couldn't have been dealing on top of the table with the other two.

with

he knew
he intended
wanted all
leave "'

I had three great people. They were all qualified to be CEOs, and they wanted to be CEOs. They really wanted it. I wanted the person who was picked to be the unquestioned leader and not burdened with two disappointed people around for three to five years. And because the pressures were going to be so great on them to go anyway, I wanted them to go on my terms, rather than theirs.

So, one day, I had an idea in the shower, which turned out to be the best idea I'd had in years. I decided that I would appoint their successors while they were still there, so I appointed the three people that they wanted to succeed them. They each had picked somebody to succeed them because we had a long talk in April. So in June, I said, "Why don't we just do it?"

By doing that, I made sure that the organization knew who their boss was going to be. The outside analysts and the investment community knew there would be stability. It stopped all the rumors because everybody knew who they were going to work for after it was over.

Now, when I first did it, their first reaction was, "Jesus, you're really throwing the gauntlet down. This is really sort of final!" And I said, "Yeah, but *I'd* rather have the gun than let *you* have it. But do you agree it's the right idea?" They all agreed, to a person, it was the right idea.

Now, everybody [on the board] had been building their own views. So when I had the board meeting in October to lay out my views—and asked Dennis Dammerman and Bob Wright, the two vice chairman, and Bill Conaty to lay out their views—it started just rolling. And director after director was unanimous in the call.[28]

Again, what's striking is the length of the process: six years to the final choice, including four years to prune to three. As at Marks & Spencer, some rotation among jobs provided different experiences for the candidates. But as opposed to the Reg Jones–led precedent, no new layer of organization was created, and the candidates stayed in the field managing businesses. To the extent that they were competing, they competed on the basis of performance, rather than politics in corporate headquarters. And, significantly, Welch had his board members—individually or in groups—visit the candidates at their businesses, with an agenda controlled by the candidate. In this instance, the board members formed their own direct opinions. Note, though, that in this approach, there is no systematic means of sounding out candidates on their view of the environment that lies ahead. Presumably, board members elicited comments on that front during their one-on-one conversations.

The description of pruning by Lou Gerstner of IBM provides a useful addition to this discussion; it exemplifies a pattern that by now should be becoming clear:

> At my urging, the board early on established a rigorous process for considering management development. It was supported by two great HR staff I had recruited who had my confidence and that of the board. They provided institutional memory.
>
> Every October, the board would talk management development from 4:00 to 6:00 p.m. And it doesn't take very long into one of those discussions for some director to say, "Well, now, what happens if you get hit by a beer truck? What are we going to do?" So it was natural that as early as two years after I was there—that would be 1995—that we were talking at our board session on management development about succession.
>
> We would cover my direct reports, plus a few others (about twenty people who were in key jobs)—how they were doing, what we thought their future potential was, and where they might wind up. We would talk about a second category, too: emerging leaders who might someday be in one of the top three or four positions in the company and what we were doing about accelerating their development. And always a session on women and minorities—what we were doing to increase the pipeline coming up.
>
> I think that over a period of about four years, the board really got to know these people. At the same time, I really got

DRs plus 20

4 Yrs.

knght

to know how *I* felt about them—how they had done against some expectations that we had set, new jobs they took on, new responsibilities. By 1998, I had narrowed the candidates down to three who might replace me from inside. I began a program of making sure those individuals regularly made presentations to the board. As well, there were board trips where the directors got to spend time not just with those three but with others.[29]

I want to add one more example: Chuck Knight's management of succession at St. Louis–based technology and manufacturing giant Emerson. Knight himself had arrived at Emerson via an unusual route. As a leading consultant for his father's firm, Lester B. Knight, he had conducted more than forty studies for Emerson, including the last one: selecting the next CEO. Those projects introduced Knight to all the businesses and key managers of Emerson. So when he was chosen, he certainly was an outsider but effectively an Inside Outsider.

Knight was CEO of Emerson for twenty-seven years, during which time total annual return to shareholders averaged an amazing 15 percent. For Knight, succession was simply one more process that needed to be managed well.

I include Knight and Emerson for two reasons. First, their story provides a clear example of the way that passing the baton can start out as a horse race. Second, although Chuck Knight sought counsel from his board and others, he personally managed the process. As Knight recalls:

> In 1995, I went to the board. Now, this is five years before the fact. I said, "Look, I don't have any given retirement date in mind, but I think it's time to start the succession process." And the first thing we talked about was the question of not going outside of the company for a candidate. We discussed whether we had enough talent inside for the job. And we did. And I identified the five people who I wanted to go through an evaluation process, and I committed to keep the board informed on progress. They agreed. At no time in the process

did they meet with the candidates on the subject of succession. I felt that would be a distraction that might create a problem when we got down to the final decision, which the board, of course, would have to make. The board did, though, routinely meet with these individuals on other matters and had significant exposure to each of them.

I contacted a very talented consultant in Boston, who was referred to me by IBM, and who also works for Pepsi, and others. She and her group have established three parameters around which they have a database of CEO performance. One measure is the desire to achieve, another is the ability to work with people, and the third is what they call the "power motive."

All five of our people agreed to be evaluated on this basis. I wasn't sure they'd all agree to it, but they did. After evaluating the five, she sat down with me and we discussed their results on those three parameters. At that point, she predicted that one of the individuals was not the correct fit, and by the end of the process she was proven right.

One candidate, Bill Davis, chose to leave early. He was the oldest of the group, and he wanted to accept another offer if we were not prepared to move quickly. I told him that we were not yet ready to make a CEO selection, and he accepted the top job at R.R. Donnelley. That left four candidates.

The outside evaluations were only one way we were determining their fitness for the CEO position. For example, I developed a series of strategic questions for each individual to answer. One question was, how would you change the management process? Another was, what would your organizational structure for Emerson look like?

One thing I hoped to identify in the succession process was a leadership team of people who would have at least five- or ten-year perspectives with Emerson, so that the new CEO would not have to go into a dramatic reorganization. It would already be in place. So one of the questions was, who do you think should be in what positions? Getting responses from different candidates was very interesting. I also asked

Amyot

them, what is your perception of what I should do? Who
would you pick to be CEO if you went down in a plane—
who do you think would be a good CEO if it couldn't be
you? And finally, I asked how would you see the leadership
transition taking place if I continued as chairman?

I have a home in Michigan, and I had each of them come
up, individually. We began with dinner with my wife, and we
chatted informally. The next day, we'd begin meeting after
breakfast, and talk about their answers to these questions.
And we would talk as long as we wanted to.

Now, I have to tell you, this was extremely helpful. I
would talk to them at dinner the night before, and by the
next morning, I already had an idea of what was on their
mind. It was enlightening.[30]

This process continued for two years, with Knight having conversations with the four candidates that largely focused on his list
of questions. Not surprisingly, during this long process, he learned
a great deal about each of the candidates, including their opinions
of their peers. It was clear, for example, that not all of the candidates believed that each of the others was up to the task: "But they
were guessing who else was in the group, because I never talked
to them all together."

At one point, Knight promoted one of the candidates, George
Tamke, to the newly created position of co-CEO. Eventually,
though, Tamke made the decision to leave Emerson, and Knight
agreed with that decision. Tamke became a principal at Clayton,
Dubilier & Rice.

As the process continued to unfold, Knight talked regularly
with the board and met with the compensation committee of the
board, advising them of significant developments. Meanwhile, of
course, the pressures of business provided another proving ground.
As Knight recalls:

During this five-year period, one of our most important
business groups encountered some problems. Two executives

were given the chance to fix the business, and one of the two was one of the CEO candidates. Neither succeeded.

Then David Farr took on the challenge, and in two years he turned the situation around. Obviously, the board was watching, and they realized that it was a major accomplishment. He walked in there after two really heavy hitters had come up short, and did the job in an amazingly short period of time. So that influenced me a lot, because this was our biggest business and the key to overall company performance as we went forward. So David and I had a long series of meetings, and he made a really, really strong presentation on his views of the management process, and the direction and organization that he thought were right for the company.

Throughout the long process, Knight had been convening an informal group that consisted of long-term board members, two officers of the company, his outside PR executive, his outside St. Louis personnel consultant, and the consultant from Boston. That summer, the group reached a consensus that David Farr was the right choice. According to Knight:

> Once I'd made my choice, I recommended it to the board, and they agreed. This was in the fall, and we had talked about naming a new CEO early in the following year. But I felt it was time to *move*, and not put it off until year-end. The board and I were discussing the issue, and our annual corporate planning conference was coming up soon. This was a time when we assembled our top management—four hundred people—in St. Louis. So I suggested to the board, "Let's do it then." And we did. I had the pleasure of announcing our new CEO to our four hundred leading managers, and it was extremely well received. I remained as chairman for four years, and then became chairman emeritus.
>
> That was six years ago, and David and his team have done an outstanding job. And we have not lost any of the key people in our operations since then.

Now let's look briefly at the next formidable challenge that arises after the consensus is reached and the candidate is installed: the transition.

Smoothing the Transition

Let's assume that—as was true in several of the case studies presented in this chapter—you've settled on an absolutely outstanding candidate. You've found a Welch, an Immelt, or a Farr. So what happens next? Although managing the transition is not, strictly speaking, a part of the process of finding a great CEO, it certainly can affect the new CEO's chances of success, especially in the first few critical months. So a successful succession depends, in part, on a well-managed transition.[31]

The basics are obvious, but like so many things in management, success lies in the details. To begin with, if the baton is being passed, a clear date needs to be communicated—as does the implication of the change for the company. Board members play an important role here because they hold the power to elect the officers of the company.

Handling the aftermath of a horse race can be a little more complicated. It's typical to tell the winner the good news first and then impose a vow of silence on him or her until the other horses get the bad news. Eventually, the public needs to hear the decision—almost always from the incumbent CEO, not from the board or the winner.

If the board fires a CEO and that executive refuses to leave quietly, things can get awkward quickly. Inexperienced board members are often amazed to discover just how much havoc a spurned and burned CEO can wreak. One of the reasons why departing CEOs can receive huge severance sums—despite manifestly poor performance—is that the board has decided to buy a peaceful exit.[32]

These scenarios make for embarrassing headlines, but by this point, the horse is long out of the barn. We need to focus here on how to do things right—or, at least, *better*. One of the most important issues has to do with the time between the announcement and the installation of the new CEO. All too often, many months go by between these two events. And, all too often, there is confusion about who's doing what moving forward. For example, is the outgoing CEO going to stay on the board as a member? As chair? For a specified period or indefinitely?

The work of transition varies widely. As you might expect, it reflects the temperament of the departing CEO, the role of the board, and whether the new successor is an insider or an outsider. But let's start with some general propositions.

For an insider, transition consists primarily of:

- Learning about parts of the business that years near the top did not provide

- Developing a clear understanding of the corporate-level finances

- Learning about the management of key constituencies (e.g., the board, sources of finance, etc.)

- Establishing him- or herself as the company's leader

- Developing an agenda that incorporates key judgments about which matters facing the company are urgent and which can be allowed to gather some dust

For an outsider, by contrast, transition usually constitutes an almost overwhelming learning experience. For most, it is like drinking from the proverbial fire hose and includes challenges like:

- Learning about the people

- Learning about the finances

- Learning about the businesses

- Developing some kind of agenda that introduces the individual to the organization

Let's look at insider transitions first. Three of my interviews involving insiders provided very different approaches to this challenge and begin to hint at how wide the range of approaches truly is. These approaches reflect not only the personality of the incumbent but also the way the company in general is managed.

When I discussed transitions with Jack Welch, his advice for the departing CEO was typically pithy: "Get out. All you can do is get in the way."[33]

But, of course, this is only the punch line, made possible by all the years of work that had preceded getting out of the way. Welch had run GE for two decades, and his potential successors had all run enormous businesses within the company. The result, as indicated earlier, was that his candidates had had plenty of exposure to the CEO job. They had spent time with the board, presented their businesses to banks and Wall Street analysts, interacted with government officials relevant to their business, and, in many ways, were ready to step up.

As chairman-elect, moreover, Jeff Immelt had access to the senior members of Welch's team and to the leaders of the corporate staff. In fact, Immelt chose to retain certain key members of Welch's core team—most interestingly, Bill Conaty, the head of the executive development function.

Lou Gerstner approached transition from a different vantage point. As a successful outsider, he was going to pass the baton to an insider, Sam Palmisano. Early in the transition process, Palmisano served as chief operating officer, thereby demonstrating that he had the ability to run an $80 billion company.

During that time, Palmisano met with directors both individually and in social settings. Meanwhile, Gerstner asked John Thompson, a very talented IBM executive then nearing retirement, to serve as vice chairman. He gave Thompson a series of strategic questions to examine. With adjacent offices, Gerstner, Palmisano, and Thompson met weekly to discuss matters and, in the process, introduced Palmisano to the wide range of external and strategic issues for which he would be responsible as CEO. Gerstner decided that it would easier for Palmisano to engage a peer on these matters than to engage his boss—and, at the same time, Gerstner was there taking part in the discussion. In effect, Palmisano was getting a personal tutorial in the skills of an outsider.

Later—after the board had agreed to select Palmisano, and with Palmisano's blessing of the arrangement—Gerstner stayed on as nonexecutive chairman for nine months, spending increasingly less time at the job over that period. Gerstner's view, then and now, is that there is real value to the incoming CEO in having his or her predecessor available during the first critical months. After all, that predecessor not only has an unparalleled understanding of the business but also has a stake in seeing his or her successor *succeed*.

This conviction probably grows, in part, out of Gerstner's own experience of transitioning into IBM. He asked a retired senior executive, Phil Rizzo, to return to the company to provide guidance on strategic matters and administrative inheritance. Rizzo, by Gerstner's account, played a critical role in Gerstner's intensive learning phase at IBM: "The person I relied on most during [the] early days was Paul Rizzo . . . Paul had been a senior executive at IBM [and was a director] for twenty-two years. After retiring, he became dean of the Business School at the University of North Carolina, and was building a new house in that state. The last thing he needed was to come back to IBM—but he did, because he loved the company, and he didn't want to see it die."[34]

Emerson's Chuck Knight took still another approach to managing transition: he chose to stay on as nonexecutive chairman of the board for two years. Yes, he passed the baton, but he continued as chairman to help David Farr, the new CEO. In retrospect, he believes that his presence permitted Farr to concentrate on Farr's own priorities and not have to worry about the board and "all the other peripheral stuff that goes on."[35] This, in fact, was typical of modern transitions at Emerson, in which the outgoing CEO gives up the tough part of the job—the day-to-day operations—but retains some of the governance and ceremonial functions. In other words, at no point in the process is there a complete break in the continuity of leadership.

Surveys reveal that Emerson's approach is fast disappearing. The increasingly common practice in the United States is for the incumbent to step down and leave the board. In some circumstances, though, this hurts the company. Exceptions tend to arise in privately controlled or family companies, where the position of board chairman is a central mechanism in the exercise of control. In Europe, the opposite is true. There, it is not unusual for the chief executive to step up to the position of board chairman.

Lou Gerstner's creative deployment of Paul Rizzo touches on the central challenge of almost all outsiders. They really don't know what is going on, and, unless they're extraordinarily lucky, they may not learn some of the most critical facts for months. This may not be the result of malice or recalcitrance; the ongoing management team may simply have a poor understanding of the situation. In his book, Gerstner describes how shortly after his arrival he decided to start cutting the price on IBM mainframes—the company's principal profitable business—against the strongly held views of his financial staff. The others were "right" in the sense that the short-term hit from the price cuts would aggravate an already dire situation. But Gerstner was "more right." Mainframes still were the core of IBM's business, market share was dropping fast, and only painful price cuts would stabilize that share.

Because, as indicated earlier, learning is the outsider CEO's first, second, and third priorities, conventional wisdom might argue for holding off on a decision like slashing mainframe pricing. But something had to be done—and done fast. After all, that's why the company felt compelled to go against the odds and choose an outsider.

IBM was lucky, and Gerstner was lucky—and gifted, of course. But this brings us back to my central prescription: you need to manage your company and your succession in ways that minimize your reliance on luck. You've done that when you've picked an Inside Outsider. You can move forward quickly without the need for a Rizzo and without the risk that you are making major commitments to the world of yesterday.

The Role of the Board:
Another Measure of the Company

Obviously, the role of the board in key corporate processes is a topic of great contemporary interest. There is near-universal agreement—among hardheaded CEOs and governance theorists alike—that a principal responsibility of the board is CEO succession.

One reason for this rare unanimity, of course, is that under the corporate law of most countries, the board of directors or its equivalent has the legal requirement to elect the CEO. Beyond the letter of the law, though, there's also a good-governance consensus: *expecting the board to select the CEO is a good way to handle succession.* But is it true? What can the board contribute to the succession process other than the legally required signatures? It can provide help with judgments about the future environment and with independent assessments of people.

I believe that when it comes to the challenge described earlier in the chapter—developing an independent view of which way the world is headed—the board can contribute significantly. In fact, if board members are well chosen, they can probably make an invaluable contribution, based on their own experience with the technologies and markets on which the company depends. Of course, they are in a position to request independent studies that focus on key questions. They can keep asking about the future and keep assessing the talents of prospective successors. And, finally, they can get senior executives (and their fellow board members) out into the field.

A scientist on the board, for example, may suggest that certain executives visit his laboratory. A retailer may invite product designers to visit new outlets representing important trends. In the 1980s, some board members with firsthand experience of world-class Japanese competitors dragged reluctant executives to visit leading Japanese factories. (This scene was replayed in the

1990s; only this time, the head-in-the-sand executives were dragged to Shanghai Pudong to see the future in China.)

Conversely, of course, there is always the problem of the director whose knowledge is out of date. Even today, there are amazingly large numbers of directors (otherwise quite astute) who do not really understand the potential of the Internet. They tend to see it as a substitute channel for information or commerce, rather than an entirely new space in which products and services are reconfigured by the interaction of vendor and customer. In such cases, CEOs have to manage the process by which the board is tutored about the future—in effect, teaching their teachers—to be sure that the board's learning is up to date. But this is merely another part of the delicate process whereby a CEO manages his or her board.

Which brings us back, once again, to the proposition with which I opened this chapter: the idea that succession necessarily reflects the process by which the company is managed. If the board is engaged in the company on an ongoing basis, then it is in a position to contribute—not just when the final choice is being made, but also throughout the entire development process. Through their compensation committee, board members can insist on learning about the people who are running their company.[36] They can request data that goes beyond a simple ranking to describe strengths and weaknesses. (For example, they can read and discuss with the CEO and the head of executive development the reports from a "360 system" and similar processes.) Over time, this sort of information provides a cumulative picture of the progress that the company and its executive officers are making.

Board members can also request meetings with the top cohort. They can form their own opinions of those individuals through presentations of studies and projects, as well as in the context of strategic retreats. Some companies insist that major capital projects be presented to the board by their sponsor or the sponsoring team—often a very useful exercise. And those presentations may be followed by capital audits two or three years later, at which time the proponents explain what actually happened in the wake of the investment.

When divisions or groups are geographically dispersed, it is useful for boards or subsets of the board to visit these businesses and meet with their managers on site. Visits of this sort also help develop a picture of how that manager relates to his or her subordinates.

As the board learns, it becomes more useful to the CEO. Strengths and weaknesses within the executive corps may stand out starkly when viewed by committed outsiders. The CEO often knows why someone is in a job, despite his or her weaknesses; the CEO focuses on the complexities of the individual circumstances. Directors are more likely to focus on the weakness itself and its inevitable consequence to the organization—and if those directors are doing their job, they will object to an important slot being occupied by someone who can't deliver.

The converse is also true: directors may see the strengths of a quiet leader who has been overlooked by the CEO. Similarly, the strengths of a midlevel leader whose personality grates on the CEO may be more apparent to outsiders than to the irritated CEO.

The board can also help the CEO by keeping the executive development process high on the agenda. As I emphasized in chapters 1 and 2, a modern CEO is desperately busy just keeping operations on track and leading the crafting of corporate strategy. A very typical weakness of these busy people is to put the recruiting and development of the executive corps low enough on their agenda that it falls off entirely and becomes someone else's job—or no one's job at all.

As often as CEOs say, "People are our most important asset," they manage as if people are a factor input—that is, something to be bought, used, and discarded when run down. These CEOs tell me that they *know* that they should send several of their key people to executive development programs but that there just isn't time. What this usually means is that the CEO hasn't carved out time in his or her schedule to figure it out and make it happen.

This is a problem a board can address. Members can insist that a development program be put in place and make its implementation one of the objectives on which incentive compensation depends. They can also make it clear that a review of the program will be an important part of the board's agenda in subsequent years. My information is anecdotal, but when boards have made development an issue, directors report that there has been progress. Still, current studies indicate that the majority of companies believe that their development and review processes are inadequate.[37] What they tell me, in so many words, is that this is a big-deal problem.

It would be foolish to conclude this chapter without acknowledging that there are CEOs who get away with treating their boards as a group of friendly rubber stamps—good for Wednesday afternoon golf, but not for involvement in important decisions. In such cases, by definition, the board will contribute next to nothing to the succession process, other than validating the decisions of the CEO. This is simply a lost opportunity for the company.

Again, how you manage your company is likely to say a lot about how you manage succession—and how good a successor you're likely to come up with.

SIX

Why So Many
Companies Fail
at Succession

THE PREVIOUS CHAPTERS have laid out the basics of succession. On reflection, except for the patience and persistence required, no single step in the process seems very hard. Yet, picking up an opening theme, the process isn't working very well.

Every year for the past five years, the consulting firm of Booz Allen Hamilton (BAH) has conducted a survey of the world's twenty-five hundred largest public companies, attempting to develop a clear picture of the phenomenon of executive turnover.

The 2004 report was entitled "The World's Most Prominent Temp Workers," and it began with a provocative assertion: "The giant sucking sound heard in the business world during 2004 was the extraction of chief executives from seats of power."[1]

The rhetorical question posed by the BAH authors was whether—as a result of scandal and subsequent regulatory interventions—the corporate world had reached a tipping point. Was the power in the corporation shifting away from the CEO?

The authors answered their own question in the affirmative: "We are past that tipping point—not just in North America, but even more dramatically in Europe and Asia. More than 14 percent of the CEOs of these corporations left office in 2004. Of that group of departing CEOs, nearly a third—111 individuals, representing 4.4 percent of the total chief executive population—were forced from office for performance-related reasons or because of disagreements with their boards."[2]

The 2005 installment in the series was entitled "The Crest of the Wave." Once again, BAH's researchers found an astounding degree of turnover at the most senior ranks of the corporate world—and, once again, much of that turnover wasn't voluntary. As they put it: "Global turnover of CEOs set another record in 2005, with more than one in seven of the world's largest companies making a change in leadership—compared with only one in 11 a decade earlier . . . The rate of outright dismissals was also near its peak: Four times as many of the world's top CEOs were forced out last year as in 1995. Ten years ago, the CEO's job was all about 'stewardship' of the corporation's assets for stakeholders; today, it's all about the bottom line for investors."[3]

If you assume, as I do, that the data contained in these reports is accurate, then you have to conclude that corporate succession as it is currently practiced is a *disaster*. In fact, it's a worldwide disaster: almost one in five Japanese CEOs lost their jobs in 2005.

So why are all these train wrecks happening? The obvious culprit, as indicated earlier is a shift of power away from the imperial CEO—although it's not always clear to whom that power is shifting. I don't personally believe that this power is shifting, or should shift, toward boards of directors. As noted in previous chapters, boards are necessarily populated by part-time advisers. They can play a very constructive role in succession, but only as a special part of the set of processes by which the company is managed. Corporate power needs to reside in the hands of the individuals who, on a day-to-day basis, run the place and look out for the interests of the shareholders. Succession is one of their key responsibilities.

Another explanation is the recent wave of mergers and acquisitions (M&As). Logically, each deal winds up eliminating a CEO's position—a small but measurable part of the argument in favor of the combination, at least in some cases. And statistically, that is a source of turnover.

But the biggest category of change, by far, comprises what the BAH's researchers politely referred to as "performance-related" turnovers. In today's competitive conditions, it's hard for a company to perform at the levels investors want. When expectations are disappointed, investors are speaking. Here's the picture in the aggregate: Europe, Japan, and the rest of Asia have caught up with the United States so that turnover is around 15 percent, with performance the reason in something like 25 percent of the cases. (Mergers account for about 20 percent, and regular change accounts for the rest.)[4]

If you break these failures down further, additional interesting trends emerge. More than a third of the deposed CEOs in the United States, it seems, simply failed to make the grade. In Europe, the failed CEOs constituted more than 40 percent of all departures. And these trends have been in force for at least a decade: average CEO tenures drifting down, and the frequency of performance-based change trending up.

Let's dig a little deeper into this phenomenon and its causes.

The World Has Changed

Like everything else about succession, the negative trends just described reflect the interactions of complex forces. While much has been made of the new concern for governance—and while the BAH authors conclude that governance concerns are pivotal—my own research suggests that the underlying forces at work are larger and more fundamental. I'll cite a few of the most important ones in the next sections.

The Changing Nature of Financing

Simply put, the long-established tradition of relationship banking has been replaced by pure transactionalism, with much financing coming in the form of corporate bonds. The result? Instead of a banker with a relationship that includes a portfolio of the company's debt, there is an underwriter who earns fees for selling bonds to other institutions and the public.

This means that on the lender's end, math replaces judgment, and pressure for current earnings (those fees) replaces judicious review. The long-term vision of a company and its leader simply isn't factored in. And at a later date, if the value of the bonds deteriorates, the bondholder simply wants the money. Again, it's simply a transaction: there is no relationship between the lenders and borrowers that would provide the basis for a long-term work out.

The Changing Nature of Ownership

Meanwhile, the ownership structure of securities has changed. Resorting to some slightly exaggerated language to underscore my point, I argue that the ownership of corporate stocks has passed from the hands of stewards into the hands of speculators. Increasingly, as illustrated in table 6-1, individual investors have been replaced by institutions that trade on a short-term basis.

The size of the share-trading markets now dwarfs the size of companies. (In fact, the number of equity-oriented mutual funds now exceeds the number of publicly traded companies in the United States.) In 2006, the sum of private equity funds, venture

TABLE 6-1

Institutions' investments in the equity market and investment turnover, 1970–2005

1970	1980	1990	2001	2005
Percentage of equities held by institutions in overall equity market				
32.4%	41.4%	49.9%	56.9%	66.5%
New York Stock Exchange turnover				
19%	36%	46%	94%	102%

Source: SIFMA, Securities Industry Fact Book (2005), 63; New York Stock Exchange Fact Book, www.nysedata.com.

capital, and absolute return funds (which includes hedge funds) was estimated at $2 trillion.[5] Institutional investors hold their shares for far shorter periods. As speculators, rather than stewards, they apply increasingly short-term performance standards. If the company doesn't measure up, they sell.

In fact, some of today's institutions behave less like investors—with an eye toward the longer term—and more like raiders. In their investments, they follow analysts who are ranked quarterly for the performance of the companies they follow and who are rewarded munificently when they score highly. (See table 6-2.)

The Changing Nature of Takeovers

The changing nature of financing and ownership creates a huge market for corporate control. Almost any company whose shares aren't performing can be taken over because (1) there is enough fluid capital out there to raise the purchase price and (2) the owners-as-speculators are eager to sell if the price is right.

Look at figure 6-1. What's interesting here is the huge spike in the value of the deals that were put together in the late 1990s. Obviously, a period of retrenchment followed the dot-com bust and the 9/11 terrorist attacks. But, based on these data, it seems clear that every time enough money and greed come together in the marketplace, deals get done—and, by extension, CEO heads roll.

TABLE 6-2

Equity turnover by holder, 1990 and 2005

	1990*	2005
Trustees	17.2%	11.5%
Investment companies	5.6%	10.6%
Mutual funds	6.6%	18.6%

*The total equity investment in 1990 was $1.7 trillion. In 2005, it was $8.5 trillion.

Source: Federal Reserve Flow of Funds Accounts of the United States, fourth quarter, 2006, (Table L.213), www.federalreserve.gov.

FIGURE 6-1

Total announced worldwide hostile or unsolicited M&As, 1980–2006

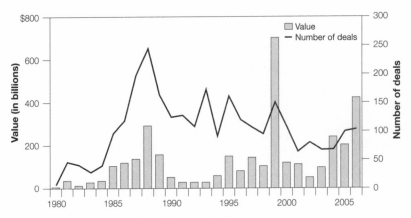

Source: SDC Platinum, a Thomson Financial product, www.thomson.com.

The Changing Nature of Competition

The changes in financing and governance is happening, of course, at a time when global competition makes it increasingly difficult for companies to perform up to expectations. In the real world, export-driven growth strategies favor newer manufacturers with (1) lower cost structures and (2) protected markets. They quickly gain market share and parlay that market share into economies of scale. Pressure on the earnings of major companies has been nothing short of brutal.

And the pressure on CEOs to perform quickly is nothing short of enormous.

The Changing Nature of CEO Compensation

Another major force affecting CEO job tenure, perversely enough, has been compensation.

Beginning in the 1990s, it became fashionable to pay for performance. In many cases, that translated into awarding large grants of stock options to CEOs so that their interests would be aligned with those of the shareholders.

Most of the obvious problems with stock options have been discussed endlessly, and I won't repeat those discussions here. But I want to add a nuanced point that comes to bear on the CEO job tenure/succession issue. What the proponents of options missed was that shareholders—who increasingly were speculators looking for a fast profit on a short investment—were increasingly willing to throw their weight around and play on a CEO's personal incentives. They would search out and cut a deal with a CEO who would, in effect, play ball with them: cut costs, drive up the earnings thereby push up the stock price and making those options more valuable with an eye toward either selling that big block of inflated stock or even selling off the entire company, perhaps generating an acquisition premium for themselves. If the financing for the transaction came from a hedge fund, the fees alone could be spectacular.

Even without unusual greed, the same problem easily develops. Recruit a CEO from a successful slot in a company where they have been a lifer. Ask them to move to a difficult situation in a new company—maybe in a new industry. They're not dumb. They can see the risk. So they want a win-win contract. They win big if they succeed. And they win big if they have to leave or sell the company (e.g., Robert Nardelli at Home Depot and James Kilts at Gillette, respectively).

Throw a criminally inclined competitor into the mix, and the results can be devastating. Recall the case of poor AT&T, which—in a doomed effort to meet WorldCom's magical numbers and thereby meet Wall Street's expectations—laid off tens of thousands and dismantled its strategy. Only later did we find out that a *real* strategy—AT&T's—was vanquished by WorldCom's phony strategy.

What's a CEO to Do?

A less-honest CEO simply looks left, looks right, cheats, and hopes for the best. But it's not a game. WorldCom's Bernie Ebbers was caught and received twenty-five years.[6]

From the point of view of honest CEOs—who make up the vast majority of CEOs out there, by the way—this is a very difficult question to answer.

Selling the company is an answer of sorts, especially for an outsider. The BAH studies cited earlier say that succession as a consequence of M&A activities went from 12 percent of all departures in the 1990s to nearly 20 percent in 2005.

The anecdotal evidence suggests that there's now a cadre of itinerant samurai CEOs, moving from one company to another to pick up yet another fat compensation package. Since the probability of long-term success in these jobs is low and, therefore, the tenure is likely to be short, the typical pay package provides a large lump-sum signing bonus, a healthy slug of stock-related compensation (options, stock appreciation rights, etc.) if there is the unlikely success, and an equally generous severance package to deal with the situation when poor performance necessitates that samurai CEO's departure. Win-win.

Truly, there is an Alice-in-Wonderland quality to these compensation packages. What happened to all that talk about pay for performance?

And what about the CEO who neither wants to cut corners nor fatten up the company like a Christmas goose? The answers aren't very comforting: develop the best strategy you can, implement the hell out of it, and cultivate good relations with the investment community and (far more important) your board. Meanwhile, and more to the main point of this book, start investing heavily in your succession planning. If you do that right, the chances of your potential successors being executives who can develop, implement, and cultivate as well as you—or better!—go way up.

What's a Board to Do?

Let's assume that the board is not a rubber-stamping body but actually has some authority and power, which it is willing to exercise. In the age of Sarbanes-Oxley, this is not an idle supposition; it is a legal presumption.

With or without the help of the CEO—depending on the circumstances of the succession—the board has to take steps to find the best possible person to take over the helm.

Well, how does the board do that? As we've seen, the people best suited to manage the process are the people on the ground. But given all the downsizing and other self-inflicted wounds, a lot of institutional memory may have been lost and along with it, internal ability. If this is the case, it's even more important for the board to step up.

You already know the choices: the board can look outside, or they can look inside. Almost certainly, they hire a search firm. While search firms are used to provide reassurance to boards during internal succession processes, they are a necessity for a board looking outside. If they do look outside, they are likely to be directed to one of the legendary people factories—GE and Procter & Gamble come to mind for generalists; Baxter, for technologists—where they will knock on the door with a large bag of money in hand and hope for the best.

What's likely to happen next? Well, the incoming CEO with a modicum of experience will find ways to cut costs during the first two or three years, thereby fattening up the bottom line somewhat. (This is especially true if the incoming CEO is a so-called turnaround artist, who is practiced at the art of corporate surgery.) After that, performance deteriorates, and it's time, once again, to get a new CEO. Most likely, the turnaround artist didn't have the time, motivation, or skills to work much on succession, so the board must look outside—again.

This time, though, the stakes are likely to be higher. The board now has at least one highly visible failure in its recent past. What follows, as a natural result, is a search for the "perfect leader," who will swing his or her sword and cut through all the company's mounting problems. This phenomenon is well described by Rakesh Khurana as a very unhappy process for the board and the company.[7] Why? According to Khurana, the perfect outside leader turns out to be imperfect at best. After he or she washes up on the beach, the cycle starts all over again, drawing on the same small and largely inappropriate talent pool.

Another consideration is how much time it takes for that outsider to wash up on the beach. Recall the relevant data from chapter 1: successful companies—companies that did well in the two years that preceded the succession—are one-third more likely to fire a new outsider than unsuccessful companies. In other words, poorly managed companies are far more likely to hang on to their outsider than are successful companies. Again, successful companies operate in particular ways and therefore think about themselves in certain ways. They want the best and invest in the best. Again, as emphasized in chapter 5, the way the CEO manages the development of leaders is the board's responsibility.

I have one last note before we turn to the problems created by success. There is a large class of transactions these days—leveraged buyouts—that have historically produced remarkable results. Those deals often involve a new CEO. Why do they do better? I discuss this more fully in the last chapter of this book, but here's the one-line answer: these companies have owners, rather than boards made up of independent directors. Usually, these private equity buyers look for the closest thing they can find to an insider—often a very experienced and successful retired CEO from the industry—and they motivate that person to build the kind of firm an owner would want.

The Cases That Produce Problems

Why do well-managed companies get into trouble when the time comes for succession? The answer lies in the downside of our opening proposition. The company has to be well managed operationally and strategically so that over time, it meets the expectations of the financial markets. But viewed from the perspective of succession, even the well-managed company creates new problems.

These fall into three categories:

- The style of the incumbent CEO

- Rapid growth

- Strategic inflection

The Style of the Incumbent CEO

Anyone who has studied successful companies has had the experience of meeting individuals who were larger than life. Even if their inherent temperament was quiet and modest to begin with, success wreaks its changes—in how they think of themselves, in how others see them, and in the kinds of input they get.

Success creates an aura of competence and, most likely, an increased level of self-confidence. (This is good up to a point, but past that point, it's problematic.) The successful CEO's calendar gets increasingly crowded as individuals and groups try to tap into his or her magic. With the best of intentions, associates start walling off the CEO, shielding him or her from "distractions." Contemporary corporate architecture compounds the problem, sequestering the CEO in a large office, often on an executive floor. The carpet is thick. The view is magnificent. The gatekeepers guard the palace, barring the door to reality.

Of course, CEOs can and do fight this tendency. Alex d'Arbeloff, founder and CEO of Teradyne, kept an engineer's cubicle for an office. Martin Sorrell, founder and CEO of WPP, has his corporate office in a mews house on a backstreet in London's Mayfair.

But even those who don't become self-impressed and who are truly dedicated to protecting the flow of unvarnished information from the outside—which helped lead to their success in the first place—can be thwarted. A member of Jimmy Carter's White House staff told me a wonderful story. The U.S. Secret Service cared so much for the president that, on at least one occasion when he went fishing at Camp David, those on service that day arranged things so that as he began casting his line, hungry fish from a trout farm were released into the water upstream. Carter, no doubt, would have been appalled, but his guardians distorted reality just to make sure that their hardworking boss had some fun.

This kind of assiduous care and feeding can cut the leader off from the rest of the organization—and from the rest of the world. Even when successful CEOs do get out in the world, it's a pretty rarified slice of life that they are exposed to. J. Irwin Miller, the legendary leader of Cummins, once noted that for both

CEOs and the queen of England, all the world smells of fresh paint.

And most CEOs aren't modest like Jimmy Carter or self-deprecating like J. Irwin Miller. They enjoy the many perks of office, as well as the exercise of power. They argue, accurately, that one reinforces the other, making it easier to lead. If you look and act invincible, you're more likely to be invincible. If you have your own elevator and your own plane, you save time. You don't get to talk to any but the chosen; you get digests of other views.

But the aura of invincibility creates a whole set of other problems. Remember that in chapter 2, when talking about Sir Richard Greenbury of Marks & Spencer, Sir Martin Jacomb remarked, "Acorns don't grow well in the shadow of great oaks."[8] When CEOs pull off the feat of appearing to be great oaks—which, of course, is gratifying and makes day-to-day life easier—then others around them can feel thwarted, diminished, and overshadowed.

It's the corporate equivalent of an ancient family dynamic. In healthy families, fathers inevitably arrive at a moment when their sons begin to challenge them and establish an independent path. For the healthy father, this moment is a curious mix of irritation and exhilaration: he *wants* his fledgling to test his wings. But there are also fathers who continue to demand obedience, even after that obedience becomes motivated by submission, rather than respect. When challenged by their sons, they react very badly, and ultimately their sons learn not to challenge, leave, or become warped.

There are CEOs like that—leaders who cow and break a whole generation of their most talented subordinates. When that happens, the board may decide that it's necessary to skip over that entire generation as potential successors. Alternatively, the board may decide to elevate a member of that oppressed cohort for a short tenure as CEO, with an eye toward finding a younger acorn that has developed away from the great oak's dense shade.

This oak-acorn phenomenon is one reason that many successful inside successions involve the appointment of leaders who have recently spent several years outside headquarters—for example, on overseas assignments. They've worked in the sunlight, where their full range of talents was visible and tested. They were aware of the imposing figure at the center of the oak universe, but they were not unduly impressed by him or her. They are, in other words, quintessential Inside Outsiders.

Rapid Growth

A second success-related problem tends to challenge the companies that have experienced rapid growth. Here, the problem as succession approaches is that the insiders who have worked tirelessly to achieve the present scale may be at the very edge of their capabilities.

Look at the underlying math. An executive who joins a company that then grows at 40 percent a year will be trying, within five years, to manage a business four times as large. Look ahead another five years, and the company is four times bigger still. When I discussed succession with Bill George, the retired CEO of Medtronic, he expressed the strong view that an insider was always a preferable choice. But then he explained how he and his board brought in an outsider to serve as chief operating officer for several years while grooming him to be George's successor. Why didn't they groom an insider? Medtronic's revenue had grown sevenfold under George's leadership. As George explains: "When we looked at the people who worked for me, we didn't see the range of capabilities that would be required to take the company to a whole new level. If the company continued to grow at 20 percent a year, they would be managing a $15 billion enterprise in three or four years. They were good but didn't have what Medtronic would need. Some were unhappy when we brought Art Collins in, but after working with him for a year or two, they acknowledged to me that they understood why we had brought him in."[9]

Scale makes a difference in terms of organization, systems, the nature of competition, and the relations with financial markets and other external constituencies. Untested talent can sometimes make the jump, but that is a risk the board may not want to take.

There is also a variation of the father-son problem here. It is always easy to attribute success to the talents of the departing CEO and underestimate the contribution and skills of the potential successor. This is especially true in the context of a functional organization, where none of the inside successors has had a chance to run a whole business with a profit and loss. The absence of general management experience, coupled with the scale issue, really drives the search process toward an outsider.

Strategic Inflection

Andy Grove defined a "strategic inflection" point as "a time in the life of a business when its fundamentals are about to change."[10] By definition, this is a time when the skill set of insiders may turn out to be ill suited to the challenges ahead. I have already suggested that the value of an Inside Outsider is that she or he may have the skills required in new circumstances. That, in fact, is how Reg Jones described Jack Welch. Jones saw a totally new set of circumstances ahead in the 1980s and thought Welch's technical training and tough personality would be well suited to the task. But it is understandable if those who have grown up inside an organization and have been crafted for one set of circumstances lack the mind-set appropriate for something really different.

It is also understandable when a board that has concluded that it faces a strategic inflection point decides that the insiders lack the skills to take the company to the next stage of development. They are implicitly discounting the value of the team they have been developing, but it is a common conclusion. Tom Neff of Spencer Stuart and Gerry Roche of Heidrick & Struggles, both CEO search gurus, spoke to the greater tendency of boards to discount the abilities of insiders when they believe the circumstances ahead will be substantially different.[11]

But all this can be managed. (That is what chapter 5 was about.) Great oaks, rapid growth, and strategic inflection are not new phenomena. They are as old as the history of organization.

And they can be recognized, and managed, as forces that simply make succession a bit harder.

Great oaks need to give potential successors some room. Overseas assignments make sense. Organization can be changed to create more general management roles. In the interests of efficiency, companies may retain the functional structure they used to grow big. But managing new business with distinct business units pays a big long-term dividend in the form of general managers who can grow business and potentially lead the company. Rapid growth needs to trigger even more attention to recruiting and developing talent. If the problem is recognized early enough, the pool can be enriched by lateral hires so that several years later, succession can be managed in a normal fashion.

Strategic inflection is harder to manage than incremental growth, since the ability to recognize big movements early is a scarce talent in and of itself. But that makes it even more important for strategy to be on the board agenda annually. The best stimulus for developing talent is the recognition that the strategy under development will require a raft of great people who are not now in the company.

These are exactly the kinds of issues that boards should be discussing with their CEO. They are part and parcel of the resource allocation process. Dealt with successfully, they create all kinds of associated benefits—including, for example, protecting the corporation against marauding speculator owners.

To recap the cold but inescapable logic: outsiders have a hard time succeeding. Insiders may have problems, too—especially if their rise reflected their ability to serve their boss's vision, rather than developing their own. Those insiders' wings have been allowed to atrophy at exactly the career junction when they should have been exercised and strengthened.

A company has to recruit, organize, plan, and invest in ways that teach its most talented people how to fly. If you skip that investment, you ultimately pay the price: you get to recruit an outsider and pray hard.

SEVEN

The Special Case of Family-Business Succession

Rarely there descends from the branches (father to son)
Human probity, and this is the will (of the one)
who gives it, because it is asked alone from him.

The welfare of a Republic or a Kingdom, therefore, is not
in having a Prince who governs prudently while he lives,
but one who organizes it in a way that,
if he should die, it will still maintain itself.

—MACHIAVELLI, *Discourses*

THE CENTRAL PREMISE of the previous chapters has been that managing succession has three key characteristics. It is:

- Critically important
- Very difficult to get right

- Very likely to reflect the way that you manage your business overall

So far, I've described succession and how it can be managed in the context of large publicly traded companies. Now I want to complicate the equation by looking at a very special context: the family business.

Why? Because families have significant or controlling positions in about a third of the large firms in the United States and Europe and about two-thirds in East Asia.[1] If we consider all publicly traded firms, the number would be over half of large firms,[2] and adding private firms would simply increase the percentage. In other words, family ownership is very important.

On an intuitive level, we grasp that managing the succession process in a family business is a good-news/bad-news story. The good news is that you know where to look for candidates and that the candidates should have a long-term perspective about the company. The bad news is that picking the right leader for the family enterprise is complicated immeasurably by relationships among siblings and cousins, by relationships between parents and children, by the challenge of managing the distribution of income and benefits across the family, and, especially, by relationships among family who are working in the company and those who are not.

Family tensions surface dramatically when it comes time to choose a successor. Brothers and sisters compete bitterly for the crown, with all the violence of unresolved sibling rivalry. Sallie Bingham forced the sale of the Bingham family newspapers rather than see her brother continue as the leader. The third generation of Pritzkers forced the breakup and sale of their father's real estate empire.

Whatever tensions exist in sibling relationships are exacerbated when one sibling is proposed to be elevated to the throne the father occupied. It is about power, money, prestige—in fact, it is about everything that people fight over.

Managing Succession in a Family Company: An Overview

As I've already explained, succession is a process that reflects the way the *company* is managed. Ideally, it begins early, perhaps a decade before the event. Succession in a family business also reflects how the *family* is managed and, in particular, how the children have been brought up. Whatever patterns have developed in the relationships get played out in exaggerated form, precisely because they've had years to be refined.

The very first questions that need to be considered—which are often ignored—are if the company should remain in family hands, and if so, why. There are only two good answers. The first is that there is a cross-generational agreement that this is a good idea. The second is that managing the assets invested in the company is the best way the family knows to preserve and grow its wealth.

If no one in the successor generation wants to manage the company, then forcing that outcome is unlikely to work. And if the successor generation can manage passive assets better than a company—or if the descendants are simply not good at business—it may make more sense for the family to monetize the company's wealth by selling it. So, for the purposes of this chapter, when I talk about "family succession," I am talking about the circumstances in which the decision has already been made to manage the family wealth through the founder's company.

This leads, in turn, to two more questions:

- Who will control the wealth represented by the family ownership?

- Who will control the management of the company (which includes not only who sits in which chair but who controls the people who sit in the chairs)?

Neither question is easy. And, in most cases, both involve the sorting out of complex family relationships.[3]

The wealth management problem can be separated from the business management question as long as control of ownership is not involved. Expressed another way, as long as the ownership of the company is private, the arrangements for the distribution of dividends, ownership, and inheritance are a matter for the family. But many forces tend to push in the direction of public ownership. Successful companies eventually outgrow even a very wealthy family's capacity to sustain them, and at that point, access to adequate quantities of capital often requires a public listing. Inheritance taxes too raise questions of valuation and liquidity that are well handled by public share ownership. Once there are public shares, though, control of the company becomes an issue, as family interests and those of public shareholders come into conflict. For example: How much of a dividend is enough? What kind of expenses are excessive? If a family member is accustomed to taking the maximum possible amount out of the company in the form of dividends or perks, what happens when the publicly held company can no longer justify that strategy?

The distribution of income, ownership, and inheritance are no small problems. Typically, the family members who are engaged in management see the need for retaining income in the firm more clearly than do the passive owners. And personal relationships are never far below the surface. The passive owners may be skeptical of the capabilities of their fellow family members as managers. Worse, they may actively distrust or even *detest* them and hate the idea that "their company" is paying good money to their incompetent relatives. The resulting fights, obviously, can be quite bloody.

If the previous generation of the family tended to distribute income on an equal basis to all of the next generation, the salaries earned by active family members can be awkward, especially in big companies where the compensation can be high. Complicating the matter are management perks such as company cars and planes.

But there are mechanisms that can be put in place to offset perceived inequities and reduce potential tensions. For example, many families establish offices that are separate from the company and that serve to make the treatment of active and passive family owners transparent and equal. A family holding company is another mechanism that can help deal with ownership and inheritance issues. It is in that forum that trade-offs between company needs for retained income and family needs for current income can be sorted out. Yes, these conflicts can be bitter, but unless they escalate into lawsuits, they can be kept separate from the management and board of the company.

But even assuming that all these matters can be resolved in some reasonable fashion, the issue of management succession remains. Let's go back to the metaphors of running a horse race and passing the baton, introduced in chapter 5. What works, and what's poison?

Running a horse race inside a family falls into the latter category: poison. It is almost guaranteed to turbocharge whatever sibling rivalry exists. To be sure, the family needs to identify the best family member to run the business, but it needs to do so in a way that builds consensus around the decision. This process has to start early and be consistent. From very early on, the company and its management need to be discussed with the children. Rules need to be established for who gets to work for the company and how progress in the company will be managed. The ground rules have to be absolutely clear. For example, is the company a meritocracy, or does some other rule apply? Out of this single decision flow all kinds of other decisions, including things like how relationships between the family managers and the professionals will be sorted out.

For the family that has decided to grow its wealth through the company, the challenge of management needs to be established early. The idea that education and training and hard work are involved must be part of the indoctrination just outlined. The notion of leadership as a privilege or an opportunity for service—rather than an entitlement—is an absolutely critical one. So is practical experience, preferably gained in contexts where a family member is not the judge and jury. First jobs outside the firm help develop younger leaders and also help establish their credibility once they join the company. And by "credibility," I mean both in the eyes of work colleagues and of nonmanaging family members.

Obviously, this is a full and daunting to-do list. But only after it has been attended to can the family move on to the equally daunting set of succession challenges outlined in chapter 5.

The Costs of Bad Succession: The Fall of the House of Bronfman

When you hear the phrase "family business," you may think "small stakes." But that's not necessarily so. The financial stakes, as well as the emotional stakes, can be enormous.

Let's deepen this discussion of family businesses with an extended case study, focusing on the Bronfman dynasty and the Seagram empire that it built—and ultimately destroyed. I'll argue that poor succession planning contributed significantly to that outcome.

Samuel Bronfman, the son of eastern European immigrants, built his tiny Montreal liquor distributorship into Seagram Company Ltd., the world's largest distillery. Sam Bronfman was a seat-of-the-pants entrepreneur—the sort of business builder who overcame his rough origins and prevailed in a tough industry. He involved both of his sons, Edgar and Charles, in the business and resolutely kept all other family members out. "I don't believe that anybody should clutter up his business with relatives," he once commented.[4]

When he died "in the saddle" in 1971, he left his family 33 percent of the stock of Seagram—a controlling interest that was worth some $671 million at that time.

The older son, Edgar, then forty-two years old, relocated to New York City to become the company's new CEO. His brother, Charles, two years younger than Edgar, kept peace in the family by remaining in Montreal and accepting a completely subordinate role—deputy chairman—and serving as head of the Canadian operations. Here, we see a typical family-business succession, although played out with less drama than some: the older brother steps into Dad's shoes, and the younger brother acquiesces. Charles focused much of his attention on outside activities, including the Montreal Expos baseball team, of which he was the principal owner.

Seeing only limited growth potential in its core business—hard-liquor consumption was on the decline—Seagram began a long process of diversification, including significant investments in oil and gas properties. To make a long and complicated story short, in 1980 Seagram got in a bidding war with DuPont for Continental Oil and ended up not only reaping a $2 billion profit on its oil properties but also owning one-quarter of DuPont's common stock.

Seagram's DuPont stake was a passive investment, but a highly profitable one. Between 1980 and 1994, the Delaware-based chemical giant's stock tripled in value, and the value of the family holding rose to $4.3 billion. Meanwhile, the $2 billion in DuPont dividends that Seagram received in that period helped pay for a massive retooling of the core distillery business.

So far, so good. We can see in retrospect that Sam Bronfman made a good choice when he made the *obvious* choice—that is, picking his oldest son. Edgar came up through the business, and although the succession process was accelerated by Sam's death, Edgar was prepared for his responsibilities.

The same cannot be said of Edgar's son, Edgar Jr. (For simplicity's sake, I'll call them "Senior" and "Junior" hereafter.) Junior was the prototypical black sheep of the family.[5] After graduating from an elite New England prep school, he declined to go to college and instead began working in the New York theater community and Hollywood, and also launched a songwriting career, working under two pseudonyms. Although Senior refused to support his son in these ventures, which he considered silly and self-indulgent, the Bronfman name opened many doors.

Overshadowed by Junior and his glittery success was his brother, Samuel Bronfman II. Sam was nineteen months older than Junior and was an odd mix of stolid and flaky. He went into the family business (stolid) but was caught up in a strange kidnapping episode in 1975, which may or may not have been staged for unknown reasons (flaky). Sam then relocated to northern California to head up the Seagram Classics Wine Company.

In 1980, evidently impressed by Junior's budding success in Hollywood, Senior called him in for a talk. He told his son—then twenty-six years old—that Junior had what it took to run Seagram. Junior was tough, creative, and independent minded—something like his father, in fact. And Junior didn't have to be in Hollywood to exercise his creative imagination; business offered ample opportunities for that.

Junior probably surprised them both by saying yes—on three conditions. First, he would begin by taking a temporary job with the company, to see if it was a good fit. Second, Junior's older brother, Sam, would have to give the arrangement his blessing. And, third, Junior would need assurances from Senior that Junior would ultimately get to run the company, assuming he proved himself.

Junior subsequently remembers his father agreeing to all three conditions. Neither Senior nor Sam recalls any discussion of Sam's blessing—a conversation that Sam would presumably remember, had it happened.

In any case, Junior began his climb up the corporate ladder. Signing on in 1982 as assistant to President and COO Philip Beekman, Junior quickly disarmed his critics inside and outside the company. Despite his near-total lack of relevant experience, he seemed to have a natural ability for business. He relocated to London to take over Seagram's money-losing European operations and soon turned that collection of businesses around. He returned to the United States in 1984 to run the core spirits business; a year later, he took over the moribund wine-cooler division. Drawing on his still-active Hollywood ties, he persuaded Bruce Willis to star in an ambitious ad campaign; Seagram's wine coolers went from number five to number one in the market.

In 1986, Senior decided to name Junior as the eventual successor to Beekman—and, by extension, to himself. Father and son posed for a *Fortune* cover story about the planned transition—which stung both Uncle Charlie and brother Sam, who objected to both the outcome and its public disclosure, which they thought was premature. (In fact, the succession was planned for some unspecified date in the future, which turned out to be almost a decade off.) But both Charlie and Sam eventually calmed down, and Sam and Junior patched up their relationship.

Even before getting formal authority, Junior began putting his stamp on the company. He bought Tropicana in 1988 for $1.2 billion, which probably was too high of a price; he also began buying premium spirits brands (like Martell cognac) and selling off low-end Seagram brands. On balance, this portfolio tweaking was generally positive and bought entrée into foreign markets that Seagram would have been hard pressed to gain otherwise.

In late 1991, Junior began looking for a major acquisition or investment for Seagram, presumably to play the role that the DuPont coup had played for his father. After conversations with a range of investment gurus, including the legendary Herb Allen, Junior settled on the communications industry as a high-growth area. Unfortunately, there wasn't much available except Time Warner. Beginning in 1993, at Junior's direction, Seagram began investing in Time Warner stock, reaching a 15 percent stake by the spring of 1994. Time Warner's board eyed Seagram warily and even erected a poison pill defense to fend off the Bronfmans, if necessary. For their part, the Bronfmans called themselves "friendly investors" and wondered aloud what all the fuss was about.

In the summer of 1994, Senior turned over the day-to-day operations of the company to Junior, who was formally installed as CEO. Senior remained on as chairman of the board but vowed not to get in Junior's way—a vow that, in retrospect, he should never have taken.

As it turned out, the Time Warner fuss was soon overshadowed by a bigger deal. In 1995, Junior, the newly installed CEO, liquidated Seagram's $9 billion stake in DuPont to buy MCA, the entertainment conglomerate.

In retrospect, it was a disaster. The DuPont stock doubled in value over the next three years; therefore, MCA (later known as Universal) cost Seagram shareholders an *additional* $9 billion.[6] Over the next few years, Junior continued buying his way into the music and film industries, with generally unimpressive results. In 2000, he led Seagram into a terrible acquisition by French conglomerate Vivendi—a $34 billion deal that was strongly opposed by Uncle Charlie and other family members—and assumed a minor executive role in that company. When Vivendi teetered on bankruptcy shortly thereafter, the Bronfman family fortune was reduced by $3 billion almost overnight.

Junior was named one of the worst managers of 2002 by *BusinessWeek*. "Probably the stupidest person in the media business," *New York* magazine opined in 2002.[7] Junior eventually left his Vivendi position and, in 2004, bought Warner Music, naming himself chairman and CEO.[8] That investment has proved modestly profitable.

What can we learn from this multigenerational saga?

The third generation is hardly in rags, but a great deal of its value has been lost. Succession was managed so that control of the company rested with one side of the family, Edgar Sr. In turn, he gave control to one son, who quickly moved a major block of resources from chemicals to entertainment, an industry dominated by entrepreneurs. It is not clear that change was needed; Edgar Jr. wasn't particularly well grounded substantively or administratively; and he appears to have lacked leadership skills, although he surely had the will to lead. Strong will, however, is no substitute for proven management ability. The successes in the modern mass entertainment industry—Sumner Redstone (Viacom, Paramount), Rupert Murdoch (News Corp, Fox), and early Michael Eisner (Disney)—built remarkable teams that worked with them over decades. Cutting losses and moving assets are not the skills needed to build a team that can create sustained value.

But there is no evidence in the Bronfman saga that these managerial issues played a role in the decision making around succession. The first problem was how Edgar Sr. and Charlie would relate. That was resolved by the older taking over the business and the younger stepping back—in other words, traditional primogeniture, to which we're about to turn our attention. The second had to do with how the ownership rights of the second brother would be handled. They were more or less ignored, in favor of a pure power play.

Primogeniture:
The Most Arbitrary Template

Primogeniture technically means being the first born, but in the legal tradition, it generally refers to the oldest son's right of inheritance. It was originally a way of keeping the family landholdings together, but over the centuries, it has come to apply to other kinds of family property, as well, including the family business.

When it comes to naming a new head for the family business, a surprising number of families start with the eldest son as the obvious candidate. (Sam Bronfman I did; Edgar Bronfman Sr. didn't.) Because the primogeniture tradition is so deeply engrained, it can make managing family relationships a bit easier by depersonalizing the succession decision: "It's not that I don't trust you, but tradition dictates that I give the business to your older brother."

Many fathers have a strong desire to pass on their legacy to a son who bears the same name, which is most often the oldest son. In addition, in most cases, the older son—who, by definition, has been around longer—has more experience, has made more of an impression on the father, and therefore becomes the logical candidate.

But there's no guarantee that the oldest son is the most competent person for the job. In one European company with which I am familiar, a sequence of three sons as CEO nearly ruined the business before control finally was passed to a very capable daughter who wanted the job all along. There isn't even a guarantee that the oldest son will be interested in the business, if and when the time comes.

In another situation in which I played a peripheral role, the father has done a brilliant job of building a world-class company. But this turned out to be something of a golden trap: the more successful and valuable the company became, the less feasible it became to effect a transition to either of his two sons. Fortunately, the father was wise enough to organize a transition from his direct leadership to a professional CEO working under his chairmanship, whereby he could exercise a stewardship role and supervise the company's strategy.

Of course, this has only delayed the ultimate issue of succession. It now appears that a very capable daughter will someday succeed her father as chair of the family holding that controls the company—which, of course, will present a new raft of challenges. For example, up until now, the children have been on a more or less equal financial footing. Now the daughter will be filling a highly responsible and demanding position for which she will have to be compensated. Will her siblings understand and accept that? Life in a family business is not easy.

Professionals for the Second Generation

Belén Villalonga has carried out a series of empirical studies of this problem. She has found that one scenario—in which the first-generation family members define a stewardship role for themselves and pass operating leadership of the company on to professional managers—often leads to the best results for the companies.[9] This is exactly the scenario I just described.

What it provides is a separation of ownership from management. Owners can take a long look at performance. They are substantively and administratively grounded, and they are in a position to see strategic issues well. They are managing for generations, so short-term blips can be ignored and intelligent risk can be accepted. In turn, with the family forces removed from inside the company, succession can be managed in the fashion described in chapter 5. Issues of control do remain, however, as explained later. But, first, let's look at an extreme countercase to the Bronfman story—a four-generation success story—to see what is involved for multigeneration succession within the family to succeed.

The Gerdau Group: Getting It Right

The Gerdau Group is a manufacturer and distributor of long steel products the largest in the Americas.[10] The company dates back to 1901, when a German immigrant named João Gerdau bought a failing nail factory. The extended Gerdau-Johannpeter clan has run the enterprise ever since, with four of João Gerdau's great-grandsons currently in senior positions at the company.[11]

Over the past ten decades, the company has grown from a producer of nails in the southern part of Brazil to a multinational with an important and expanding position in North America. Much of the work of expanding the company was carried out by the four great-grandsons, the Johannpeter brothers. Recruited to the company by their father, Curt, they started working when they were young, mainly carrying out menial tasks. Over time, their studies and their temperaments determined the more senior roles that they eventually took on.

By the traditions of primogeniture, the oldest son, Germano, would have been the logical leader of the company, but he much preferred heading the sales and marketing, deferring to his brother Jorge, whom he felt had the temperament and intellect appropriate for a job involving relationships with unions and governments. A third brother, Klaus, studied engineering and found it natural to head up the development of the company's physical plant. The youngest brother, Frederico, studied commerce and rose to be the chief financial officer.

So the brothers were all different, and they took advantage of those differences to benefit the company. At the same time, they worked hard to achieve and maintain a consensus. Toward that end, they held a near-continuous four-way conversation over the years and decades—about the business, and about themselves—so that they could move quickly and decisively.

What's interesting is how organically these relationships evolved. Curt's eldest son, Germano, started to work at Gerdau in 1951 at the age of seventeen: "I didn't have any formal instruction on how to work in a steel company. I started going to the factory with my father, and then, suddenly, I was working for the company. We hadn't formalized my position, we hadn't even discussed what I was going to do in the company, and yet it was very natural. It simply happened. I can see now that everything was so improvised. Today, we have access to a lot of information through newspapers, television, the Internet. At that time, we had to learn by doing."[12]

Three years later, Klaus and Jorge (then nineteen and eighteen, respectively) also formally joined the company—although for them, as for Germano, spending time at Gerdau was nothing new. Klaus recalled his first days at the plant: "We four were given responsibilities very early. In fact, our lives have always been linked to Gerdau. When I was thirteen years old, for instance, I spent my time sweeping the plant's floor while my father was working."[13]

In 1961, the youngest brother, Frederico (then nineteen) joined his father and three brothers at Gerdau. Together, they worked to build a completely modern business. Although control rested in the hands of the family, a group of very talented professionals was recruited, some of whom sat on the board of directors with the brothers.

In recent years, a leading consulting group specializing in talent was recruited to assess the capabilities of the management. Naturally enough, the consultants looked at the up-and-coming fifth generation, four of whom were already starting to climb the ranks of the business. Among them, the four Johannpeter brothers had a total of sixteen children, but it wasn't a given that any of them would be prepared to take over in the future—in fact, some of the fifth generation have left the company.

The same set of issues led to the retention of another major consulting group to help restructure the company as a modern multinational, in which family ownership and company leadership were separate.

Compare this with the Bronfman story. To begin, the four Johannpeter brothers sorted out active roles for themselves that reflected their personalities. The oldest deferred to a brother he thought better suited for the CEO role. And they continued to talk with each other about the company's affairs and waited for consensus before taking strategic decisions. Instead of freezing out talent, they gained the benefit of four different perspectives. We can only admire what must have been the strength of their parents as they were brought up. It is not surprising that when any of the brothers are in town, they still have Sunday lunch with their mother.

More striking are the steps they have taken to manage the transition to the fifth generation. While they have welcomed family, they have set the bar high and used outside resources to improve the chances that succession will be successful. As noted, some senior members of the fifth generation left the company. And they have built a team of nonfamily executives who play critical roles in the top management team. In a sense, they are preparing for a situation in which family may not prove to be good enough. Even this short summary of these actions highlights how unusual they are and how troubling the situations could be, if it's mishandled.

General Principles

Let's examine the general principles behind successful succession in a family business.

Separating ownership from leadership, the first step in this process, is the key challenge that faces a family wishing to retain control of the company. Why? Because it is necessary to ensure that over time, the company is well managed. Children and cousins often lack the talent, the will, or the desire to cooperate.

A wonderful description of the battles involved in this shift is Alfred D. Chandler Jr.'s account of the introduction of professional management to DuPont by Pierre du Pont.[14] Family financial interests were dealt with by a finance committee of the board of directors. Meanwhile, a standard of quality was put in place: while family were welcome to work in the company, they had to meet the same high standards as other executives.

The second step is defining the relationships among siblings and cousins. The founding generation can establish policies and legal frameworks that may well resolve problems, and there are legions of lawyers and trust officers available to provide advice. But the heart of the matter is that the founders must work to bring up a congenial group of young people in which relationships are governed by comity, even when there is conflict. Regardless of the legal arrangements, there must be consensus among the second generation. The Bible, Shakespeare's plays, and the business press all testify to how often that process breaks down.

The third step involves the establishment of policies that dictate how family who want to work for the company will be treated. Here, as you'd expect, there is tremendous variety. One CEO of his own firm described his family as so obsessed with the threat of nepotism that they drove out *all* family members: "The company had very strict policies concerning the proper preparation for entering the firm in terms of education and relevant work at other companies. The result is that none of the family works there today. None of us could get by the hurdles that were set up, although many of us have had very fine careers in business."

Another firm takes the view that any family member who wants to sign on will be found an appropriate entry-level job. What happens after that, however, is a function of the individual's progress. The problem is, of course, that young people with names like *du Pont* or *Rockefeller* are not just any employees. They are owners and have to be treated with some delicacy by the organization.

As mentioned earlier, family members often begin their careers at other companies—for example, at the banks or consulting firms that serve the business. These interested third parties may provide a kind of informal graduate education in a functional area or corporate-level activity and generally provide very useful exposure to the way another large and/or skilled organization does business. When sons or daughters return to the family company after a success elsewhere, there is a heightened legitimacy to their subsequent progress within the company.

The Upside of Family

It's common for media accounts to focus on family-business train wrecks or, at the very least, the eccentricities of the ownership class. But many executives with whom I have discussed the matter actually regard family ownership as a blessing at a time when so many public companies are driven by pressure to generate short-term profits. Many of the participants in Harvard's General Manager Program are from privately owned or controlled companies, and they speak of the satisfaction and the opportunities that grow out of this kind of long-term perspective. They know what the world is like for the companies, such as those described in chapter 6, that are controlled by speculator owners. Jorge Johannpeter, Gerdau Group's chief executive, provides an apt summary of what they find appealing: "A company needs values to survive. In the end, values come from the personal, as in a family. So participation of owners helps to build values that incorporate a long-term view. Today, the biggest problem is profit for the short term versus strategy for the long term. My shareholders want profit today. But my interest is in long-term market share."[15]

Simple comparisons of privately owned firms with their public counterparts suggest that it is not just market share that can be achieved. A *Business Week* study of family companies finds their total return on capital exceeding that of their publicly held counterparts.[16] *Business Week* attributes this generally superior performance to a number of factors, including the ability to make decisions quickly and foster loyalty. But the most important success factor, concludes *Business Week*, is having the CEO trained by a father (or other relative) who cares. I would agree that this is a great path—when it works out.

Which brings us back to succession. Using proxy data from all *Fortune* 500 firms during 1994–2000, Belén Villalonga's study shows that it is important to distinguish among family ownership, control, and management. She finds that family ownership creates value when the founder serves as CEO or, as in the case described earlier, as chairman with a professional CEO. Descendants as CEOs, on average, destroy value.[17] Edgar Sr. was unusual; Edgar Jr. was not.

BusinessWeek's assertion that plenty do better doesn't offset Villalonga's findings. The difficulty, of course, is that succession questions are compounded by family conflicts, family tendencies to smooth over those conflicts, and the difficulty of making harsh objective judgments about family members. It is almost impossible to imagine a family following the pruning process described by Emerson's Chuck Knight (see chapter 5). The family relationships would never recover.

This is not to say that tensions and rivalries within a family are necessarily a destructive thing. I think, for example, of the sort of rivalries exemplified by the Merloni brothers. Franco Merloni inherited the leadership of the Merloni business on the sudden death of his father. His company today is an industry leader in Europe. But both his brothers chose to build their own businesses, rather than work as part of a family team. Today, Vittorio (who founded Merloni Elettrodomestici, now known as Indesit) and Antonio Merloni compete with each other as important players in the European home appliance industry: Vittorio is number two in Europe; Antonio is in the second tier. Asked to think of a critical moment in his company's history, Vittorio Merloni pauses, adopts a grave expression, and cites a juncture when a key competitor could have been bought out—had his brother loaned him the money.

One of my favorite Merloni brother stories dates back to the occasion of the twenty-fifth anniversary of Vittorio's company, Merloni Elettrodomestici. Pope John Paul II attended the ceremonies held at one of the factories. He was told that the company had capacity to make 2 million machines. Brother Antonio, hearing this statistic, at first described it as being preposterous. But, when he learned it was indeed true, he immediately invested so that his company *also* would have a capacity of 2 million. That is the energy of sibling rivalry transferred into the business arena.

Great Potential; Tough to Realize

Let's close this chapter with some general reflections on succession in family businesses. Family businesses have great potential, which is often hard to realize. One reason for that difficulty is the challenge of trying to act meritocratically when every emotional impulse may be running in the opposite direction.

When the succession process begins with a generation in control of a successful company, there are distinct advantages. In particular, short-term questions of performance are likely to be irrelevant or at least far less compelling than they are for most public companies. A second advantage is that the pool is well identified. Whether the next generation will develop as managers strong enough to lead the company is a question that will only be answered in time, but it is clear where the investment needs to be made.

But as suggested earlier, everything else is a bit harder in the family context. Once the younger people are at work in the company, they need the same kind of development assignments as nonfamily managers. To reduce the parent-child tension, it helps if these younger people can work in a field that complements the first generation, so that they need not destroy the work of their elders in order to drive real change. Overseas assignments work very well in this respect. (It is the same principle of oaks and acorns that we have discussed, but respect for family elders can exacerbate the problem. At Gerdau, members of the fifth generation of Johannpeters were permitted to show their mettle on North American assignments.) So does the development of new technology, which often comes easier to the younger generation than the older one.

The pace of transition is often awkward. In a public company, if the CEO is determined to hang on to age sixty-five or older and an heir apparent succumbs to the Tonto syndrome—that is, gets tired of being second fiddle, it's a problem. But, in the worst case, that heir apparent leaves, and life goes on. Assuming the company has followed the general prescriptions laid out in this book, there is a deep pool of Inside Outsiders to draw from. But, in a family company, if the son or daughter takes off, the family succession plan goes out the window, and there's no backup plan.

And most fathers who are also founders don't like to be rushed. Think about the patricides that we've all read about in ancient history, which revolve around exactly the kinds of issues that we are discussing so gently here. I've talked earlier about the passion and intellect of business. When a son or daughter is pushing his or her father, there is extra passion mixed into the equation. And this is a baton pass that I am discussing; if a family is foolish enough to run a horse race, assume that things will be even worse.

Were a family to ask me what to do, I would advise them to try to make family succession work, since the benefits can be so great. Toward that end, I would advise them to work their children really hard along the dimensions where they have talent, all the while trying to instill notions of discipline and service. That wonderful institution, the family dinner, would be one key forum where the most important issues of the company (and the family) would get discussed. Education would play a critical role. Increasingly meaningful employment—including business trips, as appropriate—provide an introduction to the workaday world, including building relationships under difficult circumstances.

Collectively, all these processes contribute to the happy outcome of allowing children to learn their own preferences and hone and demonstrate their skills—in ways that are sometimes surprising to both them and their parents. And these processes help build a family team that works well together.

And all of this, in turn, would help increase the chances of a fruitful family succession.

EIGHT

What We Ask
of Our Leaders

There is nothing more difficult to take in hand,
more perilous to conduct, or more uncertain in its success,
than to take the lead in the introduction of a new order of things.

—MACHIAVELLI, *The Prince*

A S WE CONCLUDE this book, it may be useful to step back
from our topic—effective leadership transition—and scruti-
nize it once again from a broad perspective, letting the passion back
into the discussion.

Succession in the leadership of human organizations, broadly
defined, has always been of great interest and importance to people both inside and outside of those organizations. Historically,
of course, succession mostly involves the leadership of a nation
or a church—and, in those contexts, the story tends to be about
imperfect and violent succession.

Political successions in democracies are relatively peaceful
transitions in the sense that in most cases, no one actually dies.
But they can be gently violent, nonetheless. In the typical U.S.
presidential election, for example, espionage and dirty tricks run

rife, friendships are conditional, and resources are mobilized toward one goal: winning. The reputations of disabled war heroes are trashed. The measure of a proposed smear is not whether it is a fair and honorable tactic but whether it will gain traction and not blow back to damage its perpetrator. Money flows to wherever it may buy advantage. Even physical confrontation can be called into play, as in Florida in 2000, when Republican election workers from all over the country converged on that critical state and used physical intimidation to force a temporary postponement of a recount. It was this postponement that gave the U.S. Supreme Court time to validate Florida's vote, allocate the state's electoral votes to George W. Bush, and make Bush the victor in the succession struggle.

Whatever your politics, it wasn't pretty. Nor was Watergate and its aftermath, in which several remarkably talented White House staff ended up in jail.

Succession: Passion and Payback

Controversial successions have their natural follow-ons: purges.

In the wake of a contested transition, those holding positions in the bureaucracy and military are removed—one way or the other—to make way for those whose loyalty to the new leader is beyond question. Some are killed, some exiled, and some deprived of all means of influence. After the purges comes a phase of consolidation of power, in which the rulers—still quasi-legitimate, at best—test and compel obedience. In the reign of the Tokugawa in Japan, noblemen governing in the provinces were compelled periodically to relocate their families to Edo, the imperial capital, so that their fealty to the Shogun would be assured.

I raise these other contexts of succession to underscore the continuing and common element in all these struggles: *passion.* Succession in companies is less violent, but it's still a battleground of great passion and intensity. The bigger the prize, the more likely it is that several brilliant type A alpha males or females are plotting to storm the corner office. Typically, several of the senior executives who report to the incumbent CEO are among the plotters. They've been in that corner office, and they've already thought about how they would redecorate it.

Some sense for how this works is conveyed by *Business Week*'s description of Henry Paulson's ascent to the CEO's job at Goldman Sachs in 1999. Note the references to pain, oustings, and coups:

> Monday, Jan. 11, was a painful day for Jon S. Corzine, the leader of Wall Street's most prestigious investment bank, Goldman, Sachs & Co. That morning, from his unassuming office at 85 Broad Street in the heart of New York's financial district, Corzine called clients and regulators to tell them his astonishing news: He was no longer chief executive of Goldman Sachs. . . .
>
> Insiders and competitors alike say Corzine was ousted in a coup within Goldman's all-powerful five-man executive committee. Corzine was forced aside by a troika of senior bankers: his co-chief executive, Henry "Hank" M. Paulson Jr.; Goldman's top investment banker, John L. Thornton; and Corzine's protégé, Chief Financial Officer John A. Thain. "Everyone liked Corzine. No one likes to see someone ganged up on," says one insider.
>
> Yet talk to Paulson, now Goldman's sole chief executive, and all is running like clockwork in Goldman's executive suite.[1]

As that passage suggests, becoming CEO is usually the end of one campaign and the beginning of another. That alpha male or female got the coveted job and now has to *do* something with it. The first step, commonly, is the formation of a team of executives who will work together with the new CEO to provide coherent leadership for the company. Consolidation of power in the corporate context can be extremely difficult. It is likely to be incomplete because internal challenges to the new leadership tend to take a certain amount of time to develop. The challengers' inability to resort to violence, in most cases, makes rebellions heat up more slowly. And passive aggression works very nicely as a mode of resistance. It is easy for a new CEO distracted by a host of serious challenges to misread cooperation from disgruntled senior executives that is really: perfunctory. In many companies, consolidation comes as the victor's former rivals for the CEO job leave for leadership positions elsewhere. Think of GE, for example, where four of Jack Welch's rivals left for top jobs in other companies and where, in the next succession, Jeff Immelt's two rivals were relieved of responsibility by Welch in the process of anointing Immelt.

Some chief executives go to great lengths to hold on to their disappointed former rivals—in part to retain access to their demonstrated talent and in part to keep an eye on them. The classic example from politics is Abraham Lincoln, who assembled a cabinet of ambitious overachievers, most of whom saw Lincoln as a weak and naive country boy whom they could dominate.[2] From the business realm, Immelt has worked hard to retain the top executives in the cohort just behind him.

With or without the departure of key executives, forming a new team is challenging. Especially where new directions are contemplated, finding the appropriate talent often involves going outside the company. For example, at Brown Group, after the election of Ron Fromm as CEO in 1999, the following appointments of outsiders were made:

2000   A new general counsel

2002   A new president for the largest division, followed
       by a new number two for that division, a new head
       of HR, and several other new staff

2003   A new chief operating officer

At Brown, Fromm was an Inside Outsider. He was number two in the retail division, which in the hundred-and-two-year history of the company had never produced a CEO. The process of bringing in outsiders to reshape the team took five years.

At Marks & Spencer, outsider Luc Vandevelde was brought in as chairman to resolve the failure of the inside candidate. Once he concluded that his CEO was ineffective, he took the job himself and replaced half of the top management team with other outsiders in the space of a year.

Whether or not new people are brought in, there are almost always reorganizations on some scale or another. As discussed in chapter 4, the effective management of succession almost always involves organizing the company so that the principal candidates are given jobs of roughly equivalent influence and visibility as a means of proving themselves. As the pruning takes place, the rivals are given increasing control over the operations of the company.

Following succession, of course, the organization lines must be redrawn to facilitate the development and implementation of new strategy. As we have seen, whether the new strategy involves a turnaround or growth in a new direction, new configurations of executives will be involved. Consultants may or may not be brought in as the strategy and structural context of the company are revised.

A good description of the magnitude of the new CEO's task is provided by Siemens CEO Heinrich von Pierer, the quintessential Inside Outsider. He had a long career at Siemens but also served as an elected member of the city council in his hometown of Erlangen—not the usual background for a German CEO. He also boasted of being the only CEO in Germany who was a member of a "works council."

> In 1989, when the Berlin Wall came down, we were excited to be celebrating the reunification of Germany. We did not realize something more important: The collapse of the Eastern Bloc was more or less the beginning of globalization. And a global marketplace at that time meant that prices really came down. That's a nice mild phrase to describe what happened. Prices started falling in '89, and the decline became more brutal over time. The prices in some of our businesses dropped by 50 percent in three years.
>
> A year or so after I took over as CEO, a friend I have a lot of respect for asked me, "Do you know that in your

annual report, you use the term 'price erosion' 13 times? Is this an excuse?" And it came to me suddenly that it *was* an excuse, as if we were saying, "Our company's in bad shape because other people are behaving unreasonably." Complaining about price erosion didn't do us any good. So this comment from my friend was an awakening. He was right, and I knew that our company needed to change.[3]

Von Pierer went on to change nearly *everything* at Siemens: the cost structure, the capability for innovation, the ability to grow, and—hardest of all—the culture. As he recalls:

Some people told me when I started, "It's nice to talk about culture change, but how long do you think it will take until you really achieve something?" I said, "Well, two years." They laughed. "Young friend," they said, "it will take ten years." And unfortunately, they were right.

To me, it's perfectly obvious that an outsider lacking von Pierer's intimate knowledge of the company would have had a *far harder* time making all these substantive changes at once. Perhaps "two years" would have turned into "twenty years"—or never.

I've already discussed the pressure that is exerted on CEOs by the financial community. Sometimes, Wall Street (and its equivalents around the world) gives advice that from the outside looks sensible, but from the inside looks terrible. Along the way, Siemens's von Pierer got lots of guidance from the financial community. For example, they strongly recommended that he sell the medical systems and power-generation equipment businesses. These two divisions, von Pierer later observed, ultimately turned out to be central pillars of the company's dramatic revival:

If we had listened to the financial analysts during the 1990s, we would have sold off most of the company by now.

Even in the midst of crisis, I knew our medical business was stronger than they could know, so I didn't listen to them . . . Then the power business went through a crisis. Again the financial people told me, "Don't invest." It was a good thing

I had some experience in the business. They said, "There's no growth in power." I said, "Wait a bit. There's overcapacity now, but this goes in waves" . . .

In secrecy, we made the decision to keep the power business and buy Westinghouse Power Corporation, which turned out to be a real success story. In fact, it was one of the smartest moves we made in my time as CEO. So this shows the wisdom of financial markets, you know?

I have been arguing this key proposition for many pages now. An outside perspective is necessary for the insider who will drive strategic change. And surely Siemens and von Pierer illustrate again the virtues of the Inside Outsider. Over the twelve years of von Pierer's leadership, 1992–2004, Siemens's revenues grew from €41 billion to €75 billion, and net income grew from €1 billion to €3.4 billion. Meanwhile, the firm's center of gravity shifted to include the United States and Asia—an enormous transition for a formerly traditional German company.

Note the references to ten years for cultural change and twelve years to reorient a major manufacturing enterprise. This kind of work takes *time*. It would almost certainly take an outsider more time. It also takes skills, including skills that an outsider probably doesn't have or probably can't take the time to acquire.

The Right Stuff

Let's return briefly to the criteria outlined in chapter 3 for picking leaders:

- Has a critical view, can see the need for change   *1*
- Is substantively grounded, knows the issues   *2*
- Is administratively grounded and plugged in   *3*
- Has leadership skills, wants to lead   *4*

To borrow a phrase from Tom Wolfe, this is the "right stuff" that you're most likely to find in an Inside Outsider.

If you think back to Heinrich von Pierer's account of his early years, he had to accept the idea that Siemens was not succeeding because it was fundamentally ill suited to the world in which it was competing. The company had to change—or more accurately, *parts* of the company had to change. Von Pierer had enough experience with the company's businesses to understand which ones (like medical systems) were badly managed gold mines, which were in cyclical troughs, and which could be strategically improved through alliances. To make the required changes in costs and culture, he had to understand far more. He had to understand the people of the company and how to speak to them. And, finally, he had to be willing to work at his agenda for more than a decade, constantly talking to groups and individuals who had to accept disagreeable changes in their lives for the good of the company. In short, it was hard, grinding, brutal work.

There is a tendency in reporting the achievements of executives like von Pierer to emphasize the cost cutting and repositioning that they achieve. But for the most part, when these executives are interviewed about their accomplishments, pruning the corporate tree is *not* what they talk about. As we've seen, von Pierer emphasizes his unwillingness to sell off the power business. Lou Gerstner was ultimately celebrated for rejecting the plans that were already in place when he arrived on the scene to reduce the integration of IBM. Mike Armstrong, who ran AT&T, has described the fierce pressure he was under to cut his costs and abandon the strategy he had put in place.

This is as close as it comes to making an individual decision as a CEO, and it can get very lonely. And this, in turn, brings us to a fifth attribute of the leader:

- Has the toughness to maintain his or her personal perspective in the face of resistance from key colleagues

For the Inside Outsider's virtues to be realized, in other words, he or she has to be willing to act personally on the conclusions to which his or her understanding of the organization and the need to change have led.

A good example is provided by Frank Dangeard, the CEO of the French company Thomson. He described for me the critical period after a successful turnaround during which he settled on the new strategic direction for the company:

> So we were looking at businesses and trying to find businesses that were still relevant to our core competencies but were stronger, were more cash generative, were maybe less volatile. And we had one or two very small businesses inside Thomson, which were B-to-B type businesses, where we felt these characteristics could be developed.
>
> We spent a lot of time thinking about: Is our core competency the end consumer? Are we actually about consumer electronics? In which case, why not do what Philips does, buy a shaver company or go into PCs or go into mobile phones? Is this really where our brands, where our technology skills, where our [intellectual property] portfolio applies?
>
> And the more I thought about it—*because, I have to admit, this was a very lonely journey*—all my colleagues, whether keepers of the RCA brand or keepers of the Thomson brand, saw themselves at the center of the universe of consumers. And I remember very well the executive committee . . . where I told them, "You guys are completely wrong."[4]

CEOs also tend to emphasize the hard work involved in persuading the organization of the necessity of change. Part of the difficulty, it must be admitted, lies in the outside perspective of the newcomer or the Inside Outsider. If the newcomer talks the talk of the outsider, the insiders are predictably threatened.

As Alfred North Whitehead remarked, "Routine is the god of social organization."[5] Up and down the ladder, people want to protect their routines and stay in their grooves. On a somewhat higher level—but operating in the same corner of the brain—managers want to protect the status quo because they don't want their skill set rendered irrelevant. And if the organization has a history of past success, people are less likely to embrace a very different formula. "It is one thing to feel confident," as Winston Churchill once put it, "and it is another to impart that confidence to people who do not like your plan, and who feel the same confidence in their knowledge as you do in yours."[6]

The so-called change literature speaks about the importance of a "burning platform."[7] Urgency—the smell of smoke in the air—does help in some cases. But it can also be paralyzing. What successful new CEOs do is help their people understand how markets and technology have changed—without scaring them to death and without destroying the god of routine (at least, prematurely or gratuitously). After all, it's these very people who then devise the policies and programs that allow the company to move forward. Without their engagement, the CEO is John Sculley at Apple: proud, polished, and eventually irrelevant. The new vision stays a vision and is never implemented.

The right stuff is hard to find. One reason why we see so many corporate crises today is that there aren't many executives who have the elusive balanced mix of talent, energy, experience, and substantive knowledge and skills. The insiders lack the outside dimension, and the outsiders aren't insiders and can't fill the gap. The saga of the not-very-portable GE executives related in chapter 1 is telling. Yes, they were all great general managers. But more than half of them lacked the substantive and administrative knowledge needed to bring those talents to bear in fundamentally new contexts. Recall my metaphor of the musician: it is not enough to be a great violinist if the task at hand requires a horn player—or a maestro. And, sometimes, taking a great violinist out of a great orchestra diminishes that violinist.

Just being an insider doesn't guarantee the right stuff, of course. Many otherwise wonderful insiders lack the willingness or simply the capability to change their inheritance so that they and their organizations can succeed. A good example of the problem is provided by Intel, where talented insiders have been working for a decade to break out of the powerful administrative and strategic inheritance of Gordon Moore and Andy Grove.

Craig Barrett, the CEO who succeeded Grove, understood better than most the dilemma in which he found himself. In fact, he coined the phrase "creosote bush" to describe the way the systems and processes of Intel's core microprocessor business killed off new things before they could flourish. Time will tell whether he found an antidote for those poisons. Case studies suggest that he may have been too much the insider and not enough the Inside Outsider. For now we can observe that growth at Intel is slower but that its competitors are falling back.

The Infinite Learning Curve

Leadership has—or ought to have—an infinite learning curve. Here's one good question to ask a potential CEO: "Do you have the fortitude to keep learning?"

Learning requires both self-confidence and intellectual curiosity. Confidence is important because you have to be able to say, confidently, that you don't yet know everything there is to know. Curiosity is important because it is the raw fuel of learning. There's a stage of childhood development in which a child's favorite word is *why*. Somehow, great leaders retain that childlike openness and inquisitiveness.

What's the other side of the coin? For many people, the uncertainties of a job make them insecure. They get the job and realize that their chances of actually mastering it are quite limited. Under those circumstances, a common pattern is to seek control— by which they mean eliminate surprises.

One of the executives I interviewed put it this way:

> I've seen situations where the people with the title *president* or *CEO* are insecure in their position. And, sometimes, times are difficult. The company isn't doing well. News of problems for the CEO usually comes from below, so the CEO may focus on loyalty, rather than who is the best candidate for the job. They want to know "who's watching my back?" They want people in key positions who they feel comfortable with.

But the organization sees it. They see you picking cronies, rather than the best performers. And they start thinking, "Maybe this *isn't* a meritocracy."

Putting loyalty above competence produces at least two negative results: the team is weaker, and the organization concludes that there is no organizational justice—no rational system whereby rewards will be doled out. Performance suffers, and a vicious spiral develops as insecurity is heightened.

As the same executive noted: "As people get more senior, they get more insecure. They have no coaches, no one to talk to. Good managers learn that they have to have junior coaches. They seek out younger people in the organization who will give them honest feedback."

What happens when someone *can't* learn—or *won't* learn?

Well, one answer is that they sell—especially if their compensation package includes stock options or the equivalent, such as stock appreciation rights. In such cases, the personal reward for turning off the curiosity switch, deciding that you can't help this particular company, and finding a strategic buyer can be huge. James Kilts earned $175 million in three years for selling Gillette to Procter & Gamble. The incentive for Kilts was irresistible, especially since he had learned the benefits of such sales when after a decade at RJR Nabisco, he personally earned $65 million for selling Kraft Foods to Philip Morris. So why *not* sell?

Under these circumstances, it is not surprising to see the current statistics on CEO tenure in public companies. In chapter 6, I introduced some of the data from Booz Allen Hamilton's annual study of CEO turnover in global companies. Forced turnover is up 300 percent since 1995. "Underperformance," wrote the researchers, "—not ethics, not illegality, not power struggles—is the primary reason CEOs get fired."[8] See figure 8-1.

In fact, the "performance related" category in the figure may be understated, in the sense that the "merger driven" category probably includes mergers prompted by CEOs who see no other way out. And I'd bet that many CEOs in this "merger" category discovered, to their dismay, that their learning curves were finite.

FIGURE 8-1

Global rates of CEO succession, by reason for succession, 1995–2004

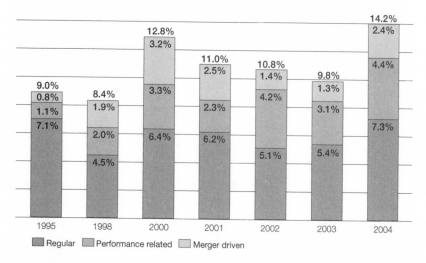

Source: Reprinted by permission from *strategy+business*, the award-winning management quarterly published by Booz Allen Hamilton, www.strategy-business.com.

The Right Stuff Goes Wrong

If you frequently find yourself dealing with people who are imperious or self-important—or if you yourself are sometimes inclined that way—I recommend that you commit to memory Percy Bysshe Shelley's *Ozymandias*:

> *I met a traveler from an antique land*
> *Who said: "Two vast and trunkless legs of stone*
> *Stand in the desert . . . Near them, on the sand,*
> *Half sunk a shattered visage lies, whose frown,*
> *And wrinkled lip, and sneer of cold command,*
> *Tell that its sculptor well those passions read*
> *Which yet survive, stamped on these lifeless things,*
> *The hand that mocked them and the heart that fed;*
> *And on the pedestal these words appear:*
> *My name is Ozymandias, King of Kings,*

Look on my works, ye Mighty, and despair!
Nothing beside remains. Round the decay
Of that colossal wreck, boundless and bare
The lone and level sands stretch far away.

We put enormous burdens on our leaders. And those burdens change the people who bear them. On the positive side of the ledger, these individuals grow. They overcome obstacles and build self-confidence. Their personalities develop; their repertoire of communication, persuasion, and administrative skills broadens; and their relationships with constituencies that are important to their company grow deeper and become more extensive. If their organization is of reasonable size and if they succeed along key dimensions, these leaders will become the subject of flattering stories in the business press. They may even become celebrities.

This is all very gratifying and generally harmless.

Then there's the negative side of the ledger. Shelley's *Ozymandias* captures one entry. Successful CEOs not only get great press notices; they often come to *believe* them. In the worst case, the initial face of leadership—self-assured, but still welcoming— becomes the "sneer of cold command."

These CEOs knew, at one point, that change was necessary. They tried several things, and—magically—some worked. (The ones that *didn't* work have most likely been forgotten about.) These executives pursued ad hoc avenues vigorously and achieved great outcomes; a decade later, they were lionized by *Fortune* or the *Financial Times*.

Under these circumstances, it is easy to mistake the repertoire of ad hoc moves for strategic principles—for eternal verities, rather than a group of policies that worked well for a period of time. Marks & Spencer's Clinton Silver described the problem as "confusing successful practices with underlying principles."[9] At Marks & Spencer, the clearest example was "buying British." As long as Britain was the textile capital of the world, being the largest customer of the best suppliers was a sound policy—the right way to provide good quality and value. But as soon as the Asian textile powers mastered quality *and* speed, then buying British was a sure route to loss of market share.

Greenbury may have understood intellectually that change was needed, but when he achieved leadership his focus was first on improving internal efficiency and then to preside over geographic and product-range expansion based on proven Marks & Spencer principles. He continued to view the company as a leader, even as new competitors—such as the Spanish Inditex's retail chain Zara—were penetrating the U.K. market. He saw the steady improvement of profits as evidence of the success of his strategy, was celebrated in the financial and business press for his achievements as a leader, and was knighted by the Queen. He led an important government commission on governance. All in all, heady medicine.

Intel's Andy Grove captures this critical problem in his wonderful book *Only the Paranoid Survive*:

> Senior managers got to where they are by having been good at what they do. And over time they have learned to lead with their strengths. So it's not surprising that they will keep implementing the same strategic and tactical moves that worked for them during the courses of their careers—especially during their "championship season."
>
> I call this phenomenon the inertia of success. It is extremely dangerous and it can reinforce denial."[10]

Success also carries a price because of its impact on a CEO's calendar. Unless CEOs are very careful, they can quickly find that the demand for speeches, service in the community, and even participation in internal processes take time away from the activities that were at the core of their early success. Often, those early successes grew out of talking with important customers, meeting with new recruits, getting steeped in the technology in the company of engineers, or getting a dose of the marketplace in the company of salespeople. The impromptu visit to the nearby university campus, with ample time to get a window into developments in relevant technologies, gives way to the charity ball or the convening of the blue-ribbon panel.

Yes, part of the job is telling the company's story again and again.[11] But another part is listening to people who might have something new to say.

One leader I interviewed spoke of the change that came when he "reached the sixtieth floor," as he put it. "It was very quiet. The offices were huge and beautifully furnished. The views were magnificent. In two weeks, I realized that I didn't have a clue what was happening in the business." This kind of isolation is reinforced by the delights of limousines, private planes, and country clubs.

Again, Andy Grove has a powerful way of stating the problem: "Do people seem to be 'losing it' around you? Does it seem that people who for years had been very competent have suddenly got decoupled from what really matters? Your genes were right for the original business. But if key aspects of the business shift around you, the very process of genetic selection that got you and your associates where you are might retard your ability to recognize new trends."[12]

Grove speaks of the value of listening to "Cassandras," who send warnings in e-mails from the periphery of the business: "There is a fine distinction here. When I say, 'Learn what goes on at the periphery of your business,' it means something different than if I had said, 'Learn what goes on in your business' . . . When I absorb news or information coming from people who are geographically distant or who are several levels below me in the organization, I will triangulate on business issues with their view, which comes from a completely different perspective."[13]

The question comes down to whether the CEO's calendar has room for people who are geographically or organizationally distant. If it does not—if it is too crowded with pomp, circumstance, and self-celebration—it may render that CEO unable to pick up on strategic shifts in the environment.

Sumner Redstone of Viacom was notorious within his company for talking about the most serious company matters with all sorts of people. As Tom Dooley—formerly Redstone's executive vice president in charge of finance, corporate development, and communications, and a key confidant—put it: "Despite his reputation, Sumner is a very consensus-oriented manager. He wants to hear all sorts of points of view before he makes his decision, and usually he'll couch it in a way where if somebody has a real issue, he'll stop and say, 'Wait a minute. Does so-and-so have a point here?' He's very good at looking at all sides of the issue."[14]

Unfortunately, Redstone's willingness to listen in all directions is unusual—particularly for a leader who's been in the job for more than a few years. Think about it: for all their perks and privileges, CEOs need a healthy dose of humility—or even a streak of masochism. They must organize their lives to let in criticism and challenges to their wisdom—the more painful, the better. (It's a little like leaving the sunroof open on your car as the clouds are opening up.) When CEOs hear such information, they have to resist the temptation to treat it as griping or insurrectionary rumblings and instead test it and file the good stuff away for future use.

But what if the alternative is a good day of golf with friends or with the CEO of a top customer? What if the alternative is a retreat at Herb Allen's place with fifty other titans of industry? Would you rather spend a day at the beach or at the dentist?

It takes discipline to seek out and listen to the periphery. This is why there is a natural limit to the effective tenure of CEOs. At some point, adulation drives out reflection.

Breaking the Mold

My main point, at the end of the day, is that succession has to be managed so that there is at least one qualified Inside Outsider to choose from. If there isn't, the company may find itself in a bind. The insiders are often not ready to lead change, and the outsiders are often not able to lead or sustain it.

What's to be done in that case? Having admitted in advance that we're already making the best of a bad situation, let's look at a clue that's provided by the buyout industry. While not well regarded by many in practice and in the academy, some buyout groups have had considerable success buying divisions of large companies, installing new management, and providing the capital so that the newly independent firm can grow.

There are two aspects of the buyout industry's business model that help explain this success. First, in almost all cases, the acquirers achieve majority control of the business. In effect, they have taken it private. That means that until they liquidate their investment, they have an owner's perspective, not a speculator's. In the most mercenary terms, it will be hard to sell if they haven't fixed it.

Second, when they install a CEO, that person almost always has industry knowledge. Rather than recruit a star from GE, they are far more likely to hunt and hire a successful manager from the exact same industry who, for one reason or another, is available to take the job.

So what can we say about this type of hired guns? At least four things:

- Because of the way they've been hired, they have to take a critical view. They can see the need for change.

- The very reason they've been hired is that they are substantively grounded; they know the issues.

- The power of the owner makes up for knowledge of the administrative inheritance that the incoming CEO lacks. But this is always a key issue. These CEOs' success in the same industry usually means they know at least something about the company they are about to lead.

- Not least important, they're getting the rare chance—a chance they may never have had before—to lead a company in an industry they know well, with the financing to make growth happen and with an equity position their success will make them wealthy. So they have a strong incentive to lead.

In other words, while lacking insider credibility, they have approximations to the characteristics of an Inside Outsider.

Contrast this circumstance with most outside successions. Executives are hired for their performance running a business that is likely to have been *very different* from the one they are stepping into. The contract that is negotiated is usually not tied (or tied sufficiently) to the long-term success of the company. They are joining a company that's in some kind of trouble. In most cases, they are hired by part-timers worried about the stock market's short-term assessment of performance and consequently are insecure. And for all these reasons, they have the incentive of a hired gun. Get in, do what you can, and when trouble appears, cash in and leave.

The board that has done its homework knows the company has its stable of Inside Outsiders: chomping at their bits, kicking their stalls, waiting for a turn around the track. But what about the typical company—the one that doesn't have eager, well-qualified contenders? How avoid the hired gun?

The answer is, "Start ten years ago."

That is, obviously, a somewhat facetious prescription—only slightly more actionable than "pick your parents well"—but you get my point. A board that *hasn't* set up succession planning this effectively needs to recognize its shortcomings and break the mold of traditional hiring practices. The board should instruct their search consultant to find them the kind of manager a buyout firm would choose—and then, having found him or her, negotiate a contract with the individual that looks a lot like a buyout firm's contract.

If go outside . . .

Alternatively, the board should look inside for the strongest manager they can find and give him or her the CEO job. Then they have to pull out the organizational stops and figure out how to help that new CEO succeed. For all the reasons described in previous chapters, that won't be easy. The new CEO will need to reframe relationships and establish credibility while learning. He or she will need to reestablish the confidence of senior executives who are friends while asking them to change. Most of all, the

CEO will need *time* to grow personally and to perform. The growth part may well involve executive education, reaching outside to consultants for industry information, competitive analysis, executive assessments, and even personal coaching. He or she will probably need measures other than share price to be weighed against, so that he or she can be rewarded for accomplishments that don't show up on—or actually drag down!—the bottom line.

Nor can the board sit back and exhale once the CEO starts gaining traction and the company seems to be progressing. That's precisely the moment—when the platform isn't burning and when no one feels particularly hungry or threatened—when the board needs to start investing in the development of leadership talent at every level of the company.

Investment turns out to be a two-step process. In step 1, as part of the early work of the new CEO, the board needs to work with the outsider or the insider to build the capability to manage succession. In many cases—maybe even most cases—that means hiring a chief talent officer who can partner with the CEO to help drive the process. Step 2 comprises developing a way of managing that generates Inside Outsiders who are great candidates for succession—my chapters 4 and 5, if you like.

The conclusion, in other words, is that there is no shortcut to providing strong leadership for a company. We have examined the process of succession up close and personal and find it daunting, more or less what Abraham Lincoln was worried about when he spoke of not wanting to change horses in midstream. In today's world, it's always midstream—just sometimes, the water is deeper and the current is swifter.

If you accept the logic of the argument here and understand the evidence provided by some of the most outstandingly successful executives of the past half century, then you will have bought into a very powerful proposition. Leadership matters greatly today not because the leader is all powerful and makes the only decisions that count but because our modern corporations have scale and complexity that demand great management. The talents of many must contribute for there to be sustained success.

Managing so that the contributions are welcomed is also managing so that new leaders can develop. The company that is investing in the growth of Inside Outsiders has planning, resource allocation, and compensation processes that encourage open debate, measured risk taking, and even entrepreneurial behavior. The company that can produce Inside Outsiders is open to change precisely because it has people around who recognize the changes in markets, technology, and competition. When you have the next CEO ready within, you have a company alive to change and ready to succeed.

Chapter 1

1. For a compelling journalistic treatment of the decline and demise of Westinghouse, see Steve Massey, "Who Killed Westinghouse?" *Pittsburgh Post-Gazette*, March 1, 1998, http://www.post-gazette.com/westinghouse.

2. Why? In large part because once pensions were defined in terms of contributions rather than benefits, pensioners looked to their 401(k)s to make up the difference. They need performance in order to eat.

3. Jim Collins, *Good to Great* (New York: HarperBusiness, 2001).

4. Jeffrey L. Cruikshank, *Shaping the Waves* (Boston: Harvard Business School Press, 2006), 345.

5. I found the most useful academic study to be Noam Wasserman, Bharat Anand, and Nitin Nohria, "When Does Leadership Matter? The Contingent Opportunities View of CEO Leadership," working paper 01-063, Harvard Business School, Boston, 2001.

6. Louis V. Gerstner Jr., *Who Says Elephants Can't Dance?* (New York: HarperBusiness, 2002), 60–61.

7. For those who are curious, here is the problem: research has shown that firm performance itself affects the timing and process of CEO change, and the forces that influenced firm performance continue to linger well after a successor is in place. The same forces confound the timing relationship between CEO turnover and firm performance. Poor prior performance, combined with regression to the mean, will bias the results toward finding a positive effect due to new CEOs. Survivor bias is endemic in samples for studies that depend on publicly available financial data, and studies on CEO succession and firm performance are no exception. More serious is the issue

that, in a typical sample of firms that have experienced CEO succession, about 88 percent, on average, tend to be insider succession and 12 percent tend to be outsider succession. This makes for small outside-succession samples (about twenty-five in a sample of two hundred companies) and further clouds the reliability of the results for outside succession.

8. Chuck Lucier, Rob Schuyt, and Edward Tse, "CEO Succession 2004: The World's Most Prominent Temp Workers," *strategy+business,* Summer 2005, http://www.strategy-business.com/media/file/sb39_05204.pdf.

9. Collins, *Good to Great,* 251.

10. Rakesh Khurana, *Searching for a Corporate Savior: The Irrational Quest for Charismatic CEOs* (Princeton, NJ: Princeton University Press, 2004).

Chapter 2

1. The quotation from Harry S. Truman can be found in Richard E. Neustadt, *Presidential Power and the Modern Presidents* (New York: Free Press, 1990), 10. Italics added.

2. Quotations from Ken Andrews in this section can be found in his book *The Concept of Corporate Strategy* (Homewood, IL: Dow Jones-Irwin, 1971).

3. Most people mistakenly think that "passing the buck" and "the buck stops here" refer to money. According to the Truman Library, the terms derive from poker, which Truman loved to play. The "buck"—which, in the early days, was often made from a buck's horn—was the dealer's marker. If someone "passed the buck," he was declining to serve as the dealer. Mitford M. Mathews, *A Dictionary of Americanisms on Historical Principles,* vol. 1 (Chicago: University of Chicago Press, 1951), 198–199.

4. For examples of Ogilvy's work, as well as more historical details, see the Center for Interactive Advertising's Web site at http://www.ciadvertising.org.

5. Joseph L. Bower, "WPP: Integrating Icons to Leverage Knowledge," Case 396-249 (Boston: Harvard Business School, 1996).

6. Ibid, 5.

7. The hiring process included an extended interview with founder David Ogilvy. "Charlotte and I talked for seven hours," he later said, "and found nothing to disagree about." Dabney Oliver, "The Steel Magnolia of Advertising: Charlotte Beers," http://www.ciadvertising.org/studies/student/00_spring/theory/dabney/public_html/CBFrame.html.

8. Martin Sorrell, interview by author, tape recording, New York, July 2005.

9. This quotation, and the remaining ones from Charlotte Beers in this section, are taken from Bower, "WPP."

10. David B. Yoffie and Johanna M. Hurstak, "Reshaping Apple Computer's Destiny—1992," Case 393-011 (Boston: Harvard Business School, 1992).

11. Doris Kearns Goodwin, *Team of Rivals* (New York: Simon & Schuster, 2005).

12. Spindler, in turn, was replaced by a board member (Gil Amelio), who was replaced by Steve Jobs himself: the return of the prince.

13. Another class of situations in which outsiders have fared better is buyouts. When private equity groups buy a company, they often use a search firm to identify a new CEO—with great success. Why does this happen? Research suggests that the reason lies in the simple objective provided to the CEO by the board: manage for cash to reduce debt. A second reason is the active participation of a board that represents the owners.

14. Joseph L. Bower, "Jack Welch: General Electric, The People Factory at Work—Picking My Successor at GE," video, product number 304-808 (Boston: Harvard Business School, 2004).

15. William E. Rothschild, *The Secret to GE's Success* (New York: McGraw-Hill, 2007), 189.

16. Those familiar with these contracts will recognize that the candidate accepted the loss of his incentives if he was fired "for cause," meaning fraud or the equivalent, but insisted on having the benefits if relieved of his duties "not for cause," meaning poor performance as CEO.

17. Marks & Spencer, "Our History," Marks & Spencer Web site, http://www2.marksandspencer.com/thecompany/whoweare/our_history/index.shtml.

18. Joseph L. Bower and John Matthews, "Marks & Spencer: Sir Richard Greenbury's Quiet Revolution," Case 395-054 (Boston: Harvard Business School, 1994).

19. Joseph L. Bower, "Sir Richard Greenbury: Events Leading to Succession," video, product number 302-812 (Boston: Harvard Business School, 2002).

20. Joseph L. Bower, "Marks & Spencer Update: The Crisis of 2000," September 27, 2001. Harvard Business School video tape library, tape number 7785.

21. Rothschild, *The Secret to GE's Success*, 192.

22. Ibid.

23. Ibid.

24. This has been the case at my own institution, Harvard Business School, where presidents have regularly skipped a half generation of scholars to find the school's next dean.

Chapter 3

1. The quotation from Winston Churchill can be found in *The Second World War, Volume 1: The Gathering Storm* (London: Cassell, 1948), 526–527.

2. Ibid.

3. Churchill's views were especially unpopular among Britain's political and nonpolitical leaders who sought to deliver on the Wilsonian notion that World War I was the war to end all wars.

4. Doz and Kosonen's forthcoming book is entitled *Strategic Agility*. These summary statements come from Yves Doz and Mikko Kosonen, interview with author, November 2005.

5. Yves Doz and Mikko Kosonen, telephone conversations with author, November 2005.

6. Boris Groysberg, Andrew N. McLean, and Nitin Nohria, "Are Leaders Portable?" *Harvard Business Review*, May 2006, 92.

7. Rakesh Khurana, *Searching for a Corporate Savior* (Princeton and Oxford: Princeton University Press, 2002), 171–172.

8. William George and Andrew N. McLean, "Anne Mulcahy: Leading Xerox Through the Perfect Storm (A)," Case 405-050 (Boston: Harvard Business School, 2005).

9. Joseph L. Bower and Sonja E. Hout, "Interview with Philip Casey at AmeriSteel, Video," video, product number 302-809 (Boston: Harvard Business School, 2001).

10. Winston Churchill, speech to the House of Commons, London, 1925.

11. The predilection of the present leadership of the United States to listen only to the members of a small and closed circle when debating strategy drives many in the business management community to distraction.

12. Marcus Sieff, interview by author, London, 1975.

13. Clark G. Gilbert and Joseph L. Bower, "Disruptive Change: When Trying Harder is Part of the Problem," *Harvard Business Review*, May 2002, 97–99.

14. Clark Gilbert, "Change in the Presence of Residual Fit: Can Competing Frames Coexist?" *Organizational Science,* Jan/Feb 2006, 156.

15. Clark Gilbert, "Unbundling the Structure of Inertia: Resource Versus Routine Rigidity," *Academy of Management Journal*, October 2005, 751.

16. "Face Value: A Post-Modern Proctoid," *The Economist*, April 15, 2006, 68.

17. Ibid.

Chapter 4

1. The quotation from Tom Neff can be found in Tom Neff's speech to the National Association of Corporate Directors/Aetna Directors conference, New York, September 28, 2005.

2. Society of Human Resource Management, "At What Levels of Your Organization Are There Succession Plans in Place?," December 2003, results reported in Susan Meisinger, "The King Is Dead, Long Live the King!" *HR Magazine* 49, no. 6 (2004).

3. Dan Ciampa, "Almost There: How Leaders Move Up," *Harvard Business Review*, January 2005, 46–53.

4. Henry Schacht, interview by author, New York, May 2000.

5. Joseph L. Bower, James B. Weber, and Sonja E. Hout, "Kenan Systems," Case 301-101 (Boston: Harvard Business School, 2001).

6. Christopher A. Bartlett and Andrew N. McLean, "GE's Talent Machine: The Making of a CEO," Case 304-049 (Boston: Harvard Business School, 2005), 4.

7. Ibid.

8. St. John's College, "Student Life," St. John's College Web site, http://www.sjca.edu/asp/main.aspx?page=1006.

9. It's interesting to speculate what will happen now that these well-endowed institutions are using more of their wealth to seek out and provide scholarships to highly talented young people from poor families. Logically, their "gatekeeping" function, and resulting power, should only increase as the "product" improves.

10. For example, see Boris Groysberg, Ashish Nanda, and Nitin Nohria, "The Risky Business of Hiring Stars," *Harvard Business Review*, May 2004; and Boris Groysberg and Ashish Nanda, "Can They Take It with Them? The Portability of Star Knowledge Workers' Performance: Myth or Reality?" working paper 05-029, Harvard Business School, 2004.

11. William Finnegan, "The Terrorism Beat," *The New Yorker*, July 25, 2005, http://www.newyorker.com/fact/content/articles/050725fa_fact2.

12. That colleague is Dorothy Leonard. See Dorothy Leonard and Walter Swap, *When Sparks Fly: Harnessing the Power of Group Creativity* (Boston: Harvard Business School Press, 2005).

13. This is a paraphrase of Albert Szent-Györgyi's definition of discovery from his *Bioenergetics* (New York: Academic Press, 1957).

14. Peter F. Drucker, *The Practice of Management* (New York: Harper, 1954). The date is significant because it precedes the Ford Foundation's and the Carnegie Foundation's reports that recommended that schools and companies adopt management and behavioral science.

15. These have been called "disruptive innovations." Clayton Christensen and Joseph L. Bower, "Disruptive Technologies: Catching the Wave" *Harvard Business Review*, January 1995, 43.

16. Joseph L. Bower, "Kenan Systems," video, product number 302-805 (Boston: Harvard Business School, 2002).

17. Joseph L. Bower, "Jack Welch at GE, 1981–2001: The Evolution of a Chief Executive," video, product number 304-814 (Boston: Harvard Business School, 2004).

18. Christopher A. Bartlett and Meg Glinska, "Enron's Transformation: From Gas Pipelines to New Economy Powerhouse," Case 301-064 (Boston: Harvard Business School, 2001).

19. Field research by the author in the 1970s.

20. Clayton Christensen, "Hewlett-Packard: The Flight of the Kittyhawk (A)," Case 606-088 (Boston: Harvard Business School, 2006).

21. My colleague Clayton Christensen has called an important version of this problem "disruptive technologies." See Bower and Christensen, "Disruptive Technologies," 43.

22. A. G. Lafley Jr., interview by author, tape recording, Boston, May 2005.

23. General Electric, "Careers at GE: Student Opportunities: Entry-Level Leadership Programs," GE Company Web site, http://www.gecareers.com/GECAREERS/html/us/studentOpportunities/leadershipPrograms/entry_level.html.

24. Ibid.

Chapter 5

1. Richard F. Vancil, *Passing the Baton* (New York: McGraw-Hill, 1987).

2. This is not unusual. One way to start building the cohort of potential leaders is to use the admissions offices of schools that aim to develop the

kind of leader you are seeking. Pay top dollar for the people you like, and then you've got a program started. This is exactly the kind of process described in chapter 4.

3. Henry Schacht, interview by author, tape recording, New York, May 2000.

4. Joseph L. Bower, "Interview with Philip Casey at Ameristeel," video, product number 302-809 (Boston: Harvard Business School, 2001).

5. Jim Robinson, "Presentation to an MBA Class: James Robinson," (presentation, Harvard Business School, Boston, 1996), http://video.hbs.edu/videotools/play?clip=robinson_1996_cl.

6. Jack Stafford, interview by author, Edgartown, MA, August 2005.

7. Harvey Golub, interview by David Garvin, video recording, Boston, October 2000.

8. Ken Auletta, *Greed and Glory on Wall Street* (New York: Random House, 1985).

9. A. G. Lafley Jr., interview by author, Boston, May 2005.

10. Ibid.

11. Henry Schacht, interview by author, tape recording, New York, May 2000.

12. Ibid.

13. Jeff Immelt, interview by author and Christopher Bartlett, video recording, Boston, February 2003.

14. This extract is my paraphrase of a list provided to me by A. G. Lafley Jr.

15. A. G. Lafley Jr., interview by author, Boston, May 2005.

16. Harvey Golub, interview by David Garvin, video recording, Boston, October 2000.

17. Scott W. Spreier, Mary H. Fontaine, and Ruth L. Malloy, "Leadership Run Amok: The Destructive Potential of Overachievers," *Harvard Business Review*, June 2006, 72.

18. Jim Collins, *Good to Great* (New York: HarperBusiness, 2001), 39.

19. Joseph L. Bower and Sonja E. Hout, "Entrepreneurial Insights (Multimedia Case)," video, product number 306-703 (Boston: Harvard Business School, 2006).

20. Ibid.

21. Reginald H. Jones, address to the Advanced Management Program, Harvard Business School, Boston, April 15, 1982.

22. Rakesh Khurana, *Searching for a Corporate Savior: The Irrational Quest for Charismatic CEOs* (Princeton, NJ: Princeton University Press, 2004).

23. At the time of this writing, in winter 2007, Nardelli is gone, and it

is not at all clear that his formidable management skills were appropriate to the needs of The Home Depot.

24. In the academic literature, *strategic context* has exactly this meaning. It is the shaping influence on the ideas expressed in managers' business strategies and the assumptions that underlie component propositions.

25. Retaining a search firm may also limit that firm's ability to fish for candidates in your waters.

26. Joseph L. Bower, "Sir Richard Greenbury: Events Leading to Succession," video, product number 302-812 (Boston: Harvard Business School, 2002).

27. Jones, address to the Advanced Management Program, April 15, 1982.

28. Joseph L. Bower, "Jack Welch: General Electric, The People Factory at Work—Picking My Successor at GE," video, product number 304-808 (Boston: Harvard Business School, 2004).

29. Louis V. Gerstner Jr., interview by author, tape recording, New York, July 2003.

30. This quotation and the ones that follow come from Chuck Knight, interview by author, tape recording, New York City, February 2006.

31. Michael Watkins has written a useful manual for new leaders: *The First 90 Days: Critical Success Strategies for New Leaders at All Levels* (Boston: Harvard Business School Press, 2003).

32. Most recently, a panel of arbitrators told the board of MassMutual that it could not fire its CEO for cause, despite the CEO's inappropriate moves to benefit his retirement account and his affairs with two company employees. Joann S. Lublin and Scott Thurm, "How to Fire a CEO: More Bosses Are Getting the Boot, but It's Harder to Sack Them Without Paying for the Privilege," *Wall Street Journal*, October 30, 2006, B1.

33. Jack Welch, interview by author, Boston, March 2005.

34. Louis V. Gerstner Jr., *Who Says Elephants Can't Dance?* (New York: HarperBusiness, 2002), 36.

35. Chuck Knight, interview by author, tape recording, New York City, February 2006.

36. The exact name of the committee varies from company to company. For example, some call it the "compensation and development committee." But the committee responsible for compensation is supervising the most central part of the development and motivating of managers.

37. Jeffrey M. Cohn, Rakesh Khurana, and Laura Reeves, "Growing Talent as if Your Business Depended on It," *Harvard Business Review*, October 2005, 62–70.

Chapter 6

1. Chuck Lucier, Rob Schuyt, and Edward Tse, "CEO Succession 2004: The World's Most Prominent Temp Workers," *strategy+business,* Summer 2005, http://www.strategy-business.com/media/file/sb39_05204.pdf.

2. Ibid.

3. Chuck Lucier, Paul Kocourek, and Rolf Habbel, "CEO Succession 2005: The Crest of the Wave," *strategy+business*, Summer 2006, http://www .strategy-business.com/media/file/sb43_06210.pdf.

4. Ibid.

5. This number is accumulated from three data sources: Thompson Financial Database, the NVCA 2006 Yearbook, and the 2006 Hedge Fund Industry Research Report.

6. See, for example, "Ebbers Sentenced to 25 Years in Prison," MSNBC .com, July 13, 2005, http://www.msnbc.msn.com/id/8474930.

7. Rakesh Khurana, *Searching for a Corporate Savior: The Irrational Quest for Charismatic CEOs* (Princeton, NJ: Princeton University Press, 2004).

8. Joseph L. Bower, "Marks & Spencer Update: The Crisis of 2000," September 27, 2001. Harvard Business School video tape library, tape number 7785.

9. William W. George, interview by author, Boston, January 2006.

10. Andrew S. Grove, *Only the Paranoid Survive* (New York: Currency Doubleday, 1996), 3.

11. Tom Neff, interview by author, tape recording, New York, October 2005; Gerry Roche, interview by author, tape recording, New York, August 2005.

Chapter 7

1. Mara Faccio and Larry H.P. Lang, "The ultimate ownership of Western European corporations," *Journal of Financial Economics,* September 2002, 365–395. Ronald C. Anderson and David M. Reeb, "Founding-Family Ownership and Firm Performance: Evidence from the S&P 500," *The Journal of Finance*, June 2003, 1301–1329. Belén Villalonga and Raphael Amit, "How do Family Ownership, Control and Management Affect Firm Value?" *Journal of Financial Economics*, May 2006, 385–417. For firms in East Asia see Stijn Claessens, Simeon Djankov, and Larry H.P. Lang, "Separation of Ownership and Control in East Asian Corporations," *Journal of Financial Economics* (October/November 2000): 81–112.

2. Belén Villalonga and Raphael Amit, "How Do Family Ownership, Control and Management Affect Firm Value?" *Journal of Financial Economics* 80 (May 2006): 385-417.

3. The classic citation on family succession is Kelin Gersick et al., *Generation to Generation: Life Cycles of Family Business* (Boston: Harvard Business School Press, 1997). The authors develop their analysis using a simple model involving ownership, family, and business.

4. See Frank J. Prial, "Whiskey Chasers," review of *The Bronfmans*, by Nicholas Faith, *New York Times Sunday Book Review*, June 25, 2006.

5. Much of the detail of the Bronfman story is from Ken Auletta, "Rising Son," *New Yorker*, June 6, 1994. (Available online at http://www .kenauletta.com/risingson.html.)

6. See David Plotz, "Edgar Bronfman, Edgar Bronfman: Overrated Father, Misunderstood Son" Slate.com, April 26, 1998, http://www.slate .com/id/1862.

7. Prial, review of *The Bronfmans*, by Nicholas Faith. Michael Wolff, "Meet Barry Buffet," *New York* magazine, September 2002, quoted in Prial, review of *The Bronfmans*, by Nicholas Faith.

8. To be fair, Junior has made a success of Warner Music and has probably rebuilt his own fortune substantially. See Devin Leonard, "Warner Music: A Big Hit for Bronfman," *Fortune*, May 11, 2006, http://money .cnn.com/magazines/fortune/fortune_archive/2006/05/15/837693/.

9. Villalonga and Amit, "How Do Family Ownership, Control and Management Affect Firm Value?", 385-417.

10. Joseph L. Bower, Luiz Felipe Monteiro Jr., and Sonja E. Hout, "Gerdau (A)," Case 302-016 (Boston: Harvard Business School, 2001).

11. Larry Rohter, "From Brazil, an Emerging Steel Giant," *New York Times*, August 30, 2001. (Available online at http://www.raizesdosul.com .br/gerdau_nyt_eng.htm.)

12. Joseph L. Bower, "Ameristeel/Gerdau: The Brothers Build a Multi-national," February 9, 2001. Harvard Business School video tape library, tape number 8221.

13. Ibid.

14. Alfred D. Chandler, Jr., and Stephen Salsbury, *Pierre S. Du Pont and the Making of the Modern Corporation* (New York: Harper & Row, 1971).

15. Bower, Monteiro, and Hout, "Gerdau (A)."

16. Unsigned, "Family, Inc.," *BusinessWeek* (November 10, 2003), 110–114.

17. Villalonga and Amit, "How Do Family Ownership, Control, and Management Affect Firm Value?"

Chapter 8

1. Leah Nathans Spiro with Gary Silverman and Stanley Reed, "The Coup at Goldman; How the Fight Over Going Public and a Banker-Trader Clash Helped Topple Jon Corzine," *Business Week* (January 25, 1999): 84.

2. See, for example, Doris Kearns Goodwin, *Team of Rivals* (New York: Simon & Schuster, 2005).

3 Heinrich von Pierer, Thomas A. Stewart, and Louise O'Brien, "Transforming an Industrial Giant: Heinrich von Pierer," *Harvard Business Review* (February 2005), 114–122.

4. Joseph L. Bower, "The Acquisition of Technicolor by Thomson," December 3, 2004. Harvard Business School video tape library, tape number 12132.

5. Alfred North Whitehead, *Adventures of Ideas* (New York: Free Press, 1967), 90.

6. Winston Churchill, speech to the House of Commons, London, 1925.

7. For a discussion of the change literature, see Michael Beer and Nitin Nohria, eds., *Breaking the Code of Change* (Boston: Harvard Business School Press, 2000).

8. Chuck Lucier, Rob Schuyt, and Edward Tse, "CEO Succession 2004: The World's Most Prominent Temp Workers," *strategy+business*, Summer 2005, http://www.strategy-business.com/media/file/sb39_05204.pdf.

9. Joseph L. Bower and John Matthews, "Marks & Spencer: Sir Richard Greenbury's Quiet Revolution," Case 395-054 (Boston: Harvard Business School, 1994) and Joseph L. Bower and Sonja E. Hout, "Marks & Spencer Go Global, A Video Case Study," video, product number 395-524 (Boston: Harvard Business School, 1995).

10. Andrew S. Grove, *Only the Paranoid Survive* (New York: Currency Doubleday, 1996), 127.

11. The past chairman of MIT's board of trustees, a friend of mine, told me of a dinner at which a leading CEO sat with some of the luminaries from MIT's alumni. "He didn't ask a good question all evening" was my friend's worried comment.

12. Grove, *Only the Paranoid Survive*, 108.

13. Ibid., 110.

14. Joseph L. Bower, Thomas Eisenmann, and Sonja E. Hout, "Viacom: Carpe Diem," Case 396-250 (Boston: Harvard Business School, 1996).

INDEX

AAWE (aptitude, attitude, willingness to learn, experience), 87–88
administrative inheritance
  advantages of being plugged in, 69
  described, 68
  disadvantages of not being plugged in, 69–71
Ameristeel, 70
Andrews, Ken, 22, 23
Apple Computer. 31–36
  Sculley's inability to implement a vision, 72–73
aptitude as a hiring criterion, 87–88
attitude as a hiring criterion, 88, 91

Barnard, Chester, 124, 127
Barrett, Craig, 211
baton-passing concept, 120–124
Beers, Charlotte, 26–31, 34, 52–53
Blockbuster, 66
board of directors
  dilemma facing boards, 5
  role in changing negative trend in CEO retention, 172–174
  role in succession process, 161–164
  succession process challenges, 132–137

Bridgewater, Dolph, 41
Bronfman family, 186–189
Brown Shoe. 41–45, 49–50
building Inside Outsiders
  building leaders and, 82–84
  coaching and, 114–115
  culture of performance and, 115–117
  evaluation and feedback importance, 110–112
  managing succession (*see* succession management)
  paying for performance and, 82
  providing education in processes (*see* education in business processes)
  recruiting new leaders (*see* recruiting new leaders)
  training importance, 112–114
  typical succession process, 83

Casey, Phil, 70, 122
CEO job
  attributes that lead to success, 51–53
  business climate challenges, 23–24

CEO job (*continued*)
  characteristics of a good CEO,
    16–18
  critical nature of having a succes-
    sion plan, 36
  dilemma facing boards, 5
  failure of some U.S. companies to
    evolve, 6–7
  investors' expectations and, 4
  key elements in picking leaders,
    36–38
  lack of succession plans in
    companies, 14–15
  responsibilities of, 21–23
  scope of leadership challenge, 23
  shortcomings that lead to failure,
    53
  sporadic nature of outsider success,
    38–39
  talent management responsibility,
    2–3
  team management skills needed, 36
  track records of promoted insiders,
    11–14
  typical tenure, 4
Chandler, Alfred D., Jr., 195
Christensen, C. Roland, 95
Churchill, Winston, 59–61
  leadership skills, 71
coaching, 85–86, 99–100, 101–102,
  114–115
Collins, Jim, 5, 11, 44, 131
compensation, CEO, 170–171
Corzine, Jon S., 203
Cummins, 121

DaimlerChrysler, 70
Dangeard, Frank, 209
d'Arbeloff, Alex, 76, 175
Dooley, Tom, 216
Doz, Yves, 66
Drucker, Peter, 96
DuPont, 195

education in business processes
  developmental opportunity tied to
    strategy, 107–109
  leadership development and,
    109–110
  necessary conditions for, 103
  planning involvement, 104–105
  problems when strategy is based on
    targeted outcomes, 105–107
  senior management's role in
    guiding managers, 108–109
education pools for recruitment,
  88–91
Emerson Electric, 152
Enron, 105
executive search firms, 140–141
experience as a hiring criterion, 87, 88

family-business succession
  added dimension of relationships,
    182
  advantages and disadvantages of a
    family business, 199–200
  benefits of family ownership, 197
  considerations in succession
    management, 185–186
  general principles for success,
    195–197
  good succession example, 193–195
  hiring professionals and, 192–193
  primogeniture tradition, 191–192
  private firms' success with
    succession, 198
  wealth control and business man-
    agement decisions, 183–185
Farr, David, 155, 159
Fiorina, Carly, 10, 65
Fontaine, Mary, 130
Fromm, Ron, 42–45, 52, 204

General Electric (GE)
  horse race metaphor and, 124

importance of leadership, 5
leadership training, 111–112
recruitment approach, 88, 89, 137
success under Welch, 3
surprise at Welch's selection, 40,
    51–52
George, Bill, 177
Gerdau Group, 193–195
Gerstner, Lou
    American Express and, 123
    insider attributes, 8–9
    start as an outsider, 52
    success at IBM, 39
    transition process advice, 158, 159,
        160
Gilbert, Clark, 77
Goldman Sachs, 203
Golub, Harvey, 123–124, 130
Good to Great (Collins), 5, 11, 44,
    51, 59
Greenbury, Richard, 45–47,
    143–145, 215
Grove, Andy, 134, 215, 216
Groysberg, Boris, 91

Hewlett-Packard (HP), 10, 65, 106
Home Depot, 138
horse race metaphor, 124–128
Hurd, Mark, 10

IBM, 8–9, 151, 158
Immelt, Jeff, 52, 127–128, 148, 158,
    204
Ingle, Bob, 78
Inside Outsiders
    administrative inheritance,
        68–71
    described, 15–16
    developing (see building Inside
        Outsiders)
    example of Churchill (see
        Churchill, Winston)

insiders' common fear of the
    unknown, 77–80
insiders' inability to see need for
    change, 74–76
insiders' misunderstanding the
    drivers of change, 76–77
knowledge requirements of (see
    knowledge requirements of
    Inside Outsiders)
leadership and, 71–74
outsiders versus, 5, 8–10, 54–56
preferred choice for business
    success, 39–40
sporadic nature of outsider success,
    38–39
track records of promoted insiders,
    11–14
integrity as a hiring criterion, 130
Intel, 33, 139, 211
Internet, 77–78

job description. See CEO job
Johannpeter, Jorge, 197
Johnston, Larry, 67
Jones, Reg, 51, 124, 135, 137,
    145–148, 178. See also Welch,
    Jack

Kelly, Raymond W., 93
Kenan Systems, 87–88, 89, 102
Khurana, Rakesh, 13, 137, 173
Kilts, James, 39, 212
Knight, Chuck, 152–156, 159
knowledge requirements of Inside
    Outsiders
    ability to address strategic issues,
        64–65
    ability to call upon a wide range of
        relevant knowledge, 65–67
    financial and strategic processes,
        62–64
Kosonen, Mikko, 66

Lafley, A. G., 79–80, 109, 125–126, 128–129

Lazarus, Shelly, 28

leadership
    building Inside Outsider leaders, 82–84
    communicating a vision, 72–73
    education in business processes and, 109–110
    key elements in picking leaders, 36–38
    possessing a desire to lead, 73–74
    post-succession (*see* post-succession leadership)
    recruiting new leaders (*see* recruiting new leaders)
    required skills, 71–72
    succession process challenge, 132–137

Lintner, John, 131

Malloy, Ruth, 130

managing for performance, 105

Marks & Spencer, 45–51, 64, 66, 100, 143–145, 214–215

McNerney, James, 39

Medtronic, 101, 177

mentoring and coaching, 85–86, 99–100, 101–102

Merloni, Antonio, 198

Merloni, Franco, 198

Merloni, Vittorio, 74, 75–76, 133–134, 198

Microsoft, 5, 33

Miller, Irwin, 121, 122, 175–176

Moore, Gordon, 36

Mulcahy, Ann, 69

Myles's Law, 98

Nardelli, Robert, 138

Neff, Tom, 81, 178

negative trend in successions
    board of directors' role, 172–174
    CEO compensation and, 170–171
    competition and, 170
    current state of executive turnover, 165–167
    financing and, 167–168
    need for CEO honesty, 171–172
    ownership and, 168–169
    takeovers and, 169, 170

Nevin, John, 9

newspaper publishers, 77–78, 79

Nisenholtz, Martin, 78

Oates, Keith, 47, 49, 145

Ogilvy, David, 26

Ogilvy & Mather. 26–31

Only the Paranoid Survive (Grove), 215

Palmisano, Sam, 54, 158, 159

Passing the Baton (Vancil), 120

Paulson, Henry, 203

Perez, William, 138

Phillips, Graham, 26

post-succession leadership
    ability to push new plans forward, 208–211
    executive-level purges and, 202–205
    failure of some U.S. companies to evolve, 6–7
    insiders' common fear of the unknown, 77–80
    insiders' inability to see need for change, 74–76
    insiders' misunderstanding the drivers of change, 76–77
    new strategy implementation challenges, 205–207
    problems caused by a celebrity status, 213–217

recognition of an infinite learning curve, 211–213
primogeniture tradition, 191–192
Procter & Gamble, 109, 125, 128–129

recruiting new leaders
  characteristics to consider, 87–89
  determining how much you are willing to pay, 92–94
  hiring today for tomorrow, 94–95
  identifying the kinds of people you want, 89–92
Redstone, Sumner, 66, 216
Rizzo, Phil, 159
Robinson, Jim, 123
Roche, Gerry, 178
Rose, Stuart, 48, 52, 64

Sahin, Kenan, 87, 89
Salsbury, Peter, 47, 48, 49–50, 53
Schacht, Henry, 86, 121, 126–127
Sculley, John, 53, 72–73
Seagram, Inc. See Bronfman family
Searching for a Corporate Savior (Khurana), 137
Sieff, Marcus, 72
Siemans, 205–207
Smith, Darwin, 10
Sorrell, Martin, 26, 175
Spreier, Scott, 130
Stafford, Jack, 123
succession management
  gaining experience coordinating across all levels, 100–102
  goal of grooming the insider, 84–85
  goal of innovation, 102
  having a perspective of each part of the company, 98–99
  lateral and vertical moves to develop expertise, 97–98
  learning the value of each part of the company, 99–100

succession plan
  board's role in, 161–164
  critical nature of having, 36
  key elements in picking leaders, 36–38
  lack of in companies, 14–15
  necessity of planning ahead, 219–221
succession process
  ability to anticipate and react to change and, 131–137
  aftermath (see post-succession leadership)
  baton-passing concept, 120–122
  baton-passing-related problems, 122–124
  board's role, 161–164
  central role of age in, 144
  challenge for the leadership of a company, 132–137
  companies' susceptibility to grooved thinking, 139–140
  current CEO's retirement plans and, 142–143
  current state of executive turnover, 165–167
  developing leaders (see building Inside Outsiders)
  executive search firms' value, 140–141
  in family businesses (see family-business succession)
  Gerstner's description of pruning, 151–152
  Greenbury's approach, 143–145
  horse race metaphor, 124–128
  incumbent CEO's style and poor outcomes, 175–177
  Jones' pruning process at GE, 145–148
  key qualities to look for, 128–130
  Knight's approach at Emerson, 152–156

succession plan (*continued*)
  negative trend in (*see* negative
    trend in successions)
  perils from looking outside, 137–138
  planning for succession (*see*
    succession plan)
  rapid company growth and poor
    outcomes, 177–179
  search criteria example, 136
  strategic inflection as a reason for
    poor outcomes, 178–179
  strategy of thinking like a buyout
    firm, 218–219
  transition process for an insider,
    157, 158–160
  transition process for an outsider,
    157, 160
  typical process, 83
  Welch's process at GE, 148–151

Teradyne, 76
training new leaders, 112–114
Trani, John, 67

Vancil, Richard, 40, 120
Vandevelde, Luc, 48, 53, 64

Villalonga, Belén, 192, 198
von Pierer, Heinrich, 205–207

Watson, Thomas, Jr., 93
Welch, Jack
  comment on succession
    management, 104
  comments on insider selection,
    39–40
  Jones's pruning process at GE,
    145–148
  outsider perspective, 10, 51–52,
    178
  selection as CEO, 3, 124–125,
    140
  selection process at GE and, 135,
    137, 145
  transition process advice, 158
  Welch's process at GE,
    148–151
Westinghouse, 3
willingness to learn as a hiring
    criterion, 87, 88

Xerox, 106

ACKNOWLEDGMENTS

This book began in the 1980s. At Harvard Business School in 1985 we appointed a new professor, Michael Jensen, who began to argue the merits of agency theory, a view that a corporation was a nexus of contracts between principals (owners) and agents (managers). His thinking soon led him to question the value of diversified companies and to praise the disciplining consequences of debt. It was consistent with much thinking on Wall Street, that saw the breaking up of conglomerate enterprises by leveraged buyouts as a wonderful way to make money while serving society. Jensen also argued that top managers held inadequate holdings of their companies' shares, an idea that has led to or legitimized the boom in stock options for CEOs—but that is another book.

I begin my acknowledgments with Michael Jensen because it was to answer his critique that I began a study of more than a decade focused on corporate value added—in other words, what the corporate office added to the value being created by a group of operating businesses. It seemed obvious that the multibusiness firm was alive and well all around the globe at the end of the twentieth century. It was worth exploring why. Only at Harvard Business School do you get to explore a question that big in a context where it is easy to get access to important companies and their managers and to the funding to stay at it for a long time. So the second step in the acknowledgment process is to thank the dean at that time, Kim Clark, and the several directors of research who supported and funded my explorations.

As I began to form my answers into the outline of a book, I began discussions with editors at Harvard Business School Press, the publisher of *The CEO Within*. It is fair to say that they were supportive of me, but not of the book. On the other hand, when I indicated that one clear contribution of successful corporate offices was the management of CEO succession, they jumped. I am a true academic, but I am not insensitive to audience reaction. Their encouragement focused me on what was becoming very apparent: the companies that were able to outperform peers over long periods of time were all able to manage CEO succession, and those CEOs were almost always insiders. And that, with a few important additions, is the story of this book. So thanks to Melinda Merino, Julia Ely, and the team at HBS Press.

I also want to thank the many CEOs who were enormously cooperative in their willingness to give me time and to share their histories and views with candor. In particular, interviews with Charlotte Beers, Bill George, Lou Gerstner, Rick Greenbury (Sir Richard Greenbury), Andy Grove, Chris Hogg (Sir Christopher Hogg), Jeff Immelt, Chuck Knight, A. G. Lafley, Shelly Lazarus, Vittorio Merloni, Gordon Moore, Henry Schacht, Martin Sorrell, Jack Welch, and others who stayed anonymous contributed significantly to the set of ideas laid out in this book as well as the telling illustrations for my arguments. I have also drawn from a series of case studies that I developed over the course of that decade of research and from the research of others who studied succession—especially my late colleague Richard Vancil.

Several colleagues read early drafts and offered helpful criticism and suggestions. Thanks to Tom Eisenmann, Boris Groysberg, Rakesh Khurana, and Jay Lorsch. Chris Allen helped with the statistical analysis of CEO succession. In the writing and editing of the manuscript, Jeff Cruikshank was invaluable in helping me find a voice that kept the message clear, the evidence organized, and the pace pleasant. All authors should have the good fortune of having as helpful an editor.

In the final steps of production, Virginia Fuller assisted with the footnotes, and Katherine Farren helped with the final manuscript.

As with all projects of this sort, responsibility for the defects belongs with the author.

Joseph L. Bower

JOSEPH L. BOWER, the Donald Kirk David Professor of Business Administration at Harvard Business School, has been a faculty leader in general management at the school for more than forty years. An expert on corporate strategy, organization, and leadership, he has devoted much of his teaching and research to challenges confronting corporate leaders in today's rapidly changing hyper-competitive conditions. Presently, he is focusing on corporate value added—the contribution that corporate groups make to their operating divisions—as well as on the management of CEO succession.

Bower is the author or coauthor of several books, including *From Resource Allocation to Strategy* (which was named the best book of 2006 by *strategy+business* magazine), *When Markets Quake: The Management Challenge of Restructuring Industry*, and *The Two Faces of Management: An American Approach to Leadership in Business and Government*. He is also the author of several *Harvard Business Review* articles.

In addition to teaching, consulting, and conducting research, Bower is a director of Anika Therapeutics, Brown Shoe, Loews Corporation, the New America High Income Fund, and Sonesta International Hotels Corporation; and he's a trustee of TH Lee, Putnam Emerging Opportunities Portfolio. He is also a lifetime trustee of the New England Conservatory and trustee of the DeCordova Museum and Sculpture Park.

The CEO Within is the result of a decade's research on corporate value added and Bower's board experience with nine CEO successions.